POLICY RESPONSES TO

SOCIAL EXCLUSION

TOWARDS INCLUSION?

Edited by

Janie Percy-Smith

OPEN UNIVERSITY PRESS
Buckingham • Philadelphia

Open University Press
Celtic Court
22 Ballmoor
Buckingham
MK18 1XW

email: enquiries@openup.co.uk
world wide web: www.openup.co.uk

and
325 Chestnut Street
Philadelphia, PA 19106, USA

First Published 2000

A catalogue record of this book is available from the British Library

ISBN   0 335 20473 2 (pb)   0 335 20474 0 (hb)

Library of Congress Cataloging-in-Publication Data
Policy responses to social exclusion / edited by Janie Percy-Smith.
     p.   cm.
   Includes bibliographical references and index.
   ISBN 0–335–20473–2 – ISBN 0–335–20474–0
   1. Marginality, Social–European Union countries.   2. European Union countries–Social policy.   3. Social work administration–European Union countries.   I. Percy-Smith, Janie.
HN380.Z9 M265 2000
305.5'6'094–dc21   99–088206

Typeset by Graphicraft Limited, Hong Kong
Printed in Great Britain by Biddles Ltd, Guildford and King's Lynn

POLICY RESPONSES TO
SOCIAL EXCLUSION

CONTENTS

LIST OF CONTRIBUTORS

Tom Burden is a principal policy analyst at the Policy Research Institute, Leeds Metropolitan University. For many years he has also worked as a tutor, author and consultant for The Open University. He has written five books including *Features of a Viable Socialism* (Harvester Wheatsheaf, 1990) and *Social Policy and Welfare* (Pluto Press, 1998). He is currently finishing a book on New Labour's social policies.

Professor Mike Campbell is the founding director of the Policy Research Institute at Leeds Metropolitan University. He is currently working on UK labour market issues for the European Commission; skills policy for the DfEE; and on the role of the Third System in local development.

Gabriel Chanan is Director of Research at the Community Development Foundation. He has written widely on community development, arts and education. He has recently been involved in European research examining the role and activities of community organizations.

Tricia Hamm is a research officer at the Policy Research Institute, Leeds Metropolitan University, where she is involved in a wide range of community-based research. Her main area of interest is equal opportunities and diversity.

Murray Hawtin is a senior policy analyst at the Policy Research Institute, Leeds Metropolitan University. He was a social worker, community development worker and housing worker before joining the Policy Research Institute in 1992. His main areas of research interest are social housing and residents' involvement in the community.

Jo Hutchinson is a senior consultant with the economic development consultancy, Segal Quince Wicksteed. Her research and consultancy work focuses on the social elements of regeneration activities, in particular the development and management of partnerships, local labour market and skills issues, and community economic development.

Jane Kettle is a senior lecturer in planning and housing at Leeds Metropolitan University and a member of the Centre for Urban Development and Environmental Management. She is a fellow of the Chartered Institute of Housing and is currently vice-chair of The Ridings Housing Association Ltd in Leeds.

Ged Moran is a senior lecturer in the Faculty of Health and the Environment at Leeds Metropolitan University. He has previously worked as health liaison officer for the London Borough of Greenwich and for Leeds City Council. He has written and researched extensively on the health role of local government.

Dr Janie Percy-Smith is a principal policy analyst at the Policy Research Institute, Leeds Metropolitan University, where she is engaged in a wide range of research relating to local governance, social exclusion, community needs and community development.

Professor Ian Sanderson is a principal policy analyst in the Policy Research Institute, Leeds Metropolitan University. He has undertaken extensive research and consultancy in the fields of evaluation and public services management, local labour markets and community needs. He has a particular interest in management and policy issues in local government and has published widely in these areas.

Mike Simpkin has extensive experience of social work in health-related settings. He is now Public Health Strategy Officer for Leeds City Council, and until recently was on the executive of the UK Health for All Network. He writes here in a personal capacity.

Fiona Walton is a research officer at the Policy Research Institute. She has worked extensively in the fields of labour markets, local economic development and education and training. In particular she has undertaken research into skills issues, the National Targets and young people's transition from education to the labour market.

1 INTRODUCTION: THE CONTOURS

OF SOCIAL EXCLUSION

Janie Percy-Smith

Introduction

This introductory chapter provides a context for the discussion of policy responses to social exclusion in the subsequent chapters. It begins with an overview of the origins and development of social exclusion as a concept and discusses the ways in which social exclusion is defined. From this discussion of definitions I then derive a series of dimensions of social exclusion which are related to the subject matter of the subsequent chapters. In the final section I begin the discussion of policy responses to social exclusion by drawing out the cross-cutting themes and issues which characterize and inform the policy initiatives discussed in the later chapters of this book.

The origins and development of social exclusion as a concept

The term 'social exclusion' originated in the social policy of the French socialist governments of the 1980s and was used to refer to a disparate group of people living on the margins of society and, in particular, without access to the system of social insurance (Room 1995; Jordan 1997; Burchardt *et al.* 1999). However, when the term began to be used in the European context it referred more to the European Union (EU) objective of achieving social and economic cohesion. Economic cohesion has been a key goal for the EU since the early treaties establishing the European Economic Community, but social cohesion really came to the fore with the negotiations around the Maastricht Treaty. The term social cohesion refers to the 'reconciliation of a system of organisation based on market forces, freedom of opportunity and enterprise with a commitment to the values of internal solidarity and mutual support which ensures open access to benefit and protection for all members of society' (Geddes 1998: 20). Social cohesion therefore requires improvement in the living conditions of those regions or groups within the EU that are worst off so that they are closer to those of the regions that are better off (European Commission 1997).

Social exclusion is now written into the Maastricht Treaty and is an objective for the European structural funds (Room 1995: 1). Some writers have commented that the term social exclusion was preferred to the term poverty in European circles because of the difficulties on the part of some member states at that time to apply the term poverty to their own countries (see Lee and Murie 1999: 3). Indeed the EU poverty programmes which had been in existence since 1974 were brought to an abrupt halt in 1994 when the Council of Europe rejected a new poverty programme. Since then, it has been argued, social exclusion rather than poverty has been the main focus of EU social policy and, furthermore, the approach to social exclusion has, in practice, reflected a more limited concern with labour market exclusion (Geyer 1999: 161).

The Social Exclusion Unit

In the UK the concept of social exclusion came to the fore with the setting up by the government in 1997 of the interdepartmental Social Exclusion Unit. The Social Exclusion Unit only encompasses England: social exclusion and poverty are devolved responsibilities and, in Scotland, there is a separate 'Scottish Social Inclusion Strategy'; in Wales, 'Building an Inclusive Wales'; and in Northern Ireland, 'Targeting Social Need in Northern Ireland' (see Northern Ireland Office 1998; Scottish Office 1999; Welsh Office 1999). The Social Exclusion Unit was charged with reporting to the prime minister on how to 'develop integrated and sustainable approaches to the problems of the worst housing estates, including crime, drugs, unemployment, community breakdown, and bad schools etc.' (Social Exclusion Unit 1997: 2). Since then a range of policy initiatives have been developed by the Social Exclusion Unit and other policies have been redirected towards the social exclusion agenda.

The Social Exclusion Unit (1998: 9), in developing new policy responses to social exclusion, noted the failure of previous attempts to deal with the problems and identified the reasons for failure as follows:

- The lack of effective national policies to address 'the structural causes of decline'.
- A failure to effectively engage local communities.
- Too great an emphasis on physical regeneration at the expense of creating opportunities for people.
- The failure to develop a 'joined up' approach to the issues.

The Social Exclusion Unit's report identifies three 'strands' to its response to social exclusion. The first strand comprises the 'New Deals' for the unemployed, lone parents and the disabled together with actions to address failing schools, crime and public health. The second strand comprises new funding programmes to support the regeneration of poor neighbourhoods, in particular the New Deal for communities, but also the latest round of the Single Regeneration Budget and Sure Start. The third strand is aimed at ensuring coherence and a 'joined-up' approach and involves the work of 18 cross-cutting Policy Action Teams involving cross-departmental groupings and outside experts. The work of the teams falls under five broad themes:

1 Getting the people to work: focusing on maximizing the contribution of the New Deal in the poorest areas; addressing barriers to employment; and developing innovative ways of assisting re-entry into the labour market.
2 Getting the place to work: focusing on effective neighbourhood and housing management so that issues such as crime and antisocial behaviour are addressed.
3 Building a future for young people: focusing on Sure Start to provide more integrated help for children at risk and other measures to motivate children and young people in relation to education.
4 Access to services: focusing on ensuring access to services in the poorest areas.
5 Making the government work better: focusing on improving the way government at all levels responds to social exclusion.

The government's strategy for tackling poverty and social exclusion is summed up in its first annual report on poverty and social exclusion, *Opportunity for All*, using the language of universalism: 'Our strategy is based in the principle that everybody has the right to participate in society, and the opportunity to achieve their full potential' (Department of Social Security 1999: 30). This statement raises issues around how social exclusion is defined, to which we now turn.

Defining social exclusion

Social exclusion has been defined in a number of different ways which may include all or some of the following elements: disadvantage in relation to certain norms of social, economic or political activity pertaining to individuals, households, spatial areas or population groups; the social, economic and institutional processes through which disadvantage comes about; and the outcomes or consequences for individuals, groups or communities. The following, quite comprehensive, definition comes from the European Commission:

> Social exclusion refers to the multiple and changing factors resulting in people being excluded from the normal exchanges, practices and rights of modern society. Poverty is one of the most obvious factors, but social exclusion also refers to inadequate rights in housing, education, health and access to services. It affects individuals and groups, particularly in urban and rural areas, who are in some way subject to discrimination or segregation; and it emphasises the weaknesses in the social infrastructure and the risk of allowing a two-tier society to become established by default. The Commission believes that a fatalistic acceptance of social exclusion must be rejected, and that all Community citizens have a right to the respect of human dignity.
> (Commission of the European Communities 1993: 1)

This definition is interesting for a number of reasons. First, it emphasizes the multiple factors associated with social exclusion; second, it refers to the dynamic nature of exclusionary processes; third, it includes within its scope policy failure to adequately address social exclusion and its consequences; and finally it endorses the view that citizens within the EU have 'the right to a certain basic standard of living and to participate in the major social and occupational institutions of the society' (Room 1995: 6). Thus, social exclusion occurs when citizens are denied these social rights or they are not fully realized and, furthermore, in such circumstances citizens are likely to experience more generalized disadvantage.

Burchardt et al. (1999: 230) offer the following, more restricted, definition of social exclusion: 'An individual is socially excluded if (a) he or she is geographically resident in a society and (b) he or she does not participate in the normal activities of citizens in that society'. In developing this definition they consider including a condition relating to the issue of 'agency' – that is, whether or not the exclusion is self-imposed or voluntary. Ultimately they decide not to do so because of the difficulties associated with deciding when self-exclusion is really voluntary. For example, individuals may decide to exclude themselves as a result of a history or previous experience of exclusion or discrimination. Can this, then, really be deemed self-exclusion? Burchardt et al. then raise the question of whether individual choice should in any case be paramount, especially when self-exclusion has negative consequences or is problematic for society more generally. Examples here might include those who decide to 'opt out' of paid work and are dependent on state benefits or those who choose alternative lifestyles which are regarded as problematic by mainstream society. This issue relates to the moral agenda which is widely perceived as underpinning policies to address social exclusion (see below).

The way in which the Social Exclusion Unit has defined social exclusion does not refer to citizenship rights, rather it utilizes a definition that is much closer to the concept of disadvantage: 'Social exclusion is a shorthand label for what can happen when individuals or areas suffer from a combination of linked problems such as unemployment, poor skills, low incomes, poor housing, high crime environments, bad health and family breakdown' (Social Exclusion Unit 1997: 1). This definition is very much focused on outcomes and makes no reference to the processes that create the problems identified in the definition.

The term 'social exclusion' is sometimes taken as being more or less synonymous with poverty or disadvantage. However there are important differences. The concept of poverty is, as noted by Burden in Chapter 3, primarily concerned with the distribution of resources: a poor household is one in which the resources available, especially income, fall below a particular level. Policies to alleviate poverty are typically focused on the redistribution of resources to individuals or households in need. The concept of disadvantage is arguably more complex, focusing on the interaction between lack of material resources and the provision of social services and supports. Thus, policies to address disadvantage are typically concerned with the distribution of a range of goods and services as well as resources (Oppenheim 1998: 12).

By contrast, social exclusion is generally defined in such a way as to include a number of characteristics which are not usually referred to in definitions of

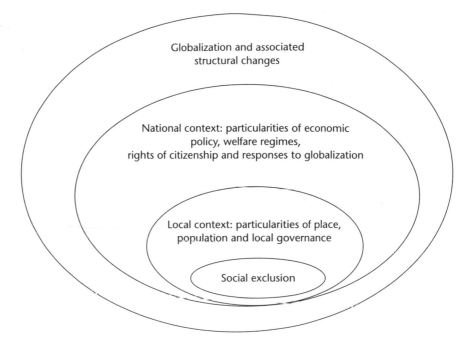

Figure 1.1   Social exclusion in context

poverty or disadvantage. The first is that social exclusion is seen in a wider context. In particular it is seen in the context of globalization and the structural changes brought about by globalization. Parkinson (1998: 1) describes these processes in the following terms:

> Rapid changes in the economic environment caused by international-isation and industrial and corporate restructuring have transformed the character of local economies. They have brought a more fragmented labour market, a decline in manufacturing and a rise in the service sector, high levels of structural unemployment, an increase in part time, insecure and low paid employment, a shift in the balance of male and female employment and a growing gap between the highest and lowest household incomes. These changes are not only found in cities where the economy is in decline or during periods of recession. They are also a feature of booming economies.

However, although social exclusion can be seen as a consequence of global phenomena, it is nevertheless affected by the *national* context, notably the particularities of national economic policies, welfare regimes and rights of citizenship, and indeed the *local* context – particularities of place, population and local governance (see Figure 1.1). Madanipour *et al.* write:

> Welfare regimes in each country reflect different principles of social organisation and normative bases. Different cities are differentially placed within the European economic and social space, some experiencing growth

and others in long-term decline. Urban socio-spatial structures vary. In some, social exclusion and spatial segregation are virtually synonymous. Others exhibit a more fine-grained pattern of differentiation. In some places, ethnicity and race form fundamental dividing lines in socio-spatial structures. In other places, cultural and kinship networks are more significant. Finally, specific patterns of local governance and welfare state provision affect local patterns of social exclusion.

(Madanipour *et al.* 1998: 9; see also Cousins 1998: 130–1)

While the causes of social exclusion may be structural, its effects can be ameliorated or exacerbated by the attitudes, activities and policies of governmental bodies. For example, despite the increasing importance of combating social exclusion within the EU and the focus on unemployment as a key part of the overall strategy, at the same time the push towards economic cohesion is resulting in some member states reducing social expenditure and thereby increasing the risk of poverty and exclusion.

The second key feature of social exclusion is that it can be seen as a process or set of processes rather than a static condition and, moreover, a set of processes largely outside the control of the individual. This avoids the 'trap', typical of at least some policies aimed at addressing poverty, of blaming the individual for their own plight. This has important implications both for the analysis of social exclusion and also for policy development.

The third key feature of social exclusion is that it is necessarily a 'relational' concept. Groups and individuals are socially excluded from other groups and individuals, and society as a whole. Thus:

structural processes affect the whole of society in ways which create barriers which prevent particular groups from forming those kinds of social relationships with other groups which are essential to realising a full human potential. It is not that some groups 'exclude' other groups, but that processes affecting the whole of society mean that some groups experience social boundaries as barriers preventing their full participation in the economic, political and cultural life of the society within which they live.

(Madanipour *et al.* 1998: 17)

This has the advantage of allowing a broader focus, not only on those who are excluded, but also on the systems that they are excluded from (Oppenheim 1998: 14). In particular it allows for policy responses which seek to change institutions and institutional processes rather than solely seeking to change socially excluded individuals, groups and communities.

Social exclusion can also be defined in terms of a lack of 'social capital' and, increasingly, the idea of developing social capital is being incorporated into policies and programmes to address social exclusion. Putnam (1993, 1995) defines social capital in terms of four features of communities: the existence of community networks; civic engagement or participation in community networks; a sense of community identity, solidarity and equality with other community members; and norms of trust and reciprocal help and support. There is increasing interest in, and research evidence relating to, social capital as an 'antidote' to social exclusion. In other words, there is evidence linking the extent and strength of community networks, the degree of community and civic participation and norms of trust and reciprocity with good health (see, for example, Gillies 1997; Kawachi *et al.* 1997; Campbell *et al.* 1999), effective and responsive public services and strong political institutions (see, for example, Boix and Posner 1998) and local economic development and economic prosperity (see, for example, Putnam 1993; Wilson 1997). Thus, developing social capital can create the conditions in which it is easier to address other aspects of social exclusion. This might be achieved by devoting resources to community development or by managers of public services considering how their activities in particular localities contribute to or negatively impact on social capital (Corrigan and King 1999: 15). However, Boix and Posner (1998: 687), in an article discussing the origins of social capital, note that 'a community's co-operative capacity is a function of the degree of social and political inequality that the community has experienced over the course of its historical development'. The implication is the obvious, but nevertheless important, point that social capital is more difficult to develop in those communities where there is little tradition of trust or reciprocity.

The growth in the use of the term social exclusion has not been universally welcomed. In particular Levitas (1996) has argued that the social exclusion discourse treats as abnormal the social divisions which are endemic to capitalist society, since the aim of policy is reintegration, primarily, to the labour market. As a result, Levitas argues, unpaid work is devalued and inequalities between paid workers are obscured. She goes on to identify three different approaches to social exclusion: the 'integrationist' approach which focuses on reintegrating those without work into the labour market; the 'poverty' approach which links the causes of exclusion primarily to low income and lack of resources; and the 'underclass' approach which blames the excluded themselves for their situation and goes on to link this to individual moral failings. Aspects of all these approaches can be found in various strands of UK policy towards social exclusion.

Towards an analytical framework

A framework for analysing social exclusion needs, therefore, to take account of these key features: that social exclusion occurs as a result of structural change but is played out through and affected by the specificity of local circumstances, policy frameworks and welfare regimes; that it connotes a process or set of processes rather than an 'end-state'; and that it is a relational concept. In addition, social exclusion is a multidimensional phenomenon and, furthermore, the various 'dimensions' of social exclusion are typically mutually reinforcing. Thus an individual or group is more likely to be vulnerable to exclusionary processes when they experience difficulties in relation to more than one of the dimensions of social exclusion.

Dimensions of social exclusion

In the first annual report on poverty and social exclusion (Department of Social Security 1999: 24–6), the 'key features of poverty and social exclusion' are identified. These are as follows:

- lack of opportunities to work;
- lack of opportunities to acquire education and skills;
- childhood deprivation;
- disrupted families;
- barriers to older people living active, fulfilling and healthy lives;
- inequalities in health;
- poor housing;
- poor neighbourhoods;
- fear of crime;
- disadvantaged groups.

A rather different approach is adopted by Burchardt *et al.* (1999: 231) who identify five dimensions of social exclusion in terms of the 'normal activities' in which it is important that citizens participate. These dimensions are as follows:

1 Consumption activity: relates to traditional measures of poverty.
2 Savings activity: includes pensions, savings, home ownership.
3 Production activity: defined in terms of 'engaging in an economically or socially valued activity, such as paid work, education or training, retirement . . . or looking after a family'.
4 Political activity: defined as 'engaging in some collective effort to improve or protect the immediate or wider social or physical environment'.
5 Social activity: defined as 'engaging in significant social interaction with family, or friends, and identifying with a cultural group or community'.

Burchardt *et al.* go on to note that an individual's ability to participate in these activities will be affected by a range of interconnected factors including: their own personal characteristics and life histories; the characteristics of the area in which they live; and the social, civil and political institutions with which they have to interact. Furthermore, they recognise that participation or non-participation on any one of these dimensions is likely to have implications for participation on the others (Burchardt *et al.* 1999: 232).

In Table 1.1 I identify a number of 'dimensions' of social exclusion which are similar to those discussed above but incorporate other aspects which I consider to be important. These dimensions are discussed briefly below but are elaborated on in the subsequent chapters of this book.

The economic dimension

While social exclusion cannot be reduced to economic factors, economic factors are undoubtedly a key aspect of social exclusion. Economic factors are taken as encompassing not only poverty, defined in terms of lack of an adequate income, but also exclusion from the labour market. This, in turn, has a number of different aspects to it that go beyond unemployment. It will certainly include length of unemployment and households in which no working-age adults are in employment. But it might also include other changes affecting the labour market such as casualization, decreasing job security and fragile attachment to the labour market. The chapters by Campbell (Chapter 2) and Burden (Chapter 3) in this volume address the issues of labour market exclusion and poverty respectively.

Table 1.1 Dimensions of social exclusion

Dimension	Indicators
Economic	Long-term unemployment Casualization and job insecurity Workless households Income poverty
Social	Breakdown of traditional households Unwanted teenage pregnancies Homelessness Crime Disaffected youth
Political	Disempowerment Lack of political rights Low registration of voters Low voter turnout Low levels of community activity Alienation/lack of confidence in political processes Social disturbance/disorder
Neighbourhood	Environmental degradation Decaying housing stock Withdrawal of local services Collapse of support networks
Individual	Mental and physical ill health Educational underachievement/low skills Loss of self-esteem/confidence
Spatial	Concentration/marginalization of vulnerable groups
Group	Concentration of above characteristics in particular groups: elderly, disabled, ethnic minorities

The social dimension

It is along the social dimension of social exclusion that the Social Exclusion Unit has, thus far, largely focused its attention. This dimension can be taken to include: the breakdown of traditional households, the rise in the numbers of unwanted teenage pregnancies, homelessness, crime and disaffected youth. One of the interesting questions here is the relationship of these social variables to the economic ones identified above. The issue of housing and homelessness is addressed by Hawtin and Kettle (Chapter 6) and other social aspects are addressed in the chapter on health by Moran and Simpkins (Chapter 5) and the chapter on socially excluded groups by Burden and Hamm (Chapter 10).

The political dimension

The main issue here is individuals' ability to participate in or influence decision making which affects their lives. This may happen in a number of different ways. Individuals may be excluded from having political rights because of their immigration status. They may exclude themselves from formal processes by not registering to vote. This may be due to inertia, apathy, transience or the wish to evade officialdom. Of those who are registered a significant proportion fail to vote in local and national elections. However, formal political processes do not encapsulate political activity in its entirety. Other forms of political activity include participation in community fora of various kinds such as tenants' organizations, school governing bodies, pressure groups, service user groups and so on. All of these bodies will have some impact on decision making and the quality of local life. Non-participation contributes to disempowerment. Disengagement from socially acceptable forms of political participation and distrust of formal channels of communication can combine with a sense of frustration and anger to create the potential, if not the actuality, of social disorder. The issue of political exclusion is addressed by Percy-Smith in Chapter 8 and community activity is discussed by Chanan in Chapter 11.

The neighbourhood dimension

Analysis of the neighbourhood dimension of social exclusion is clearly related to both the social and spatial aspects. At the level of the neighbourhood the indicators of social exclusion might include environmental degradation, a decaying housing stock, the withdrawal of local services (e.g. shops, public transport), increasingly overstretched public services and the collapse of local support networks (related to the political aspects of social exclusion, namely low levels of participation in community and voluntary activities). The neighbourhood dimension of social exclusion is addressed by Sanderson (Chapter 7) in relation to access to services on the part of excluded communities, by Hawtin and Kettle (Chapter 6) in relation to housing, and by Percy-Smith (Chapter 8) and Chanan (Chapter 11) in relation to community involvement.

The individual dimension

All of the aspects of social exclusion discussed so far impact upon the individual. The form that this impact typically takes is in terms of increasing levels of physical and mental ill health, educational underachievement and failure to acquire or update skills, and low self-esteem. Walton (Chapter 4) discusses educational underachievement and low levels of skills, and Moran and Simpkins (Chapter 5) analyse the relationship between health status and social exclusion.

The spatial dimension

The spatial dimension of exclusion is important since it typically results in large numbers of disadvantaged people living together in a decaying area. This can lead to the area itself being defined as disadvantaged irrespective of the characteristics of the individuals who live there, and becoming subject to further exclusionary process (e.g. withdrawal of local services) as a result. It also results in the area becoming highly visible which can be double-edged – on the one hand resulting (perhaps) in the area becoming the focus for policy initiatives, and on the other resulting in 'place discrimination' by employers. A focus on place also results in the large numbers of socially excluded individuals scattered throughout the rest of the population becoming largely invisible. However, social exclusion might also affect localities not because of the concentration of socially excluded individuals and households within the population but because of the nature of the area itself. For example, geographically isolated rural areas might fall into this category, or areas traditionally dependent on a single industry which is now in decline. The effectiveness of area-based responses to social exclusion is a central theme developed by Hutchinson (Chapter 9) and is also addressed by Sanderson (Chapter 7) in relation to access to services.

The group dimension

Certain groups are arguably at greater risk of social exclusion either because they differ in some way from the dominant population or because of their position within society. In the first case individuals or groups who, to some degree, do not accept the values, norms or lifestyle of mainstream society are more vulnerable if they are also affected by one or more of the other dimensions of social exclusion. Nationality, ethnicity, language and religion are obvious aspects of group difference. Less obvious aspects might include lifestyle, personal and social values or characteristics. In all of these cases there is the risk that 'difference' leads to discrimination and unequal access to the labour market. In the second case we might include groups who, because of their circumstances, are particularly vulnerable. Examples of such groups include elderly people dependent on state benefits, lone parents and young people not in education or training and without a job.

An important aspect of social exclusion is its complex nature. Thus, one cannot simply 'read off' social exclusion from the presence or absence of any one of these characteristics. It is the way in which they interrelate and reinforce each other that accelerates the process of social exclusion. So to assume that, because a young person from an ethnic minority group is unemployed, she or he is also socially excluded is to grossly oversimplify. He or she may have had a good education and be supported by strong social and kinship support networks which overcome the disadvantage of being unemployed. Similarly, having a low income does not mean that a person is necessarily outside the mainstream of society. A good example here is students in higher education, many of whom are lacking in financial resources but who, in no sense, could be considered to be socially excluded. This has important implications for both the analysis of social exclusion and the development of effective strategies to combat it. The situation of groups that are widely viewed as being vulnerable is addressed in many of the chapters in this volume, as is the impact of policy on such groups. However, the complex issues relating to socially excluded groups more generally is addressed specifically by Burden and Hamm in Chapter 10.

Indicators of social exclusion

In order to develop effective policies to respond to social exclusion it is necessary to first identify the individuals, groups or areas that are affected. In most cases this involves developing 'indicators' which act as proxies for the condition of social exclusion. This facilitates the identification of *groups* or *individuals* within the population (e.g. lone parents, disabled people) who are, on the basis of the available evidence, thought to be more likely to be at risk of social exclusion, or of *geographical areas* which exhibit certain characteristics which are correlated with disadvantage and social exclusion. Furthermore, indicators are necessary in order to establish baselines against which progress can then be measured (see Chapter 12).

However, the development of indicators is not unproblematic. Most indicators of poverty, disadvantage and social exclusion represent 'snapshots' at a particular point in time. And, as we have seen, two of the distinctive aspects of the concept of social exclusion (in contrast to poverty and disadvantage) are that first it is taken to refer to a dynamic process and second it emphasizes the interconnectedness of the various dimensions and characteristics of social exclusion. This makes social exclusion considerably harder to measure than poverty and disadvantage. It requires longitudinal data to capture the effect of time on exclusionary processes and it requires sophisticated data that demonstrates the way in which different aspects of exclusion work together to reinforce each other and exacerbate the situation of individuals, households and areas.

Most data that is available can give us an indication of groups who are at risk from social exclusion, or can be used to define spatial areas which exhibit the characteristics associated with various aspects of deprivation and disadvantage. In addition, existing data can give us a picture of particular dimensions of social exclusion. However, Robinson and Oppenheim (1998: 5–6) argue that indicators should also conform to certain criteria. They should:

- be easily understood by the public and congruent with their concerns;
- be relatively easy to quantify;
- follow international conventions;
- have a 'dynamic' dimension;
- be able to be operationalized at the local area level.

Based on these principles, Robinson and Oppenheim propose indicators for income poverty, exclusion from the labour market, exclusion in education and health.

Opportunity for All (Department of Social Security 1999) reviews progress in relation to policy initiatives aimed at addressing poverty and social exclusion in relation to three population groups: children and young people, people of working age and older people. The indicators against which progress is being measured are summarized in Table 1.2. Not surprisingly these indicators are all ones which are relatively easy to measure in quantifiable terms. However, some aspects of social exclusion as I have defined it above are no so amenable to measurement in this way. For example, I have argued that multidimensionality and interconnectedness are two key aspects of social exclusion; it is difficult to measure or assess these. Similarly I have argued that social exclusion has implications for community and political participation and is related to the concept of social capital. However, once again it is rather more difficult to identify meaningful indicators for these facets of social exclusion. Sanderson (Chapter 12) develops this theme further and proposes a possible framework for evaluating the impact of policy responses to social exclusion which takes account of these and other issues.

Table 1.2 Poverty and social exclusion indicators

Theme	Indicators

Children and young people	1 An increase in the proportion of 7-year-old Sure Start children achieving Level 1 or above in KS1 (Key Stage 1) English and maths.
	2 Health outcomes in Sure Start areas:
	  • reduction in the proportion of low birth-weight babies;
	  • reduction in the rate of hospital admissions as a result of serious injury.
	3 Increase in the proportion of those aged 11 achieving Level 4 or above in KS2 (Key Stage 2) tests for literacy and numeracy.
	4 Reduction in the proportion of truancies and exclusions from school.
	5 Increase in the proportion of 19-year-olds with at least a Level 2 qualification or equivalent.
	6 Reduction in the proportion of children living in workless households.
	7 Low income indicators:
	  • reduction in the proportion of children in households with relatively low incomes;
	  • reduction in the proportion of children in households with low incomes in an absolute sense;
	  • reduction in the proportion of children with persistently low incomes.
	8 Reduction in the proportion of children living in poor housing.
	9 Reduction in the proportion of households with children experiencing fuel poverty.
	10 Reduction in the rate at which children are admitted to hospital as a result of unintentional injury resulting in a hospital stay of no longer than three days.
	11 Reduction in the proportion of 16–18-year-olds not in education or training.
	12 Improvement in the educational attainment of children looked after by local authorities.
	13 Reduction in the rate of conceptions for those aged under 18 and an increase in the proportion of teenage parents in education, employment or training.

People of working age	14 Increase in the proportion of working-age people in employment over the economic cycle. 15 Reduction in the proportion of working-age people living in workless households, for households of a given size, over the economic cycle. 16 Reduction in the number of working-age people living in families claiming Income Support or income-based Job-Seekers' Allowance who have been claiming these benefits for long periods of time.

Table 1.2   *(cont'd)*

Theme	Indicators
	17 Increase in the employment rates of disadvantaged groups – people with disabilities, lone parents, ethnic minorities and the over 50s – and a reduction in the difference between their employment rates and the overall rate.
	18 Low income indicators: • reduction in the proportion of working-age people in households with relatively low incomes; • reduction in the proportion of working-age people in households with low incomes in an absolute sense; • reduction in the proportion of people of working age with persistently low incomes.
	19 Increase in the proportion of working-age people with a qualification.
	20 Reduction in the number of people sleeping rough.
	21 Reduction in cocaine and heroin use by young people.
	22 Reduction in adult smoking rates in all social classes.
	23 Reduction in the death rates from suicide and undetermined injury.
Older people	24 Increase in the proportion of working-age people contributing to a non-state pension.
	25 Increase in the amount contributed to non-state pensions.
	26 Increase in the proportion of working-age individuals who have contributed to a non-state pension in at least three years out of the last four.
	27 Low income indicators: • reduction in the proportion of older people in households with relatively low incomes; • reduction in the proportion of older people in households with low incomes in an absolute sense; • reduction in the proportion of older people with persistently low incomes.
	28 Reduction in the proportion of elderly households experiencing fuel poverty.
	29 Reduction in the proportion of older people whose lives are affected by fear of crime.
	30 Increase in healthy life expectancy at age 65.
	31 Reduction in the proportion of households containing at least one person aged 75 or more living in poor housing.
	32 Increase in the proportion of older people being helped to live independently.

Source: Department of Social Security (1999: 5–7)

Policy responses to social exclusion: themes and issues

The chapters in this book are concerned with the dimensions and aspects of social exclusion identified above. Each presents the context within which policy is being developed, discusses the evidence relating to the particular aspect of social exclusion under scrutiny, outlines current policy developments and provides an assessment of the effectiveness of those interventions. Despite important differences between policy areas, there are a number of themes and issues which run through many of the chapters. It is these themes that are the subject of this final section.

Definitions

The first of these themes is the importance of definitions: how social exclusion is defined can determine the scope of the policy response – what issues are to be addressed, which groups or areas are to be targeted? Furthermore, how social exclusion is defined inevitably has a political or ideological element. For example, Burden (Chapter 3) discusses the relationship between social exclusion, poverty and inequality and argues that the current emphasis on social exclusion effectively rules out policies designed to achieve greater equality through redistribution. Similarly, Moran and Simpkins (Chapter 5) note the change in emphasis implied by the shift in terminology from health *inequalities* to health *variations*.

The concept social exclusion implies exclusion *from* something – typically participation in those activities that are considered to be 'normal' or 'desirable'. This clearly has a normative element. While most people would probably agree that citizens *should* have access to adequate housing, a reasonable level of income, health care services and so on, there may be less agreement on the *level* of provision or the *terms and conditions* governing the provision of certain goods and services. This is particularly apparent in relation to labour market exclusion – undoubtedly an important element in most definitions of social exclusion but arguably given undue prominence in terms of policy responses (see Chapter 11). The prominence given to labour market reintegration is partly due to arguments relating unemployment to other aspects of social exclusion, but is also strongly linked to the importance assigned to the idea of individual independence. However, it can be argued that the primacy given to independence and labour market reintegration in policy terms has deleterious effects for those groups who are unable to be fully independent or participate fully in the labour market, and diverts attention from other aspects of social exclusion such as political exclusion (see Chapter 8).

Multidimensionality is a key element in the definition of social exclusion; it is the fact that disadvantage in relation to one aspect of life is linked to disadvantage in other areas that predisposes individuals, households and neighbourhoods to become socially excluded. The chapters in this volume document numerous examples of these linkages. For example, Campbell (Chapter 2) and Walton (Chapter 4) highlight the relationship between educational underachievement and lack of skills and long-term unemployment; Moran and Simpkins (Chapter 5) discuss the relationship between health status and socioeconomic group and note the link between suicide and unemployment; Hawtin and Kettle (Chapter 6) discuss the relationship between poverty and bad housing and also between residualized estates and high levels of crime. However, while it is relatively easy to correlate different dimensions of social exclusion it is much more difficult to analyse the nature of the relationships between variables and the psychosocial processes that underpin them. Social exclusion is, necessarily, a complex phenomenon that requires complex policy interventions.

Developing effective policy

A further theme that emerges from the following chapters is the way in which past policy interventions have created or contributed to current problems. This is particularly evident in relation to social housing (see Chapter 6). As Hawtin and Kettle demonstrate, current residualization of local authority housing can be viewed as a direct result of past housing allocations policy and the 'Right to Buy' legislation. Sanderson (Chapter 7) discusses the impact on disadvantaged localities of the marketization and deregulation of certain key public services (such as education, housing, health and transport) that was a feature of policy in the 1980s and early 1990s. And Walton (Chapter 4) discusses the way in which the introduction of school league tables has intensified the pressure on schools to exclude pupils who are unlikely to make a positive contribution to their Standard Assessment Tests (SATs) results.

What this demonstrates is the need for current policy interventions to be 'evidence based' – that is, developed in the light of a clear understanding of the nature and causes of the problem and an assessment of the likely impact of particular kinds of policy intervention. Campbell (Chapter 2) highlights this as an issue in his discussion of long-term unemployment which can be seen both as a primary economic *cause* of social exclusion and as an important *consequence* of social exclusion. He concludes: 'Problem mis-specification leads to policy mis-specification and thus to failure'. Similarly Moran and Simpkins (Chapter 5), in their discussion of the connection between health and social exclusion, note that the nature of the connection is not always clear. This gives added importance, as Sanderson argues (Chapter 12), to evaluation and assessment of what works in what circumstances. The complexity of social exclusion as a phenomenon requires complex interventions and therefore complex evaluation frameworks which take account of the need to examine outcomes not only for individuals, but also for households, communities, localities and regions. Furthermore, complex policy interventions entail multiple 'stakeholders' who may hold different views as to what would constitute a successful outcome of a policy intervention.

In seeking to develop our understanding of social exclusion we should not neglect the importance of locality in determining its precise nature and characteristics and, indeed, what might be possible or appropriate in policy terms, while at the same time recognizing the limits to what local action can achieve given the wider context and causes of social exclusion (see Chapters 7 and 11). Chanan (Chapter 11) notes that social exclusion is a 'multi-layered phenomenon' involving interaction between people and places, and Sanderson (Chapter 7) argues that locality has an important influence on whether individuals or groups can gain access to certain resources such as public welfare services. He notes the connection between 'poor services' and 'poor places'.

Joined-up working

Social exclusion is multidimensional and therefore has implications for a wide range of agencies and organizations. The need for holistic, 'joined-up' partnership and multi-agency responses to social exclusion is an important thread running through the discussion of policy in the following chapters. The partnership approach is also intended to open the way for 'policy innovation', to 'overcome the compartmentalisation of policy issues inside the domains of separate agencies' and to 'facilitate new alliances and ways of understanding and reacting to problems' (Geddes 1998: 22). Partnership is a feature of many if not most of the initiatives discussed including local Learning Partnerships, local Learning and Skills Councils, Education Action Zones, Education Business Partnerships and New Start (discussed in Chapter 4), Health Action Zones (discussed in Chapter 5), the Single Regeneration Budget and the New Deal for communities (discussed in Chapter 9). The Policy Action Teams set up by the Social Exclusion Unit to examine a wide range of 'cross-cutting' issues are likely to be important catalysts for the development of 'joined-up' thinking and policy solutions. Indeed without this there is a risk that the huge range of current policy initiatives will exacerbate fragmentation. It could be argued, as Sanderson notes (Chapter 7) that the need for partnership working arises in part as a direct result of the policy of fragmenting powers and responsibilities between agencies and the corresponding erosion of power and responsibility of local authorities that has occurred since the 1970s.

Individuals and institutions

In policy terms there is increasing recognition that the 'silo' mentality of local and central government can frustrate effective implementation of policy, and that policies need to be delivered appropriately. However, for many people in the poorest areas their interaction with public services continues to be problematic and exacerbates the powerlessness that is concomitant with their disadvantage. As Chanan observes (Chapter 11) disadvantaged people are 'pinned down' by their locality and are dependent on local services. By contrast he argues that 'included people can engage with their locality to a variable, freely chosen degree'. In the poorest areas public services are frequently overstretched and inadequate. Marketization of public services and social disinvestment contribute to a decline in social capital, exacerbating social exclusion and the marginalization of poor communities (see Sanderson, Chapter 7).

Walton (Chapter 4) also highlights the relationship between institutional factors and individuals' characteristics in her discussion of the reasons for the relatively high proportion of black boys who are excluded from schools. In this case institutional racism results in low expectations of black boys on the part of teachers, contributing to a downward spiral of low aspirations and eventual disaffection. This point is reinforced by Burden and Hamm (Chapter 10) who emphasize the importance of institutional processes in the creation of unnecessary barriers to full participation on the part of people with disabilities. Hawtin and Kettle (Chapter 6) make the point in relation to social housing that the way in which housing is provided may be as important as the provision itself. As a result they emphasize the importance of participatory approaches to housing management. In Chapter 8, Percy-Smith identifies disaffection with and lack of confidence in political organizations and processes as an important cause of non-participation, social disorder and disturbance.

Targeting

Many of the policy responses discussed in this book involve targeting particular individuals, groups or areas. The various 'zone' initiatives, which are spatially targeted, have already been mentioned and Hutchinson (Chapter 9) discusses the spatial aspects of regeneration policies. In addition, Campbell (Chapter 2) notes the targeting of labour market policies on young people, lone parents, disabled people and the long-term unemployed, and Walton (Chapter 4) notes the targeting of education and training initiatives particularly on lone parents and disaffected youth. However, both spatial targeting and targeting of groups are problematic.

First, it is very difficult to identify individuals, groups or areas who should be the focus of targeted actions. Spatial targeting, especially, is dependent on the use of indicators of deprivation and disadvantage which are combined to provide a composite deprivation 'score'. However, there are various indicators which might be chosen and ways in which they might be combined, producing significantly different outcomes. Indicators are proxies for social exclusion, not the 'real thing'.

Second, social exclusion is not an 'all or nothing' phenomenon; targeting a particular group or area will inevitably result in needy people being missed. Furthermore, as we have already seen, social exclusion is a dynamic process and, as Burden notes (Chapter 3), many people living on the margins of disadvantage fall in and out of poverty as a result of small changes in their circumstances. This suggests that risk or insecurity might usefully be included in indicators of social exclusion.

Third, targeting can exacerbate negative perceptions of particular areas or groups. For example, Campbell (Chapter 2) and Hutchinson (Chapter 9) discuss 'post-code discrimination' on the part of employers; Hawtin and Kettle (Chapter 6) discuss the possible stigmatization of people living on 'the worst estates' and of disabled people living in 'special needs housing'; and Burden (Chapter 3) discusses the stigmatizing effect of claiming means-tested benefits.

Fourth, targeting of groups in effect assumes a degree of homogeneity among members of that group. Burden and Hamm (Chapter 10) highlight the dangers of assuming homogeneity among minority ethnic groups. There are significant differences in the experiences of people from different ethnic groups which have important implications for policy. A number of other contributors to this volume stress the importance of differentiating within groups in order to meet needs effectively (see Chapters 2, 4 and 5).

Finally, targeting can conflict with the principle of universalism which is embedded in certain aspects of welfare policy (see Chapter 5 in relation to health care and Chapter 3 in relation to benefits).

Status zero

Walton (Chapter 4) questions whether current policy interventions aimed at young people are likely to reach those individuals who are most disaffected – the 'status zero' group who are not in education, training, employment or involved in any of the targeted initiatives. She notes the tendency to focus policy on those groups where the possibilities for a successful outcome are greatest. Similarly, Campbell (Chapter 2) relates the possibility of success in relation to labour market policies to the characteristics of the local economy: successful policy is more difficult in areas where there is little employment growth. Hutchinson (Chapter 9) draws attention to the tension in regeneration policy between targeting resources on those areas in greatest need and targeting resources on those areas which put forward the most competitive bid in terms of the likelihood of achieving desired outcomes. Percy-Smith (Chapter 8) notes the difficulties of involving in policy and decision making those groups who are probably most in need of an effective voice.

This issue also relates to the timescales allowed for effective intervention. Typically the problems and policies discussed in this book require long-term intervention. In relation to health, Moran and Simpkins (Chapter 5) argue that there are 'no quick fixes' for reducing health inequalities; intervention needs to be linked to long-term community development. As a result, as Sanderson argues (Chapter 12), outcomes need to be assessed over the long term. However, it may also be the case (as Chanan notes in Chapter 11) that some of the processes involved in tackling social exclusion (for example, building up community activity and networks) should be seen as an end in themselves not just as a means of delivering a specific policy outcome.

Moral agenda

The final theme that runs through this book is the moral agenda that seems to underpin many of the policy interventions discussed. This has a number of different aspects to it. First there is the importance attached to independence as a primary requirement of social inclusion. This is most evident in relation to labour market policy and is epitomized in the slogan 'welfare to work' which might be recast in terms of 'dependence to independence'. This has important implications for the status of, and attitudes towards, those who may be unable to achieve full independence – for example, people with disabilities or those who do not want 'independence' on the terms that it is being offered to them. An important example here is lone parents who are subject to enormous pressure to enter the labour market, a pressure that is not generally applied to mothers in two-parent households.

A second aspect to this moral agenda is the intolerant attitudes towards and punitive treatment of those who are considered to be deviant or non-conforming. There are clear echoes here, as Burden (Chapter 3) notes, of the Victorian notion of the 'deserving' and 'undeserving' poor. Those who wilfully refuse to conform to the activities and behaviour considered to be 'normal' or desirable may be subject to punitive interventions or interventions that are in some way conditional on 'good behaviour' (see Chapter 10). This can be seen as a threat to diversity. However, as Burden and Hamm note, there are contradictory aspects to New Labour's approach: on the one hand there is evidence of liberalization in relation to some aspects of the law relating to homosexual activity, while at the same time there is increasing emphasis on the two-parent, heterosexual nuclear family as the 'first choice' for bringing up children.

This normative element to policy raises important questions in relation to how to address those who are deemed to have voluntarily excluded themselves. There is a strand in New Labour thinking which suggests that such voluntary self-exclusion itself constitutes a social problem and as such is the legitimate target for possibly punitive action. A good example of this is the policies aimed at 'clearing the streets' of rough sleepers and beggars.

This final question – whether, how and on what terms policy interventions can reach the most excluded groups – brings us back to the definitional and normative issues raised earlier. If policy interventions are successful in integrating *some* of those who are currently excluded into the norms and activities of mainstream society, what then is the situation of those who are left behind? Will it be the case that the definitions and parameters of social exclusion will simply have been shifted in such a way that such people are constituted as a more or less permanently excluded group, an 'underclass' which is deemed to be outside the scope of effective policy interventions? This remains a question which is largely not addressed and certainly not answered by current policy interventions.

References

Boix, C. and Posner, D.N. (1998) Social capital: explaining its origins and effects on government performance. *British Journal of Political Science*, 28(4): 686–93.

Burchardt, T., Le Grand, J. and Piachaud, D. (1999) Social exclusion in Britain 1991–1995. *Social Policy and Administration*, 33(3): 227–44.

Campbell, C. with Wood, R. and Kelly, M. (1999) *Social Capital and Health*. London: Health Education Authority.

Commission of the European Communities (1993) *Background Report: Social Exclusion – Poverty and Other Social Problems in the European Community*, ISEC/B11/93. Luxembourg: Office for Official Publications of the European Communities.

Corrigan, P. and King, E. (1999) Cash in on social capital. *Local Government Chronicle*, 13 August: 15.

Cousins, C. (1998) Social exclusion in Europe: paradigms of social disadvantage in Germany, Spain, Sweden and the United Kingdom. *Policy and Politics*, 26(2): 127–46.

Department of Social Security (1999) *Opportunity for All: Tackling Poverty and Social Exclusion*, Cm 4445. London: The Stationery Office.

European Commission (1997) *First Report on Economics and Social Cohesion 1996*. Luxembourg: Office for Official Publications of the European Communities.

Geddes, M. (1998) *Local Partnership: A Successful Strategy for Social Cohesion.* Dublin: European Foundation for the Improvement of Living and Working Conditions.

Geyer, R. (1999) Can EU social policy save the Social Exclusion Unit and vice versa? *Politics*, 19(3): 159–64.

Gillies, P. (1997) Social capital: recognising the value of society. *Healthlines*, September: 15–17.

Jordan, B. (1997) *A Theory of Poverty and Social Exclusion.* Cambridge: Polity Press.

Kawachi, I., Kennedy, B.P., Lochner, K. and Prothrow-Stith, D. (1997) Social capital, income inequality and mortality. *American Journal of Public Health*, 87(9): 1491–8.

Lee, P. and Murie, A. (1999) *Literature Review of Social Exclusion.* Edinburgh: The Stationery Office.

Levitas, R. (1996) The concept of social exclusion and the new Durkheimian hegemony. *Critical Social Policy*, 16(46): 5–20.

Madanipour, A., Cars, G. and Allen, J. (eds) (1998) *Social Exclusion in European Cities: Processes, Experiences and Responses.* London: Jessica Kingsley.

Northern Ireland Office (1998) *Partnership for Equality: The Government's Proposals for Future Legislation and Policies on Employment Equality in Northern Irreland*, Cm 3890. London: The Stationery Office.

Oppenheim, C. (ed.) (1998) *An Inclusive Society: Strategies for Tackling Poverty.* London: IPPR.

Parkinson, M. (1998) *Combating Social Exclusion: Lessons from Area-based Programmes in Europe.* Bristol: The Policy Press.

Putnam, R. (1993) The prosperous community: social capital and economic growth. *The American Prospect*, 13: 35–42.

Putnam, R. (1995) Bowling alone: America's declining social capital. *Journal of Democracy*, 6(1): 65–78.

Room, G. (ed.) (1995) *Beyond the Threshold: The Measurement and Analysis of Social Exclusion.* Bristol: The Policy Press.

Scottish Office (1999) *Social Inclusion: Opening the Door to a Better Scotland.* Edinburgh: Scottish Office.

Social Exclusion Unit (1997) *Social Exclusion Unit: Purpose, Work Priorities and Working Methods.* London: HMSO.

Social Exclusion Unit (1998) *Bringing Britain Together: A National Strategy for Neighbourhood Renewal*, Cm 4045. London: The Stationery Office.

Welsh Office (1999) *Building an Inclusive Wales: Tackling the Social Exclusion Agenda.* Cardiff: Welsh Office.

Wilson, P.A. (1997) Building social capital: a learning agenda for the twenty-first century. *Urban Studies*, 34(5–6): 745–60.

2 LABOUR MARKET EXCLUSION AND INCLUSION

Mike Campbell

Introduction

Long-term unemployment is both a key characteristic and a primary economic cause of social exclusion and, in consequence, policies to reduce labour market exclusion are crucial to creating a more inclusive society. This chapter examines the main policy responses to labour market exclusion in the UK and the European Union (EU). First, I outline the nature and extent of long-term unemployment, the broad contours of the changes which have made the issue an ever-greater challenge for public policy, and its key causes. The second part of the chapter assesses current UK and EU policy, through an examination of both the policy frameworks and the concrete policy actions which have been formulated to tackle labour market exclusion. Finally, I conclude by outlining the prospects for future policy development, focusing on the gaps and weaknesses in current policy, in order to identify a range of adjustments that could enhance policy effectiveness.

The nature and extent of labour market exclusion

Exclusion from the labour market is most clearly identified empirically by the duration of people's non-participation in paid work. This represents their 'distance' from employment opportunities, both because of the 'scarring' effects of unemployment on confidence, motivation and employer perception of individuals' worth, and because of the rapid changes in the nature of work and the labour market which increasingly 'separate' those not involved in the process from those who experience it. Of course, people are only excluded in this way if they seek to be 'included' (i.e. they want a job) but are not able to be so. In consequence the meaning and measurement of what constitutes long-term unemployment becomes in itself an important policy issue.

The unemployed have traditionally been identified as those who are in receipt of unemployment benefit or, more recently, who qualify for the Job-Seekers' Allowance (JSA). However, 50 per cent leave the unemployment register within three months and 80 per cent within six months. In this sense it becomes clear that *long-term* unemployment is a much more useful measure of exclusion than unemployment per se.

This 'administrative' count of the 'claimant' unemployed is defective for at least two reasons. Some of those who are 'registered' as unemployed may not in reality be seriously seeking employment. On the other hand some who are not registered may be seriously seeking employment. In consequence a survey-based method of identifying the unemployed is superior – when individuals are asked if they are available for work and seeking it. This is the case with the so-called International Labour Organization (ILO) definition of unemployment, adopted by the UK government in 1998, and which is calculated through the Labour Force Survey. It is based on those who are available to start work within two weeks and who had looked for a job in the previous month. The number of ILO unemployed in the UK is currently about 450,000 above the claimant level – an unemployment rate differential of about 1.5 percentage points (summer 1997 figures). The 'gap' is considerably greater for women than men (around half a percentage point in the latter case but over three percentage points in the former case). However, in relation to long-term unemployment, the gap between ILO and claimant rates is much smaller, being overall around half a percentage point, or 150,000 people.

Even the ILO figures, however, do not fully capture the scale of labour market exclusion because a proportion of the economically 'inactive' (those who are not currently available for work nor have actively sought it recently) nonetheless want a job, but cannot work for a range of reasons including current incapacity, child/dependant care or 'discouragement' – i.e. believing there are no jobs available for them. Indeed there are 2.3 million people in this category (as at 1998) compared to 1.8 million ILO unemployed.

Thus, clear identification of those who are excluded from the labour market is in part dependent on who is considered to be seeking work. Moreover, these numbers vary over the economic cycle, with exclusion diminishing in booms and increasing in recession, clearly implying a relatively 'porous' definition of exclusion. There is, however, an underlying upward trend in inactivity among men since 1991. Furthermore, because exclusion is as much a process as an empirical phenomenon, there is disagreement as to what constitutes 'long-term' unemployment and thus 'exclusion' – 6 months or 12 months? Furthermore, should it be different for different groups? Moreover, most *policy* in the UK is still focused on those actually in receipt of the JSA while the EU policy framework focuses more on those actively seeking work whatever their benefit status. In this chapter I will generally focus on the ILO-defined 'excluded' for measurement purposes, as this, broadly, is the current practice in the UK and throughout the EU.

In autumn 1998 the ILO unemployment in the UK was 6.2 per cent or 1.79 million people. This unemployment rate was the sixth lowest in the EU – less than in Italy, Spain, France or Germany, but more than in the Netherlands or Denmark. Of these people, 516,000 had been unemployed continuously for 12 months or more – i.e. some 29 per cent of the unemployed, giving a long-term unemployment rate of 1.8 per cent. The numbers had fallen rapidly over the previous year – over 650,000 had been unemployed for 12 months or more in autumn 1997. The male rate substantially exceeds the female rate (unusual in a EU context). The gap between the two has been getting wider since 1990, though it did diminish a little in 1998. In terms of age, the rates are highest among men aged between 50 and 64, with the proportion who are long-term unemployed accounting for 42 per cent of unemployed 50–64-year-olds compared to just 19 per cent of 20–29-year-olds (ONS 1998). Rates also vary by social class, previous occupation and previous industry, with those formerly in manual craft and 'unskilled' occupations being particularly badly affected. Black people and those of Pakistani or Bangladeshi origin also suffer higher rates of unemployment: 20 per cent among the former and 23 per cent among the latter, compared to 7 per cent for whites in 1997 (DfEE 1998).

There is also an increasing polarization between 'work rich' and 'work poor' households. The proportion of households in which no one is economically active has risen from 8 per cent to 18 per cent in the last 20 years – the fourth highest among the Organization for Economic Cooperation and Development (OECD) countries. The proportion of the unemployed who live in such households now accounts for 60 per cent of the total (Gregg and Wadsworth 1998).

Most striking, perhaps, is the close association between qualifications and unemployment. The unemployment rate among those with a degree is 3.5 per cent, among those with two A levels or equivalent, 5.3 per cent, among those with five GCSEs at A–C or equivalent, 7.3 per cent, and among those with no qualifications, 12.4 per cent. Moreover the proportion of the unemployed who have been so for more than one year is, for example, 25 per cent among those with five GCSEs but 48 per cent for those with no qualifications (ONS 1998).

Finally, long-term unemployment varies enormously geographically. Thirty-seven per cent of the claimant long-term unemployed are concentrated in just 10 per cent of local authority districts (Campbell *et al.* 1998). ILO unemployment and inactivity are even more concentrated (Green and Owen 1998; Gregg and Wadsworth 1998).

The causes of long-term unemployment

In a market economy large volumes of job destruction and creation 'naturally' occur and will necessarily give rise to spells of unemployment for some of those changing jobs, unless labour markets operate with instantaneous perfection. However, it is the persistence of unemployment (Snower 1994) that is the real problem. Why should unemployment be of long duration? Why should the long-term unemployed find it more difficult to become re-employed? Why do employers appear to 'prefer' other potential labour resources? What failures exist in the adjustment process of the supply of labour to changes in demand which persistently exclude large numbers of the unemployed and, consequently, generate long-term unemployment?

First, of course, jobs may not be available in sufficient numbers to employ all those seeking work – i.e. there may be an insufficient overall demand for labour. This demand will be a function of international and national economic conditions, the competitive position of the national economy, productivity levels, the government's fiscal and monetary stance and, taken together, the rate of economic growth in the national economy. Slow, or even negative, growth means fewer job slots which means fewer job opportunities (vacancies) open to those without jobs. While, however, there is a relationship between economic growth on the one hand and employment growth and reductions in unemployment on the other, the relationship is less straightforward than may be expected. The pattern of growth may be more or less labour intensive, more or less dominated by particular sectors or occupations, more or less geographically concentrated and, most important of all, more or less different to previous patterns of employment in the economy. It is this process of change which is reshaping the UK labour market (see, for example, Meadows 1996; Green and Owen 1998).

These structural changes give rise to a second cause of persistent unemployment as changes in demand occur more rapidly than labour supply is able to respond, thus generating 'structural' unemployment – i.e. mismatches between the skills, job experience and location of new jobs compared to the old that are in decline. There is extensive evidence of such structural shifts and lags in the adjustment process particularly in relation to skill deficits on the part of the long-term unemployed (Campbell 1993; Balls and Gregg 1994). The unemployment rate for semi/unskilled manual workers is four times that for professional/managerial workers and is increasing (OECD 1994). Indeed, unemployment may be as much as 40 per cent higher than it would have been without occupational, industrial, spatial and age 'mismatches' in supply and demand (Layard et al. 1997).

Moreover, the speed and extent of these changes in the structure of the economy is growing. The process of globalization, the rate of technological change, the convergence of information and communication technologies, and major changes in government policies are all leading to the development of a 'weightless' economy (Coyle 1999), to rapidly growing skill requirements and to what some call the 'knowledge economy'. Certainly the labour market is tilting toward extensive increases in the demand for higher skill levels and the labour demand for low level skills is weakening. In this environment, those unemployed people with low skill levels, with experience in sectors/occupations where job losses are extensive, who live in areas of weak job growth, are at serious risk of very long unemployment spells and possibly near-permanent exclusion from evolving labour market opportunities.

Another cause may be associated with some of the long-term unemployed not searching hard enough for work. They may be registered as being unemployed but are not in reality active job seekers and, of course, some may search harder than others. This may arise because of a high reservation wage, a low replacement ratio (available wages compared to current benefits) because of low wages or high benefits, or declining commitment associated with increasing unemployment duration. There is evidence that all these factors have some impact (White 1994) though this varies by occupation, gender and, especially, age.

Recent work by the Department of Social Security (Shaw *et al.* 1996) demonstrates that many of those on Income Support see wages (for accessible jobs) as too low and see jobs as temporary and insecure. They are also aware of the additional costs of being in employment (e.g. council tax, rent, child care and work expenses). The vast majority want paid work, are flexible about travel distances and have a modest reservation wage but are worried about how they will cope in the first few weeks of a job in terms of money. One third feel trapped on Income Support by the combination of low pay and current benefits.

Another source of unemployment is imperfect information. Inadequate information on job availability may lead to 'search' unemployment, which is likely to increase as labour market turbulence rises with its associated information lags and weak labour market intelligence (Shackleton 1997). Also, asymmetric information between employers and job seekers may lead to weak job matching with employers recruiting, and workers searching, via different channels. Moreover, search intensity declines with duration of unemployment.

Another reason for the persistence of unemployment may be that policy makers, employers or unions may seek to ensure that the level of real wages does not reflect the excess supply of labour, so preventing wages falling and employment rising. Real wage rigidity may happen because employers and employees bargain to set an 'efficiency wage' – i.e. one which exceeds the supply price of labour – to aid labour retention or recruitment (Layard *et al.* 1994).

Indeed it is in the interests of 'insiders' (employers and those already in jobs) in the labour market that the setting of wage and employment levels reflects their interests rather than those of 'outsiders' (the unemployed), who become 'disenfranchised' (Lindbeck and Snower 1994). Labour turnover costs, hiring and firing costs (such as redundancy notice periods and redundancy pay), other forms of employment protection and high labour overhead costs can then become hurdles impeding the entry of outsiders to employment (and the exit of insiders from employment), and impact on hiring and retention decisions.

The number of job slots depends positively on hiring rates and negatively on retention rates. Thus high labour turnover costs and consequent low rates of turnover will reduce the volume of employment possibilities open to the unemployed. There is extensive empirical evidence for this position (e.g. OECD 1994; Snower 1994). Low labour turnover generates relatively fewer employment possibilities for the unemployed. Fewer individuals will experience unemployment in any given time period but will experience spells of longer duration.

Another reason for unemployment is that employers may discriminate against certain groups in the labour market on the basis of certain observable personal characteristics (age, ethnic group, disability, post code), and to the extent that these are disproportionately present among the unemployed, this will lead to their long-term unemployment. In addition, discrimination may operate through screening mechanisms which label the unemployed as 'inferior' to those with more recent employment experience (Atkinson and Meager 1996). Finally, domestic circumstances may prevent some people from full participation in the labour market, constraining the range of effective choices open to them. A lack of access to, or unavailability of, appropriate transport; insufficient or expensive local child care facilities or poor health are important factors here. For example, Department of Social Security (DSS) research (Shaw *et al.* 1996) demonstrates that for lone parents child care issues are the main impediment to employment and that 45 per cent of those on Income Support report a disability or health problem.

Policies for labour market inclusion

In the first part of this section we will examine the EU's policy framework. This is particularly important as the EU now has an agreed 'European Employment Strategy' which provides a detailed framework within which member states develop their policies. In the second part we will examine the current government's policies to tackle labour market exclusion.

EU policy

The 1997 Amsterdam summit added an employment 'title' to the EU treaty which gave much greater priority to labour market issues in European policy formulation. The title was specifically introduced to tackle unemployment and assist the member states in adapting to changing labour market requirements. It is often referred to as the European Employment Strategy (EES). The so-called guidelines process was introduced to implement the strategy whereby, from 1998 onwards, member states were to draw up National Action Plans (NAPs) for employment within four pillars and, from 1999, 22 guidelines, envisaged by this policy framework.

The four pillars are seen as the key objectives and *foci* for employment policy:

1 Improving employability.
2 Developing entrepreneurship.
3 Encouraging adaptability.
4 Strengthening equal opportunities.

Under these pillars are the 22 policy guidelines that member states have agreed to use as a framework for their policy actions and development. Ten of these guidelines are particularly relevant to tackling labour market exclusion and these are set out in Table 2.1 together with the specific guideline numbers the European Commission have assigned to them.

The UK's NAP sets out in a comprehensive manner the policies it is adopting and we will examine these below. The full text of the UK's 1999 NAP can be found on the DfEE web site (www.dfee.gov.uk).

There is, however, a second major element in the EU's employment policies targeted at those excluded from the labour market: the Structural Funds. As from the year 2000 the so-called 'Agenda 2000' proposals are being implemented with a new programme for the UK. The European Social Fund (ESF) will henceforth operate as the financial 'lever' of the EES, developing structural fund actions in support of the pillars/guidelines action framework and thus the UK NAP.

Table 2.1   European Employment Strategy: guidelines (GL) relevant to labour market exclusion

Tackling youth, and preventing long-term unemployment	GL1: A new start for unemployed young people before reaching six months of unemployment GL2: A fresh start for unemployed adults before reaching 12 months of unemployment
Transition from passive to active measures	GL3: Increase the number of unemployed benefitting from active measures to improve employability to at least 20% GL4: review the benefit and tax systems to provide incentives for the unemployed or inactive to seek and take up work or enhance their employability
Promoting a labour market open to all	GL9: Give special attention to the needs of the disabled, ethnic minorities and others who may be disadvantaged
New opportunities for job creation	GL12: Promote measures to exploit the possibilities offered by job creation at the local level, including in the social economy
Gender	GL19: Adopt a gender mainstreaming approach GL20: Reduce the gap in unemployment rates between women and men GL21: Develop family-friendly policies including care services for children and other dependants GL22: Give specific attention to those seeking to return to paid work after an absence

There are now to be five policy fields, as identified in the ESF regulations, within which the ESF will support actions and which will therefore be at the core of the Objective 1, 2 and 3 programmes in the period 2000–6:

1 Active labour market policy.
2 Equal opportunities for all and the promotion of social inclusion.
3 Lifelong learning.
4 Adaptability and entrepreneurship.
5 Improving the position of women in the labour market.

It can be seen that at least the first, second and fifth of these policy fields are particularly relevant to tackling labour market exclusion.

UK policy

At the heart of the UK government's approach is enhancing the 'employ-ability' of those not in paid work as the means by which they are able to be reintegrated into the labour market and connected to labour market oppor-tunities. The main focus of policy is on tackling youth unemployment and adult long-term unemployment, including those groups who are seen to be particularly disadvantaged in the labour market. The foundation is an 'active' labour market policy which seeks to move people, where possible, from 'welfare to work', from 'dependence' to 'independence'.

The so-called 'active benefits' regime provides a number of measures which begin as soon as an individual becomes unemployed and is designed to intensify as their unemployment duration increases. The rationale for this 'progressive' approach is that 50 per cent of people who become unemployed leave the register after three months and a further 20 per cent within the next three months. Most people therefore move back into the labour market quite quickly and more intensive measures to assist the 'short-term' unemployed would therefore incur extensive deadweight. However, for those individuals who are considered to be at particular risk of longer duration unemployment (e.g. those with literacy and numeracy problems, people with a disability, lone parents and those who become unemployed following large-scale redundancies), access to more intensive employability measures is available, tailored to their individual needs.

The core of the active benefits regime is the JSA regime which combines benefit payments with job search and related measures. All JSA recipients, whether young people (aged 18–24) or adults (aged 25 and above) have to demonstrate that they are available for, and actively seeking, work in order to be eligible for the JSA. On becoming unemployed an initial interview with an adviser formulates an individual action plan and checks availability for work. Further (short) interviews are conducted every fortnight, reviewing job search activity and considering job vacancies. After 13 weeks an in-depth interview is conducted reviewing job search activity and again after six months.

At this point – i.e. six months – the measures for young people and adults diverge. Young people enter the New Deal Gateway (see below). The adult unemployed now become eligible, following a six months 'Restart' interview, for a wider range of employability measures, in particular: work trials, programme centre participation (CV assistance and interview skills) and the job interview guarantee scheme. Work-based learning for adults (previously 'training for work') and basic employability training (previously pre-vocational training) kick in at this point as well.

After 12 months, individuals who remain unemployed attend a five-day 'job plan workshop' and after 18 months a series of 'job finder plus' interviews take place to reassess the individual's job prospects. After two years the adult long-term unemployed become eligible for New Deal for adults (after 18 months or 12 months in some pilot areas) (see below). The one exception to this is that, from October 1999 in several pathfinder areas, and nationally from the year 2000, those aged over 50 have become eligible for a New Deal after six months of continuous unemployment. This New Deal has more in common with that for young people than with the New Deal for adults, offering training grants, an employment credit (of £60 per week) and personal advice. The budget for it amounts to around £250 million over the three years to 2002.

The pattern of measures and subsequent labour market actions are summarized in Table 2.2. The government's flagship programme to tackle labour market exclusion is 'New Deal'.

New Deal refers to a 'family' of policies incorporating a wide range of actions: New Deal for young people, New Deal for adults, New Deal for

Table 2.2 Active labour market policy and the active benefits regime

	Period of unemployment		
	0–6 months	*6–24 months*	*24 months and over*
Young people	Action Plan Job search Measures for those at special disadvantage New Deal for some at special disadvantage	New Deal	New Deal
Adults	Action Plan Job search Measures for those at special disadvantage	Additional measures Training New Deal for over 50s	New Deal

people with a disability, New Deal for lone parents, New Deal for communities and Employment Zones. (New Deal for communities and Employment
Zones are discussed in Chapter 7 of this book.)

New Deal, with the exceptions already identified, begins at six months for
young people and 24 months for adults. The New Deal for young people has
been in operation nationally since April 1998 (see Finn 1997; Atkinson 1999).
It involves a commitment to help 250,000 young people aged 18–24 into
work in the period up to 2002. The cost of the programme is estimated at
£2.65 billion. People aged 18–24 who have been unemployed, and on JSA for
six months are offered four options:

1 A job with an employer 'subsidized' by £60 per week for six months. A
   contribution of £750 will also be made to education/training costs. Jobs
   can be taken in both the private and public sectors.
2 Work experience with a voluntary sector organization for six months.
   £750 contribution to education/training as above. Participants get an allowance, equivalent to benefit, retain entitlement to passported benefits and
   receive a grant of up to £400. There is a particular emphasis on placement
   to provide 50,000 new trained child carers.
3 Work experience with the Environmental Task Force for six months. £750
   contribution to education/training as above. Allowance, benefits and grant
   are as per the voluntary sector option.
4 Full-time education/training, primarily in relation to basic skills, for up to
   12 months, for those with current qualification levels below NVQ2. Allowance for participants are equivalent to benefit plus passported benefits.

Each of the first three options include one day per week of education or training.
Help with child care is available on all options and a self-employment option
has also now been developed as has a New Deal for musicians.

'Gateway' provision, where clients are allocated a personal adviser to assist
with job search, careers advice, guidance, assistance with exceptional problems
(e.g. homelessness or drugs) and preparation for an option, is an essential

element of the New Deal and lasts for up to four months. So too is effect-ive 'follow through' to ensure clients are assisted during their time on the option and subsequently should they not obtain employment. There is no 'fifth' option of remaining on JSA: sanctions of loss of JSA are incurred for failure to take up offered places. It is therefore effectively compulsory.

Those young people who find it particularly difficult to find work (e.g. ex-offenders, lone parents, people whose first language is not English, those with literacy/numeracy problems, those leaving local authority care, and those with a disability) but who have not been unemployed for six months are eligible for New Deal from day one of unemployment. However, the Department for Education and Employment (DfEE) estimates that only around 8 per cent of New Deal entrants are in these categories (DfEE 1999).

The Employment Service (ES) has lead responsibility for delivering New Deal but local delivery arrangements vary considerably. A range of partners can be involved: Training and Enterprise Councils (in England and Wales), local enterprise companies (in Scotland), careers service partnerships, local authorities, employers, chambers of commerce, colleges, training providers and voluntary organizations. In some areas lead responsibility has been given to a private sector organization (usually a private employment agency) and in some areas the partnerships are more inclusive than others. Each region has produced a strategic plan for delivering New Deal and each local area has produced a delivery plan to a common format. Local areas are defined as ES districts which often cover more than one local authority or Training and Enterprise Council area.

The total number of 18–24-year-olds currently unemployed is around 100,000 – a sharp fall from the peak of 403,000 in 1994. The monthly 'flow' into this 'long-term' unemployed stock is around 10,000. So far (up to March 1999) around 265,000 people have started New Deal for young people and about 70,000 young people have obtained 'permanent' employment.

New Deal for adults started in June 1998. Generally available after two years of unemployment, the exceptions are:

- Those aged over 50 (from six months).
- Certain groups considered to be at special disadvantage like ex-offenders and those lacking basic literacy and numeracy skills (discretionary 'early' access).

In April 1998, there were about 194,000 adults who had been unemployed for two years or more – 85 per cent of whom were men. New Deal for adults offers:

- A job with an employer for six months with an employer subsidy of £75 per week.
- The opportunity for up to 10,000 adults lacking basic skills to study full-time for up to a year while remaining on benefit.

In November 1998 the government launched pilots to provide 90,000 opportunities for long-term unemployed adults, who have been unemployed for 18 months or more (in some areas, for those who have been unemployed for 12 months or more). Entry before the 12 or 18 month point is available in four pilot areas for groups considered to be at special disadvantage. The pilots are testing new approaches with the detailed design of each tailored to the needs of the local labour market. Common to each pilot however is:

- a period of Gateway help, similar to that offered in the New Deal for young people;
- an intensive programme of compulsory training and work experience lasting three months for those who do not find work through Gateway;
- £60 a week subsidy to employers for those finding work, for six months.

Since its introduction, up to March 1999, 117,400 long-term unemployed adults have started on the New Deal, and 10,500 have obtained jobs. Total expenditure on the New Deal for adults is estimated at £129 million in the period up to 2002 – some 5 per cent of that devoted to the New Deal for young people. However, it is expected that provision for adults will, from 2001, become more similar to that for young people.

Central though the New Deals for young people and adults are to the policy regime, they do not apply to the 'inactive', but only to those eligible for the JSA. In consequence another crucial policy component is the New Deals for key groups who are considered to be potentially active in the labour market and who would seek and obtain employment if wider conditions were appropriate. In addition to tackling inactivity such actions seek to target those groups facing particular difficulties in accessing the labour market. The New Deals for disabled people and lone parents are the core of this approach, though it should be pointed out in addition that the 'mainstreaming' of equal opportunities in the UK means that all the above programmes should provide equality of opportunity including for the disabled and lone parents.

There are around 5 million people of working age who have a disability and they are half as likely to be in employment as those who do not have a disability. The unemployment rate for the disabled, at 10.7 per cent, is nearly double that for those who do not have a disability, and nearly 40 per cent of disabled unemployed are long-term unemployed compared to just 25 per cent of the non-disabled unemployed.

New Deal for disabled people offers a personal adviser service and has been piloted in 12 areas from September 1998. The funding of £195 million has been provided to test innovative ways of helping disabled people find and remain in work. Ten projects are underway, generally run by partnerships of private, public and voluntary sector bodies. They include information technology (IT) training, skills training in a college workshop and jobs in, inter alia, business call centres.

The government has also, from October 1998, changed the benefit rules to enable people on longer-term incapacity benefits to take up employment with a guarantee that, if they have to return to benefit within a year because of their disability, they will receive the same rate as prior to their employment, thus removing a potentially major work disincentive. In April 1999 pilots were introduced to allow those on incapacity benefits to earn up to £15 per week and/or to take trial periods in jobs without loss of benefit.

In addition the government is currently (summer 1999) considering changes to the 'supported employment programme' and, from October 1999, is introducing a disabled person's tax credit, to provide a guaranteed minimum income for disabled people moving from benefit to full-time work who are paid at the national minimum wage.

New Deal for lone parents offers a voluntary package of back-to-work help for lone parents on Income Support through personal advisers. These advisers offer lone parents:

- help to identify skills and build confidence;
- places on ES programmes designed to help them to develop job search skills;
- advice and support for the job search process;
- advice on the benefits to which they may be entitled once they are in work;
- help to find places on training programmes and funding to cover fares and child care costs while taking part in approved training;
- continued in-work support to overcome transitional difficulties.

The New Deal for lone parents was introduced in eight pilot areas in July 1997 and became available to all lone parents making a new claim to Income Support from April 1998. It was extended nationally to all lone parents who were already on Income Support from October 1998. Since it began around 40,000 lone parents have participated and 7,000 have gone on into employment.

From October 1999 Income Support has been extended for two weeks for those who move into employment to help bridge the gap between benefits and work. And, in a move similar to that for disabled people, if lone parents obtain employment which turns out to be of less than three months' duration, they are guaranteed to be no worse off than before their employment if they return to benefits. Around 40,000 lone parents are expected to benefit from this each year.

We saw above how unemployment and inactivity are often concentrated in households where no one is in employment. A New Deal for partners of unemployed people was introduced nationally in April 1999 to help address this issue. Previously, partners of unemployed people have been treated as dependants of JSA claimants and have thus been 'excluded' from ES provision. Under this New Deal, which applies to adults, partners have the option of access to a personal adviser and to the range of employability measures, if they are the partners of a job seeker who has been claiming JSA for more than six months and is claiming for their partner. They will have access to the same services as lone parents. Partners of young people will have access to New Deal for young people on a voluntary basis.

One further important measure to encourage some of the economically inactive to move into employment is the introduction in 1999, in 12 pilot areas with a view to national implementation in 2000/1, of a 'single work focused gateway' branded 'GO'. It aims to provide a coherent and seamless service from the benefit system for both unemployed and economically inactive people of working age by providing a single point of access to welfare. It is designed to assist those with the potential for work to find it and prepare for it. By having one focal point of contact to deal with the various benefits (housing benefits, JSA, Income Support and so on), benefit recipients are able to concentrate more on measures to help them find work. All new benefit recipients will have a personal adviser who will explore the opportun-ities for work and the means of overcoming obstacles – for example, child care arrangements. Following further legislation it has become a condition of receiving benefit, for all benefit recipients of working age, to attend a 'work-focused interview' in these pilot areas from April 2000.

Finally, and more generally, in addition to the largely supply-side measures to enhance employability and reintegrate the excluded back into paid work, the government is seeking to tackle the disincentives to work that arise from the interaction of the tax and benefit systems and, in so doing, seek 'to make work pay'. A range of actions that cannot be covered here are relevant to this issue, including National Insurance contribution rates, marginal income tax rates and the introduction of the national minimum wage. However, the introduction of the working families tax credit (WFTC) from October 1999 benefits around 1.4 million working families by providing a guaranteed minimum income of £190 per week for families with one member in full-time work earning the national minimum wage. It also ensures that those families with earnings of less than £220 per week (half male average earnings) do not pay any income tax. As part of the WFTC, a child care tax credit has also been introduced worth 70 per cent of eligible child care costs of up to £100 per week for one child and £150 for two or more children.

Assessment and future prospects

Eligibility and prevention

We began the chapter with an examination of the nature, extent and causes of labour market exclusion, a situation where people are distant from the labour market both historically and in terms of access to new labour market opportunities. It is crucial to understand the characteristics of the target groups identified for effective policy action and to know why people are excluded because different policies and measures tackle different causes of the problem. Problem mis-specification leads to policy mis-specification and thus to failure. The new government has adopted an 'evidence-based' approach to policy and we would thus expect new measures to be developed which reflect labour market realities. This is, indeed, largely the case, though we will assess below how effective the policies are likely to be. Nonetheless there are two fundamental prior issues.

First, the government has now adopted the ILO definition of unemployment for measurement purposes but for policy purposes most actions are targeted at the JSA registered unemployed. In terms of eligibility, therefore, many who would potentially benefit from those policies are not eligible to participate. In terms of the long-term unemployed, this difference is around 150,000 people. In addition, there is a further group of people not measured by the ILO definition, and who are classified as 'inactive', who nevertheless want a job. Here the government has begun to provide measures to assist their labour market integration, but only if they conform to certain preselected criteria – in particular, if they are lone parents or have a disability. However, the single work-focused gateway, currently being piloted, may well be the beginning of a more comprehensive and inclusive approach to labour market inclusion.

Second, should policy seek to tackle labour market exclusion after it occurs or should it seek to adopt a more preventative approach, to stop exclusion occurring in the first place? There are four important issues here. First, at what point should the intervention begin? Immediately on becoming unemployed? After six months? After one year? Or even prior to becoming unemployed? For example, the EU Objective 4 programme that was in operation in the UK from 1998–2000, assisted those who were 'at risk' from technological and industrial change. In the UK, for example, New Deal begins at six months for young people but two years for adults with, as we have seen, several exceptions. While it will be much less expensive (per person in gross terms) to intervene as early as possible, there is significant risk of deadweight because 50 per cent of those who become unemployed leave unemployment within three months in any case. This leads to the second issue. Can we then identify those who are most likely to be at risk from subsequent exclusion and target measures solely on them? This would reduce deadweight and enhance policy effectiveness (Hasluck 1997). The government remains unconvinced that this is possible (Gibbins 1997) and this is a key reason why 'policy intensity' increases with duration. However, they do, a priori, define certain groups as eligible for early action in the New Deal, as we have seen. This does appear to give rise to a contradiction within the policy regime. Third, the government believes that their active benefits regime is itself preventative. Most of its focus is on job search and the other activation measures. As job search intensity declines with duration, this is reasonable, though the introduction of additional measures for adults at six months does appear arbitrary. Finally, all these more preventative actions are, in any case, only available to those who are JSA recipients. However, the use of the European Social Fund as well as other sources of funding, like the Single Regeneration Budget, does mean that in certain localities the government's policy and measures have been adapted and developed in various ways so that *both* the target groups *and* the timing of intervention have been extended.

Likely effectiveness

How effective then are the current policies likely to be? It is, of course, too early to say in relation to many new policies but a range of studies have been undertaken which seek to assess the effectiveness of the type of active labour market policies currently in operation. I outline these findings within the framework of six policy areas which, taken together, identify the main elements of policy which are available to 'include' those excluded from the labour market: jobsearch, training, activation, job subsidies, direct employment and intermediate labour market actions. More detailed accounts appear in, for example, Campbell *et al.* (1998), Robinson (1995) and Meager (1997). More general discussions of employability and how actions to enhance it can contribute to labour market inclusion appear in Centre for Economic Performance (1998) and Philpott (1999).

First, job search. Considerable attention has been given to the assessment of the role of job search, placement and guidance in tackling long-term unemployment. Most studies focus on job search and, in particular, in the UK, the impact of Restart and job clubs in enhancing job search (see, for example, Atkinson 1994; Dolton and O'Neil 1996; White *et al.* 1997). The earlier studies of Restart show a small positive effect equivalent to a 5 per cent reduction in claimant unemployment. Duration of unemployment is reduced and participants do spend more time in jobs. However, the later studies show that the long-term effects are weaker (though still positive) than the above short-term effects. In relation to job clubs, after adjusting for deadweight, there remains a significant positive effect for women but none for men in general. There is, however, a positive effect for men who do not have vocational qualifications (White *et al.* 1997). These results show the importance of, where possible, tracking the effects of programmes through time and disaggregating their effects on different groups (e.g. women) and on those with different characteristics (e.g. those without qualifications).

One study (Atkinson 1994) examined the job search element in Training for Work and found a positive effect. In one third of cases it increased job search intensity and nearly 60 per cent of participants felt that it made them more confident. However, multivariate analysis suggests that the effect is small compared to the 'institutional' effect of local scheme managers and the effect of personal characteristics, in particular people's previous unemployment duration. Gardiner (1997) shows that job search measures are inexpensive in unit cost terms but have low levels of additionality.

White *et al.* (1997) also examined the Job Interview Guarantee (JIG) scheme and found a significant benefit for women but only for those men without vocational qualifications. Studies of individual groups on particular projects, however, show much bigger effects. Hersee's (1995) study of the impact of a six-day return to work course for lone parents showed a dramatic effect. Comparing participants with non-participants and adjusting for the different backgrounds of the two groups, it was found that participants were 2.5 times more likely to achieve a positive outcome of employment or further education/ training. It is also the case that job search and placement activity are much more likely to be successful in buoyant, rather than depressed, labour market conditions.

Second, training. Training programmes are an important and potentially valuable measure in getting the long-term unemployed back to work and have been extensively utilized in the UK (for a summary see Lourie 1997). If skills mismatch, as a result of structural change in the labour market, is a key determinant of long-term unemployment, it may be expected that programmes designed to raise skill levels or change skill mixes are likely to be effective. However, many commentators are critical (e.g. Robinson 1995; Shackleton 1995, 1997). Shackleton concludes that 'skill discrepancies are not a major factor in unemployment' and that, therefore, 'training may not need to play a great part in reducing unemployment'. Robinson concludes that convincing evidence is very limited especially for programmes that are not tightly targeted. Such a view is contrary to the position taken by many commentators (e.g. Campbell 1995) and to the position taken by the OECD (1994, 1996). These two positions are not necessarily contradictory, for, while skill acquisition is crucial to employability, the actual training programmes themselves, for a variety of reasons, may not have been effective.

Two studies in the UK on major training programmes do, in fact, demonstrate a significant positive impact (Payne 1990 on training opportunities programme; Payne *et al.* 1996 on employment training). However, as Gardiner (1997) points out, the unit cost per additional person in work is very high – more than £40,000. For employment training, the probability of a job increases by 3 per cent after one year and 22 per cent after three years, most of this being attributable to the gaining of formal qualifications and work placements. However, analysis of youth training (Dolton *et al.* 1994) shows positive effects for women but negative effects for men.

Third, activation. There are costs involved to individuals who make the transition from unemployment to work and programmes exist to defray some of these costs – for example, in relation to travel and interviews. A job finders' grant (a one-off expenses payment of between £100 and £200) has been shown to be particularly effective and inexpensive (Gardiner 1997) with the unit costs of less than £200 and an additional cost per person into work of less than £3000. Subsidies and tax incentives can also be paid to individuals to provide an incentive to take up low-paid or part-time work (Meager 1997).

It is important, however, that such activation measures do not 'push' the long-term unemployed into inherently unstable employment. White and Forth (1998) have shown that three out of four jobs taken by the unemployed are temporary, part-time, at a substantially lower skill level than previously, or of self-employed status. People were subsequently more likely to 'stick' with this kind of employment or to fall back into unemployment than to move on from the entry-level jobs to a better job.

Fourth, recruitment subsidies. There is currently extensive interest in subsidies to employers to recruit the long-term unemployed in the context of New Deal. Studies in the Netherlands (De Koning 1993, 1995) tend to show low levels of deadweight with one programme, for the three years-plus long-term unemployed, showing that two thirds of those who obtained jobs through it would not otherwise have done so. However, substitution is higher with only 15 per cent of placements constituting net employment creation. A similar subsidy for young people unemployed for two years or more displayed high levels of deadweight and very high substitution effects. Interestingly, analysis at local level suggested that differences in local implementation arrangements had 'a significant impact on programme outcomes' (De Koning 1995).

In the UK, Atkinson and Meager (1996) have assessed the effect of the Work Start pilots. They found that the deadweight effect was 53 per cent with 17 per cent of the jobs being created 'net' – the remainder being jobs that would have ultimately been created but which were 'brought forward'. They also found that the programme influenced employer selection in favour of the long-term unemployed in 46 per cent of cases. Importantly, Work Start has also had a positive impact on employer attitudes to the long-term unemployed more generally in 40 per cent of cases.

Short-term placements with employers can also be considered under this heading. Such placements are designed to provide opportunities with no commitment and little cost to employers. 'Work trials', as they are called in the UK, last for three weeks during which time the individual remains on benefit. Should the trial prove successful the individual can be taken onto a permanent employment contract. Work trials have been shown to be highly successful (White *et al.* 1997) at least in the short-term. The difference in subsequent employment rates of participants compared to those (matched) who did not participate was 34 per cent for women and 40 per cent for men. Deadweight was only around one third and the overall estimate of additionality was between 44 and 62 per cent.

The study also allowed the identification of those characteristics which influenced positive outcomes. These were found to be qualifications, work experience, health, a driving licence and a working partner.

Finally, direct employment of the long-term unemployed. Most assessments show a limited effect on participants and significant displacement, both of private sector and public sector activities. Evaluation of the Community Programme in the UK (Disney *et al.* 1992) shows no significant impact on unemployment outflow (especially for older participants), extensive deadweight and substitution effects, but limited displacement effects. An assessment of Employment Action (Payne *et al.* 1996) showed an increased probability of getting a job of only 4 per cent after three years.

However, Meager (1997) argues that 'success' for such programmes will depend on how close their work activities are to those found on the open labour market and the extent to which other measures are integrated with them. These considerations are important when examining so-called 'intermediate labour market' actions.

Work experience is a critical factor in labour market success. Many employers see long-term employment as indicative of low motivation and poor work attitudes. There is now a considerable interest in a number of organizational forms that would establish and develop new enterprises designed specifically to employ people from disadvantaged groups, often to meet local needs. Such 'reintegration' or 'insertion' enterprises are likely to be new or existing, not-for-profit organizations like community businesses, voluntary associations or cooperatives producing goods or services for the locality or region which would otherwise be unlikely to be produced. Such 'intermediate' labour markets, bridging the gap between unemployment and the open market, offer clear opportunities – a real working environment (employee status, employment contract, a wage); connections to the local community; and production of goods or services which are of value or needed by the community. Moreover there is no stigma, or subsequent 'labelling' often associated with employment 'schemes' and, if combined, as is usually the case, with training (and qualifications), counselling, job search and support, such work experience offers a package of measures to assist subsequent employment in the open labour market.

Generally the employment provided is temporary (6 or 12 months) but long enough to complete appropriate training, inculcate work habits and disciplines and increase motivation. It is possible to provide a range of services, as illustrated by the kind of services and jobs undertaken by the Wise Group and Glasgow Works in Scotland: housing maintenance and improvement; maintaining parks; supervising swimming pools; assisting in libraries; energy conservation/draught-proofing; home security; environmental improvement. The work of the European Commission's Forward Studies Unit has also been instructive in this regard, drawing attention to 19 fields of employment which provide new sources of jobs, in large part meeting local needs and where market failures prevent needs from being fully met through the market (European Commission 1997). Many of these offer substantial opportunities for social or integration enterprises to respond to these needs.

An evaluation of the UK's largest intermediate labour market, the Wise Group in Scotland, has recently been produced (McGregor *et al.* 1997). While recognizing that some of the benefits of an intermediate labour market are long-term and intrinsically difficult to measure, and that it is a 'joint product' incorporating work experience, employment subsidies, training, guidance and so on, an assessment can be made of its success and limited comparison made with other programmes. The programme completion rate is around 50 per cent, with a further 40 per cent getting jobs in the open labour market prior to the end of the programme. Fifty per cent obtain a vocational qualification (half of these at Level 1). The proportion of participants who at any time since leaving (at the time of the survey) had a job was 67 per cent and after six months it was 46 per cent. This latter figure compares to 42 per cent for the Training for Work programme in England and Wales.

There appears to be no difference in outcomes according to their pre-participation unemployment duration, and deadweight estimates (admittedly self-assessed) are relatively low. Thirty-eight per cent of participants who got a job thought that they would have done so anyway and 29 per cent of those who got a job thought that they would not have done so without participation.

Compared to other programmes, from a participant perspective, the Wise experience is superior. Two thirds of leavers said it was superior to that provided by government training programmes. Generally participants are of longer unemployment duration. Eighty-one per cent had been unemployed for more that a year prior to joining compared to 49 per cent on Glasgow's Training for Work programme. There is clearly no creaming effect, indeed there is positive action to target the more disadvantaged. Comparing, therefore, individuals of one year-plus duration, Wise achieved 46 per cent into employment compared to 35 per cent on Training for Work. Glasgow Works, an intermediate labour market run by the Glasgow Development Agency, similarly reports a higher proportion of jobs on leaving (62 per cent compared to 20 per cent) and completed NVQs on leaving (30 per cent compared to 15 per cent) than Training for Work in Glasgow.

However, the programme is substantially more expensive than was Training for Work, though account must be taken of project income (from sales of goods and services), of the social value of needs met and the more positive experience of the process itself. In considering effectiveness one also needs to consider whether the management capacity exists in other areas to undertake such a complex and demanding set of activities if such a programme were to be widened across the country. It has taken Wise several years to build up to its current level of around 500 participants at any one time. The Wise Group has franchised its operations into a number of other areas and the government's new Employment Zone pilots all have an intermediate labour market component, referred to as 'neighbourhood match'.

Conclusion

This assessment has been able to provide only a limited perspective on the likely success of current policy. This is partly because, while the results shed some light on existing policies, the latter are so new that formal evaluations of them will not begin to become available for some time, though initial indications on the New Deal for young people do appear to be positive (Atkinson 1999). Moreover, few serious evaluations have examined the effectiveness of integrated 'packages' of measures like New Deal. Such evaluation tends to focus on the effectiveness of integrating participants into the labour market, however there are a number of wider issues which need to be considered.

First, net new jobs are unlikely to be created by an active labour market policy regime. It is possible (Layard 1996), but far more important are overall macroeconomic conditions and policy as well as international competitiveness and its impact on long-run sustainable growth. Without long-term aggregate employment growth, and except under conditions of excess demand for labour, the policies examined in this chapter are likely to 'redistribute' employment opportunities towards the excluded rather than increase the total number of opportunities available. In this sense such policies create considerable 'substitution' effects. Given that employment levels have a significant impact on the level of long-term unemployment, it will be crucial to combine an effective active labour market policy with policies which stimulate employment, especially those that stimulate employment-intensive growth in occupational and skill categories accessible to the long-term unemployed.

Second, this chapter has not considered the wider issue of skills and exclusion, as this is examined elsewhere in this book. However, it is important to recognize the close link between skill levels and labour market exclusion, and place ever-greater emphasis on improving the 'basic' skills of those excluded from the labour market, their 'transferable' skills and their qualifications levels. Given the high skill intensity of jobs growth, structural changes within the labour market and the pressures unleashed by continuing globalization and technological change, especially in information and communication technologies, enhancing the skill levels of those currently excluded from the labour market will be pivotal to their likely future labour market inclusion.

Finally, labour market exclusion is highly geographically variable. Local conditions and local causes are a major contributory factor to both the existence and resolution of the problem (Fieldhouse 1996; Campbell et al. 1998; Green and Owen 1998; OECD 1998). This implies that local discretion in policy design and delivery, the operation of area-based policies like New Deal for communities and the Single Regeneration Budget and the effective implementation of the European Social Funds under the new Objective 1, 2, and 3 programmes, all have essential roles to play in moving from labour market exclusion to inclusion.

Policies to tackle labour market exclusion have developed considerably for the better in the last two or three years. However, a range of further developments are clearly required in order to ensure that exclusion is successfully and considerably reduced in the future, particularly if labour market conditions overall deteriorate in the early years of the new millennium.

References

Atkinson, J. (1994) *Getting Unemployed Adults into Jobs*, Report no. 273. Brighton: IMS.
Atkinson, J. (1999) *The New Deal for Young Unemployed People: Summary of Progress*, ESR 13. Sheffield: DfEE.

Atkinson, J. and Meager, N. (1996) *Employers, Recruitment and the Unemployed*, Report no. 279. Brighton: IMS.

Balls, E. and Gregg, P. (1994) *Work and Welfare: Tackling the Jobs Deficit*, Commission on Social Justice Issue Paper 3. London: IPPR.

Campbell, M. (1993) Local policies to beat unemployment. *Local Government Studies*, 19(4): 505–18.

Campbell, M. (1995) *Learning Pays*. London: DfEE.

Campbell, M., Sanderson, I. and Walton, F. (1998) *Local Responses to Long-Term Unemployment*. York: Joseph Rowntree Foundation/YPS.

Centre for Economic Performance (1998) *Employability and Exclusion: What Governments Can Do*. London: CEP/LSE.

Coyle, D. (1999) *The Weightless World*. Oxford: Capstone.

De Koning, J. (1993) Measuring the placement effects of two wage subsidy schemes for the long-term unemployed. *Empirical Economics*, 18: 447–68.

De Koning, J. (1995) *Strategies and Measures to Fight Long-Term Unemployment*. Amsterdam: Netherlands Economic Institute.

DfEE (Department for Education and Employment) (1998) *Labour Market and Skill Trends 1998/1999*. Sheffield: DfEE.

DfEE (Department for Education and Employment) (1999) *The UK National Action Plan*. www.dfee.gov.uk

Disney, R. *et al.* (1992) *Helping the Unemployed: Active Labour Market Policies in Britain and Germany*. Bonn/London: Anglo-German Foundation.

Dolton, P. and O'Neil, J. (1996) Unemployment duration and the re-start effect. *Economic Journal*, 106: 387–400.

Dolton, P., Makepiece, E. and Treble, J. (1994) The Youth Training Scheme and the School to Work transition. *Oxford Economic Papers*, 4: 629–57.

European Commission (1997) *First Report on Local Development Initiatives*. Brussels: DGV.

Fieldhouse, E.A. (1996) Putting unemployment in its place. *Regional Studies*, 30(2): 119–33.

Finn, D. (1997) Labour's New Deal for the unemployed. *Local Economy*, November: 247–58.

Gardiner, J. (1997) *Bridges form Benefit to Work*. York: Joseph Rowntree Foundation/YPS.

Gibbins, C. (1997) *The Early Identification Pilot*. Sheffield: Employment Service.

Green, A. and Owen, D. (1998) *Where are the Jobless?* Bristol: The Policy Press.

Gregg, P. and Wadsworth, J. (1998) *Unemployment and Non-Unemployment*. London: Employment Policy Institute.

Hasluck, C., Elias, P., Green, A. and Pitcher, J. (1997) *Identifying People at Risk of Long-Term Unemployment*. Warwick: IER.

Hersee, M. (1995) Helping lone parents back into work. *Employment Gazette*, 10(3): 109–13.

Layard, R. (1996) Stopping Unemployment, in J. Phillpott (ed.) (1996) *Working for Full Employment*. London: Routledge.

Layard, R., Nickell, S. and Jackman, R. (1994) *The Unemployment Crisis*. Oxford: Oxford University Press.

Lindbeck, A. and Snower, D. (1994) *Patterns of Unemployment: An Insider-Outsider Analysis Discussion*, Paper no. 960. London: CEPR.

Lourie, J. (1997) *Employment and Training Schemes for the Unemployed*. London: House of Commons Library.

McGregor, A., Ferguson, Z., Fitzpatrick, I., McConnochie, M. and Richmond, K. (1997) *Bridging the Jobs Gap: An Evaluation of the Wise Group and the Intermediate Labour Market*. York: Joseph Rowntree Foundation.

Meadows, P. (1996) *Work Out or Work In*. York: Joseph Rowntree Foundation/YPS.

Meager, N. (1997) *Active and Passive Labour Market Policies in the UK*, Employment Observatory Trends, no. 28. Berlin: European Employment Observatory.

OECD (1994) *The OECD Jobs Study*, Parts 1 and 2. Paris: OECD.

OECD (1996) *Pushing Ahead with the Strategy: The OECD Jobs Strategy*. Paris: OECD.

OECD (1998) *Local Management for More Effective Employment Policy*. Paris: OECD.

ONS (Office for National Statistics) (1998) *Social Focus on the Unemployed*. London: ONS.

Payne, J. (1990) *Adult off the Skills Training*. London: PSI.

Payne, J., Lissenburgh, S., White, M. and Payne, C. (1996) *Employment Training and Employment Action. Research Series*, no. 74. London: DfEE.

Phillpott, J. (1999) Behind the buzzword: employability. *Employment Policy Institute Economic Report*, 12(10).

Robinson, P. (1995) The limits of active labour market policies. *Employment Policy Institute Economic Report*, 9(6).

Shackleton, J.R. (1995) The skills mirage. *Employment Policy Institute Economic Report*, 9(9).

Shackleton, J.R. (1997) Skills and unemployment. *Local Economy*, 11(1): 229–316.

Shaw, A., Walker, R., Ashworth, K., Jenkins, S. and Middleton, S. (1996) *Moving off Income Support: Barriers and Bridges*, DSS Research Report no. 5. London: DSS.

Snower, D. (1994) *Why People Don't Find Work*, Discussion Paper no. 883. London: CEPR.

White, M. (1994) *Unemployment and Public Policy in a Changing Labour Market*. London: PSI.

White, M. and Forth, J. (1998) *Pathways Through Unemployment*. York: Joseph Rowntree Foundation/YPS.

White, M., Lissenburgh, S. and Bryson, A. (1997) *The Impact of Public Job Placing Programmes*. London: PSI.

3 POVERTY

Tom Burden

Introduction: New Labour, poverty and social exclusion

The focus of this chapter is poverty. The concern will be with those who are either in work or who are not economically active. (The unemployed and the policies designed to get them into work are dealt with in Chapter 2.) This chapter will examine the link between the concepts of poverty and social exclusion and the general approach to them of New Labour, the extent of poverty in the UK and the policies currently being employed to reduce poverty. It will end with a discussion of the factors affecting the likely success of the policies currently being developed and pursued.

The modern concept of poverty was established by Rowntree at the end of the nineteenth century (Kincaid 1973). It was based on a precise calculation of the minimum income necessary to maintain physiological efficiency. It defined what has been termed an 'absolute' or subsistence conception of poverty. This is often contrasted with the 'relative' conception of poverty according to which people are viewed as poor not in relation to a subsistence standard, but in relation to the general living standards in society. The post-war Labour government established the welfare state on the basis of the Beveridge Report of 1942 which incorporated the idea of a 'national minimum' income. Since that time, for policy purposes, the poverty line has generally been denoted by the income level below which means-tested state support became available.

This concept of poverty as a specific income standard had many advantages for policy makers since it provided:

- a scientific and objective approach to poverty;
- the means to calculate the extent of poverty with precision;
- a basis for the complete elimination of poverty;

- a theory of poverty which viewed it as caused by features of the lives of the groups with incomes below the poverty line;
- a clear guide for policy design since Income Support could be established for the groups affected.

The use of this conception of poverty as the basis for policy has important ideological and political implications since it is consistent with certain dominant values of British society, as follows:

- Expenditure on the relief of poverty can be kept to a minimum.
- There need be no wasteful expenditure on those who are not in need.
- When the issue of inequality is raised the focus of attention is solely on the poor.
- Vertical redistribution is kept to a minimum.
- The overall pattern of inequality is preserved.

The debate about poverty can be related to different political ideologies which treat poverty, its causes and the nature of effective solutions, in different ways. There are three broad positions: a right-wing view, a centre view, and a radical view (Holman 1978).

The centre view employs a poverty line which may rise with a general increase in incomes. This approach to poverty dominated policy and research throughout the period of consensus from the end of World War II until the early 1970s. Poverty was seen as an unfortunate aspect of society from which people should be protected by state action.

As the consensus began to break down from the late 1960s, a variety of new positions emerged. Both the right and the radical left attempted to redefine poverty and to suggest new ways of dealing with it. The right usually employs a conception of absolute poverty which supports setting benefits at subsistence level. It promotes a view of poverty as caused by the failings of those who experience it. They may be seen as an 'underclass', characterized by laziness, rejection of work and reliance on social benefits, which perpetuates itself over the generations through a 'cycle of deprivation'. The left tends to see poverty as a normal and ineradicable feature of capitalism. It criticizes the centre view for suggesting that poverty is a manageable problem and an eradicable feature of society. The left argue that the focus on poverty and the poor diverts attention away from issues concerned with inequality by completely ignoring the question of wealth (Novak 1984).

Even within the orthodox centre view new approaches began to emerge as the consensus broke down. The British Labour government of 1964–70 began a partial shift towards redefining poverty as 'multiple deprivation'. This included a broader range of factors such as health, housing and education as well as income. Townsend, a key figure in poverty research throughout the 1950s and 1960s, produced a massive research report in 1979 (Townsend 1979). This also moved away from a definition based purely on income: 'Individuals, families and groups in the population may be said to be in poverty when they lack the resources to obtain the types of diets, participate in the activities and have the living conditions and amenities which are customary, or at least widely encouraged or approved in the societies to which they belong' (Townsend 1979: 15). In other words, poverty involves not just a lack of income but the resulting inability to participate in a socially approved style of life.

In recent years the European Union (EU) has become a significant protagonist in the debate about poverty. The EU supports a definition which sets the poverty line at 50 per cent of average income. This relative definition means that the standard of income represented by the poverty line will vary from one member state to another and that the line will rise as average incomes rise. Within the EU the concept of poverty is now supplemented by the prominence given to the notion of 'social exclusion'. Social exclusion covers a much wider range of issues than inadequacy of income. In this respect it has some features in common with the idea of multiple deprivation. It is also close to Townsend's definition of poverty quoted above.

The concept of social exclusion is relatively more diffuse and it does not yield the same kinds of clear policy implications which flow from the idea of poverty as a deficient income. However, the concept of social exclusion does share with the concept of poverty a similar cluster of ideological and political implications. Ideologically speaking, the two concepts are perfectly compatible and policies designed to relieve poverty may be viewed as one aspect of an overall policy designed to reduce or eliminate social exclusion. However, the similarity of the concepts also means that they may be subject to the same kinds of criticism in terms of their failure to provide a basis for challenging the overall structure of inequality.

The rhetoric of New Labour highlights some issues at the same time as excluding others from the political agenda. New Labour tends to avoid the use of the term 'redistribution'. The government also prefers to talk of social exclusion rather than social inequality. Concepts such as poverty and social exclusion depict the unacceptable face of inequality in terms of the experience of those who are most disadvantaged by them. This removes attention from the other side of the scale of inequality – the massive incomes and wealth enjoyed by a minority of the population. The government has reinforced this acceptance of the overall structure of inequality with its commitment not to raise personal taxes and to remain for two years within the budgeted spending limits laid down by the previous Conservative government (Townsend 1998).

The extent of poverty

Poverty is linked to inequality. An increase in inequality will normally increase the extent of poverty. This is what has occurred over the last two decades (Hills 1998). The overall impact on inequality of the period of Conservative government since 1979 was documented in a report by the Department of Social Security published in 1998 (DSS 1998). This report showed that since 1979 the incomes of the top 10 per cent of earners had increased by 70 per cent, the incomes of average earners had increased by 44 per cent, and the incomes of the bottom 10 per cent of earners had fallen by 9 per cent. This increase in inequality was due to a number of factors including an increase in the gap between the best paid and the lowest paid workers, increased levels of unemployment, cuts in the value of benefits, increased numbers of single parent households, reduced state protection for low paid workers due to the abolition of wages councils, and greater reliance on expenditure taxes such as VAT, which hit the poor hardest.

Using the EU definition of poverty as an income below 50 per cent of the average, Department of Social Security figures show that, after the deduction of housing costs, just over 14 million people (around 25 per cent of the population) have an income below this level. Changes in the labour market, including the reduced demand for unskilled labour and the reduced rates that this kind of work could command in a period of relatively high unemployment, increased inequalities amongst those in receipt of incomes from work. By 1992 the pay levels of the lowest paid third of the workforce were lower in real terms than they had been in 1975. There was also an increasing gap between 'work rich' and 'work poor' households. Over this period the number of households with two working adults increased from 51 per cent to 60 per cent while the proportion of households with no one in receipt of income from work grew from 3 per cent to 11 per cent (Barclay 1995).

The rise in unemployment has also tended to redistribute poverty between ethnic groups. Members of the non-white population are more likely to find themselves in poverty. Over 40 per cent of West Indians were in the lowest 20 per cent of income recipients while the figure for Pakistanis and Bangladeshis was over 50 per cent. There is also some evidence of an increase in the spatial concentration of the poor. Studies of variations in social composition and social conditions in different local authority wards throughout the country show a polarization with increased concentration of deprivation in the poorer wards. This is partly a reflection of the increased inequality of income which has developed over the last two decades. It is also a reflection of housing policy, especially the privatization of a large part of the former local authority housing stock. Council housing is now increasingly restricted to those former estates with the worst housing conditions which were least attractive to potential buyers. These 'residualized' estates now contain a concentration of the poorest people (McGregor and McConnachie 1995).

It has been suggested that the dynamic processes underlying poverty have changed over the last 20 years as a result of changes in the labour market. Hutton (1995) has argued that we now live in a 30/30/40 society. Society is divided into three groups. The bottom 30 per cent of unemployed or economically inactive people occupy a marginal position in society. Large numbers of people who would previously have formed part of the workforce are now economically inactive. The economically inactive used to consist primarily of women who had withdrawn from the labour market in order to bring up their children. This category is now largely made up of men of working age who have been excluded (or have excluded themselves) from the workforce, and of single parents. The middle 30 per cent are in work although they are found in forms of employment which are insecure. Some 40 per cent of the population hold relatively secure or tenured jobs with a high expectation of a steady future income from employment. Current trends are leading to the reduction in size of this group.

Insecurity and risk play a key role in determining the incidence of poverty. It has been claimed that increasing numbers of people are at risk of redundancy, income reduction, losing their homes, family breakdown and community breakdown (Hutton 1995). While unemployment and low pay have always been a significant risk for many working-class people, especially those without significant levels of skill, casualised, temporary and short-term contract working is now again widespread throughout the occupational structure. The persistently high levels of unemployment experienced since the end of the long boom in the early 1970s have further intensified this insecurity.

It is important to understand how people move in and out of poverty over time. In a panel study of 8000 people covering the years 1990 to 1994, 41 per cent of those defined as in poverty in the first year were still in this position by the end of the study (Falkingham and Hills 1995). The groups most likely to persist in poverty are pensioners and unemployed parents including lone parents. The groups more likely to move in and out of poverty are those who are the victims of contingencies which interrupt the flow of income into the household. These can include redundancy, divorce, death of an earner in the family or the birth of a baby. The study also showed that those who do not move back into poverty often settle at an income very little above the poverty line and remain at risk of it for the future. Over a period of 12 months nearly half those defined as poor move up above the poverty line, although in the following 12 months a third of these are likely to fall below it again. One implication of this research is that very much larger numbers of people than those who fall into poverty at any one time experience it at some time and remain at risk of it, often over long periods. In other words, poverty – or close encounters with it – form part of the experience of a very substantial minority of the population.

The government does not currently possess a clear picture of the extent of poverty in Britain. However, it has proposed to hold an annual poverty audit against which its policies can be evaluated. The first of these was undertaken at the end of 1999. A useful model for this audit has recently been provided (Howarth *et al.* 1998). The report employs a range of statistical indicators covering low income and income inequality along with wider measures of social deprivation such as long-term unemployment, low birth weight of babies, lack of access to a bank account and vulnerability to crime.

One important cause of poverty is the failure of the benefits system to ensure that all those eligible for benefits actually receive them. Many benefits are now 'means-tested'. This is often justified as a form of 'targeting' – i.e. ensuring that public money is only given out to those who need it. However, means tests often limit the distribution of benefits. For example, a quarter or more of those eligible for housing benefit, family credit and free school meals do not claim them. This is due to the complexity of the procedures involved in claiming, ignorance of the benefits available, the humiliation and invasion of privacy involved in means-testing, the stigma associated with the status of claimant and the low level of many of the benefits. Means tests often also create a 'poverty trap' for those in work. Workers receiving means-tested benefits are unable to gain much extra income from a pay increase, since this will lead to loss of benefits. If there is a low income tax threshold, extra income can also attract tax and an increased National Insurance contribution. As a result, additional wage income can be reduced by up to, or more than, 100 per cent leaving many lower-paid workers trapped at a disposable income level only just above the poverty line.

Policies to alleviate poverty

New Labour arrived in office with a strong commitment to the idea of 'welfare reform' (DHSS 1998b). Some of the rhetoric around the issue of welfare reform adopted by Labour reflected the moral panic about the level and impact of welfare spending which was fostered during the Conservative period of office. Under the Conservatives, welfare spending was viewed as contributing to social breakdown and the emergence of an underclass (Murray 1994), to the growth of single parent households, and to what was seen as a massive and unsustainable level of public expenditure on the welfare state. Labour has stressed that the solution to the problem of poverty is to increase opportunities for work for those capable of it rather than simply to increase the level of benefits. The approach adopted is characterized by the slogan 'Welfare to Work'. The key aim of social security policy should be to increase employment.

Along with Welfare to Work, Labour is implementing a range of policies which will have an impact on the extent of poverty. Some of these policies are aimed specifically at those who are in the workforce. These policies are designed to compensate for the failure of the labour market and the benefit system to provide all workers with incomes adequate for meeting their needs (Lister 1998). Other policies are directed towards specific groups who are identified as being in need. This includes policies towards older people, disabled people and other groups unable fully to support themselves. The government also pursues a range of policies which are ostensibly directed towards the living standards of society as a whole, although they may be particularly significant for those in poverty. These include various forms of price regulation which have an impact on the general standard of living which people are able to achieve.

Poverty at work

Labour has established a minimum wage. It was implemented in April 1999 and set at £3.60 per hour for over 21-year-olds. Given the level of wages offered for many unskilled jobs, which can be as low as £1.50 an hour, the legislation is likely to have a significant effect. The government claims that 2 million workers will benefit. It is probable that a substantial proportion of those being paid very low rates are women and many of them should find their income is increased. However, it remains to be seen whether predictions of job losses will prove correct. Some economists have argued strongly that a minimum wage will cause employers to reduce the size of their workforce because of the subsequent increase in their direct costs. However, a higher minimum wage can reduce the indirect costs of employment. It can cut training costs by increasing the retention of workers. It can boost productivity by increasing worker motivation. It can also lower recruitment costs by making vacancies easier to fill. These reductions in indirect costs may well outweigh the rise in direct costs for many employers.

A significant element in policies to reduce poverty involves the rights accorded to people at work since these can affect the material rewards of work. In 1998 the British government published regulations designed to comply with the European Working Time Directive issued by the EU. This introduces a maximum of 48 hours for the compulsory working week. This is likely to benefit between 3 and 4 million workers. It also includes a provision for the right to three weeks' annual leave. This figure was increased to four weeks in November 1999. This benefits 2.5 million workers, mostly part-time female employees, who previously had no paid holidays at all. The government has also announced a package of measures affecting workers' rights in its White Paper *Fairness at Work* (DTI 1998). This requires recognition of trade unions where they have a membership of over 50 per cent in a company. It also abolishes the £12,000 limit on compensation for unfair dismissal bringing this into line with the awards which can be made for claims based on race, sex or disability. The White Paper also announces the right to up to 12 weeks unpaid parental leave as well as time off for urgent family reasons, in line with the provisions of the European Social Chapter.

Women

Poverty can be seen to be a particular issue for women since the proportion of women dependent on state benefits is higher than the proportion of men. Women are more likely to depend on low wages; women have often been treated unfavourably by the social security system; and women have greater caring responsibilities (Lister 1998). Women are at greater risk of poverty than men (Andersen and Larsen 1998). The distinctive position of women rests in part on their role in the labour force. The majority of women are now in paid work. However, their participation in the labour force is more uneven than that of men because of periods of child bearing and child rearing. Around two thirds of working women return to work before a year has passed after the birth of their baby. Over half of all mothers with children under 5 are in paid employment. Becoming a mother can itself be a cause of poverty because of restrictions in the rights to benefits. Around 360,000 employees become pregnant every year but 50,000 of these have incomes which are too low for them to pay National Insurance contributions so they are not entitled to National Insurance maternity benefits.

Women are more likely than men to work in low-paid jobs and in part-time employment. The wages received by women remain substantially lower than those received by men. The hourly wages of women were still 20 per cent below those of men in 1997. Probably the lowest paid and the least protected section of the workforce are the million or so home workers who are mostly women and who work long hours with few benefit entitlements. Little is known about this group although a report has documented rates of pay as low as 30p an hour (Phizacklea and Wolkowitz 1995).

Women not only receive less pay than men but their pension entitlements are also less. The increase in divorce and the expansion of the number of single parent households has further disadvantaged women. Given the commitment of the present government to improve conditions for women it is interesting to note that their policies for the pay of public sector employees have worked to the disadvantage of women. Since women form the majority of the education and health workforces, the government's decision to 'stage' their pay increases in 1997 (in order to keep overall expenditure at the levels budgeted by the former government) contributed to an increase in the difference between the pay of men and women that year – the first time this gap had widened for a decade.

Lone parents

Around a quarter of all families in Britain are now headed by lone parents. This is a very high level in comparison with other EU member states. It is also a relatively recent situation which mainly emerged in the 1980s and 1990s. Lone parents in Britain are very likely to be economically inactive, to have low levels of educational attainment, and to experience a high risk of unemployment. There is a strong connection between lone parenthood, unemployment and poverty. Despite the moral panic over teenage mothers, only 4 per cent of lone parents fall into this category. However, it is evident that marriage is less popular than it once was and 38 per cent of lone parents have never been married.

The New Deal for lone parents was introduced nationwide in April 1998. It forms part of the Labour government's Welfare to Work programme. Under the programme lone parents with school-age children will be invited to the local Job Centre for help and advice on jobs, benefits, training and child care. Under the proposals in the Welfare Reform and Pensions Bill published in February 1999 lone parents are required to attend an interview to discuss their options for work. Those who refuse three interview requests will not have their claims processed or will have their benefits cut. These proposals are being implemented in a pilot project in 12 areas which began in the middle of 1999. A nationwide system is being implemented in the year 2000.

The Conservative government believed that it would be able to make absent fathers pay for the upkeep of their children and that this would be a means of providing financial support for single mothers (Smith 1997). The Child Support Act was passed in 1991 and the Child Support Agency (CSA) was set up in 1993. Its role was to take over the administration of child maintenance payments. In 1998 Labour announced plans to simplify the operation of the CSA. It reported that only 13 per cent of cases were resulting in the CSA collecting the full amount from the fathers. A fixed percentage of net income would in future be paid depending on the number of children who were being supported. Where the net income was less, less would be paid. These changes will take effect in 2001.

Children and families

The government has emphasized its commitment to the elimination of child poverty within 20 years. Support for families with children is an explicit aim of government policy on social security (Goode *et al.* 1998). It has introduced a number of measures which are designed to help achieve this goal. Family credit is to be replaced by a new income-related benefit called working families tax credit (WFTC) for those working 16 hours a week or more. This is designed to improve work incentives for the poorest households by reducing or eliminating the poverty trap. The basic weekly credit will be £48.80 with additional payments for children depending on their age. While family credit was paid directly to mothers, the WFTC can be included as a tax allowance in the main earner's pay packet or it can be given to a non-working spouse as a cash benefit. Critics have complained that in families where the woman does not have an independent income, male earners may not allow the choice of a payment direct to the woman to be made. It is expected that around 1.4 million working families will receive this benefit, half a million more than received family credit. The new benefit will give families an extra £24 a week compared to family credit.

One of the most important of the new policies which are designed to support the family is the children's tax credit. This replaces the married couple's allowance and will be worth around £8 per week to families with children from April 2001. A childcare tax credit will be available to households receiving the WFTC. This is an income-related benefit through which families are to be enabled to pay for child care.

The disabled

The Department of Social Security in 1998 estimated that there were 8.6 million disabled adults in Britain. Spending on the disabled has increased from £4.1 billion in 1982 to £23.5 billion in 1997. There is a complex array of benefits for disabled people. Incapacity benefit (IB, formerly invalidity benefit) was claimed by 2.4 million people in 1997. Disability living allowance (DLA) is paid to those under 65 who need care or who have restricted mobility. This benefit is not means-tested. It goes to 1.8 million people. Both IB and DLA are paid on a sliding scale according to the level of disability. Attendance allowance was received by 1.2 million people aged 65-plus in 1997.

Labour has established a disability working tax credit which is designed to encourage disabled people to find work. This will guarantee an income of at least £150 a week for a disabled person working full-time. The government believes that many of those currently in receipt of incapacity benefit are not actually incapable of work and are in receipt of benefit as a means of subsidizing what is, in effect, an early retirement. Only those who have worked recently and have paid National Insurance contributions will in future be entitled to claim incapacity benefit. In addition, the benefit will be reduced for those claimants in receipt of private pensions or private health insurance payments, by half the value of these payments. Those who are judged to be severely disabled will receive higher levels of benefit. There will also be extra assistance for severely disabled children.

Older people

In the last 20 years Britain has moved increasingly towards maintaining the incomes of the elderly through the use of means tests while the basic flat rate pension has been allowed to fall in value through a failure to uprate it in line with economic growth (Vincent 1996). The extent to which the basic state pension fails to provide an adequate living standard is illustrated by the fact that it is set at £6 below the level at which Income Support is payable. Many older people also lack savings. The annual Family Resources Survey (DSS 1997) shows that 20 per cent of pensioner couples and 34 per cent of pensioners living alone have no savings. In February 1998 a report on the adequacy of existing pension arrangements (NatWest Bank 1998) found that only 21 per cent of those in work are on course to receive a pension of £179 a week, which the report calculates as the minimum which older people require for a comfortable retirement.

There is a significant gender dimension to the issue of the living standards of older people (Arber and Ginn 1995). Half of all women over 65 are widowed. Only a third of older women have any pension of their own apart from that provided by the state. The majority of women rely on the pensions of their husbands for financial security in retirement. Where women do have a pension of their own it is normally around a third of the value of the average male pension. Of those pensioners who receive means-tested Income Support, three quarters are women and many more female than male pensioners live on incomes around the poverty level.

The increase in separation and divorce has important consequences. Around 200,000 people get divorced each year. Under the Pensions Act 1995 part of the pension available to one party in a divorce can be earmarked for the other party but they have to wait until the pension-holder retires before they get the money. After April 2001 women will benefit from legislation which will give them a share of any pension received by their former husband when a divorce takes place.

After a long period of internal debate Labour finally came up with a proposed minimum retirement income to be set at 20 per cent of average earnings. This proposal was implemented in the March budget of 1999 as a minimum income guarantee of £78 for single pensioners and £121 for couples. This is well below what a full-time worker paid at the level of the minimum wage would receive. The existing state pension is to be retained although its spending power will not be increased. The State Earnings Related Pension Scheme (SERPS) is to be abolished and replaced by a new second state pension. Incentives are to be provided through a government subsidy to encourage people to take out 'stakeholder' pensions. This will be backed up by means-tested income support. A major problem with this is that up to 0.75 million pensioners do not currently claim the income support to which they are entitled. A radical element of the proposals involves providing pension tax credits for 4 million carers and disabled ex-workers in order to provide them with the pension they would otherwise not have received.

Reducing living costs

One way in which the government can influence the living standards of the poor is through the various forms of regulation which it can impose on the private sector. In the case of the privatized utilities, the government has considerable powers to influence their operation, including their pricing policies, through the regulatory systems established at the time of privatization. These policies are particularly important for poorer people since they generally spend a higher proportion of their income on the products of the privatized utilities than those who are better off.

It is government policy that the energy sector should develop plans to ensure that low income customers benefit from any price reductions resulting from increased competition. It has proposed that the regulators should have a statutory duty to protect the interests of consumers. The government, through the energy minister, has expressed concern about the failure of gas companies to reduce prices for 1 million customers using pre-payment meters. Such customers are unable to take advantage of reductions given to those paying by direct debit. The water industry has also been a source of complaint. Since privatization in 1989, water charges have risen 36 per cent and sewerage charges by 42 per cent. In September 1998 new guidance was issued to the water regulator on charges for the period 2000 to 2005. These require a 10 per cent reduction in water bills as well as improved services. It remains to be seen what changes will be made (Drakeford 1997).

The government has taken some action which it believes may eventually lead to reductions of prices in shops. It has initiated an investigation into the trading margins of supermarkets. Supermarket prices are believed to be comparatively high in Britain. A reduction in prices would benefit poorer people since supermarkets in poor areas tend to charge higher prices than those which operate in middle-class areas. The government has also asked the Office of Fair Trading to investigate the price differentials between Britain and other countries on a range of other products. These include cars, electrical goods including personal computers, some clothes, furniture and carpets.

Some significant initiatives have taken place in the area of financial services. Around 6 million households do not have a current bank account. The government has shown some interest in dealing with what has been referred to as 'financial exclusion'. This describes the situation where people lack access to basic financial services such as banking and credit. In many inner-city areas bank branch closures have made access to banks difficult. At the same time, because poor people find credit difficult to obtain, they are often forced to take on loans at very high rates of interest from various loan merchants. Since the Consumer Credit Act of 1974 which abolished the 48 per cent ceiling on annual interest rates, there is no limit to what consumers can be charged. Many poor people find themselves paying rates much higher than 48 per cent for credit. A recent Office of Fair Trading report (1999) did not recommend any radical action in the form of setting limits to interest rates or outlawing various kinds of credit offered on a door-to-door basis. However, it did recommend that banks should offer simple accounts to vulnerable customers such as the elderly, disabled people, ethnic minorities and those with fluctuating or low earnings. The government has also shown some interest in what is called 'community banking'. In the USA this is secured by a legal requirement that banks should meet the credit needs of the entire community. In addition, a task force has been established to explore how the banks might work more effectively with credit unions. In some other countries such as Ireland and the USA, these have proved a successful way of providing credit for poorer people.

The government has taken firm action to deal with the mis-selling of personal pensions. The total value of pensions mis-sold has been estimated at £11 billion. For example, when mass redundancies took place in the mining industry in the late 1980s, sales people from many large pension firms went to the affected areas and undertook intensive campaigns to persuade recipients to use redundancy money to purchase personal pensions. Others were persuaded to opt out of occupational pension schemes. There are also concerns that other financial products such as endowment policies have been similarly mis-sold. The Treasury economic secretary named the firms involved in mis-selling soon after Labour took office in 1997 and set them clear targets for compensating those customers who were affected. Many are now receiving compensation.

The system of regulation of financial services has also been reformed with the establishment of a unified regulatory agency, the Financial Services Authority (FSA), which has taken rather firmer action than its predecessor organizations. In 1999 the FSA said that it would publish 'best buy' tables for a range of private pensions, endowments, unit trusts and individual savings accounts which would detail the costs and charges levied. This small reform could actually have a substantial effect on the operation of financial services in Britain which has been plagued by poor quality products giving massive commissions to sales staff and huge profits to the companies while at the same time failing to match returns which customers were promised when they purchased the products.

The government has also introduced a new system of tax-free savings called Individual Savings Accounts (ISAs). These will replace existing tax-free saving schemes such as TESSAs (Tax Exempt Special Savings Accounts) and PEPs (Personal Equity Plans). The government hopes to encourage an increase in savings, particularly by less well-off people. It will also encourage people to use the ISA scheme through a system of 'CAT' marks which will identify those schemes which meet stipulated standards on charges, access, and terms.

Discussion and conclusion

A significant feature of the rhetoric employed by New Labour in relation to the benefits system involves the claim that it has failed. The precise character of this failure is not always clear although what appears to be meant is that despite the welfare state many people are still poor, and many of the benefits which are dispensed go to the relatively well off who may be viewed as not requiring them. It is also occasionally claimed, though by no means as frequently as it was by Conservative spokespeople, that expenditure on social security is excessively high. However, Labour appears to wish to reduce this by reducing unemployment rather than by cutting benefits across the board. It is worth noting that the actual level of benefits in the UK is relatively low by general European standards.

The approach of New Labour to poverty does represent a significant shift away from the policies pursued by the Conservative government in some areas. There has been a return to a commitment, albeit a rather muffled one, to full employment. On occasions, the chancellor has quoted the phrase 'a high and stable level of employment' which was included in the White

Paper of 1944 on full employment which heralded the post-war commitment to this policy.

A significant innovation introduced by Labour involves the widespread use of tax credits as a means of establishing a minimum level of income for various categories of recipient. Tax credits have been employed for single parents, child care, working families, people with disabilities, carers and old people.

New Labour has given a central place to policies which are designed to link the right to receive benefit with the requirement that recipients should co-operate with attempts to place them in training, education or work. However, Income Support policies have always reinforced the incentive to work, and benefits have been kept well below wage levels. Since the Victorian poor law, recipients of unemployment relief have on occasions had to demonstrate that they were seeking work. Policies have also consistently been employed to reduce the necessity for state assistance by imposing the obligation to maintain those without resources on 'liable relatives'. The CSA is a recent manifestation of this principle.

Labour has also continued to view benefit fraud as a central problem. In the Green Paper of July 1998 (DHSS 1998a) the estimate of the value of fraud was given as £7 billion, which was up from a figure of £4 billion in a government estimate made earlier in the year. The volume of resources committed to combating fraud is substantial. The Benefit Fraud Inspectorate has around 5000 staff and there are probably around another 5000 local authority staff involved in anti-fraud activities, particularly in relation to housing benefit. The concern with fraud was a consideration in the reform of the system of benefits for single parents and disabled people.

Possible barriers to success of the reforms

One line of criticism which has been levelled at the plans put forward by the Labour government concerns the complexity of the system which they are constructing. The range of benefits for families with children is extremely complex. This means that the proposed beneficiaries will have great difficulty in understanding the level and types of benefits to which they may be entitled given their family circumstances. Similarly, the proposed arrangements for pensions, or for benefits for the disabled, could hardly be described as simple.

Some of the reforms also rest on assumptions about changes in people's behaviour which will be brought about by changes made by the government in the structure of the incentives with which they are faced. For example, the success of plans to provide adequate pensions will depend on whether or not the stakeholder pensions prove sufficiently attractive to large numbers of people in the mid-range of earnings for them to take them up. Similarly, the high hopes vested in improvements in training and the promotion of life-time learning require people individually to seek out and take up the opportunities which are on offer.

Most importantly, the overall approach of New Labour appears to rest on a number of questionable articles of faith about the nature of the economic process and about the economic capabilities of government. These are as follows:

- The globalization thesis, according to which international economic processes set serious limits to government action, is accepted.
- The government appears implicitly to accept an optimistic view of the way in which this global economy will operate. The emergence of serious economic crises in the new 'Tiger' economies of South-East Asia in 1997 was both a shock and surprise to many commentators. Policies do not seem to cater for even the possibility of the older capitalist economies of Europe and North America being engulfed by a similar crisis.
- The government holds the belief, which has been shared by several past governments over the last three decades, that the economic cycle of boom and bust is now under control.
- The government accepts the monetarist belief that the main tool of economic management should be manipulation of the interest rate by the Bank of England. It views this as the means by which it is possible to maintain a target level of inflation. It is also assumed that this will provide an economic environment which will encourage and facilitate economic growth.
- The job creation policies of the New Deal assume that if the skill levels of the labour force are improved then somehow this will stimulate the demand for skilled labour and so increase employment opportunities.

The implications for poverty and social exclusion

New Labour appears determined to do little to modify the existing level of inequality in Britain. However, it is this that has always formed the main barrier to the success of schemes designed to reduce poverty. There is clear evidence in relation to health that the extent of inequality is itself a major cause of social deprivation resulting in illness and premature death among the poor (Wilkinson 1996). The government appears to believe that the existing level of inequality has to be maintained as the basis for economic efficiency. Perfectly respectable arguments can be adduced that lead to the opposite conclusion – that economic advance would be encouraged by shifting the control of social resources so that poor people had more access to them. It is certainly the case, as the experience of World War II showed, that egalitarianism is an essential element in policies designed to secure social inclusion (Calder 1969).

Where changes are being made by New Labour, as with the minimum wage and the use of tax credits to raise the income of various groups, the new target levels of income are low. Where more significant commitments are made, as in the case of the abolition of child poverty, the timescale is substantial – in this case 20 years. The restrictions which Labour has placed upon itself in relation to avoiding policies which have explicit redistributive aims, and of broadly maintaining current levels of public expenditure, are, therefore, likely to pose problems for its attempts to alleviate poverty and increase social inclusion.

It may be asked, finally, what sort of society does Labour intend to create through the pursuit of its policies to alleviate poverty? Certainly, a central role in this will be played by the process of welfare reform, although it is not yet clear precisely where this will end. One possible finishing point is what has been described as a 'wage earners' welfare state'. This would be consistent with the emphasis which has been put on Welfare to Work and on the use of means tests and tax credits, which limit benefits to those with incomes which the state judges to be deficient. In Australia and New Zealand, policies of this kind are familiar. In these countries, benefits act as a safety net rather than an enhancement of the living standards of all (Easton 1980). Insurance schemes are not widely used. Social improvement is mainly undertaken through policies on wages and workers' rights rather than social benefits. However, this approach has marginalized the poor, unemployed, single parents and ethnic minorities, who are not represented in the bargaining process. Whether this is the direction in which Britain is going remains to be seen.

References

Andersen, J. and Larsen, J.E. (1998) Gender, poverty and empowerment. *Critical Social Policy*, 18(2): 241–58.

Arber, S. and Ginn, J. (1995) *Connecting Gender and Ageing*. Buckingham: Open University Press.

Barclay, P. (1995) *Inquiry Into Income and Wealth*. York: Joseph Rowntree Foundation.

Calder, A. (1969) *The People's War*. London: Cape.

DHSS (Department of Health and Social Security) (1998a) *Beating Fraud is Everyone's Business*. London: The Stationery Office.

DHSS (Department of Health and Social Security) (1998b) *New Ambitions for our Country: A New Contract for Welfare*. London: The Stationery Office.

Drakeford, M. (1997) The poverty of privatization: poorest customers of the privatized gas, water and electricity industries. *Critical Social Policy*, 17(2): 115–32.

DSS (Department of Social Security) (1997) *Family Resources Survey*. London: HMSO.

DSS (Department of Social Security) (1998) *Households Below Average Income*. London: The Stationery Office.

DTI (Department of Trade and Industry) (1998) *Fairness at Work*. London: The Stationery Office.

Easton, B. (1980) *Social Policy and the Welfare State in New Zealand*. Auckland: Allen & Unwin.

Falkingham, J. and Hills, J. (1995) *The Dynamics of Welfare: The Welfare State and the Life Cycle*. Hemel Hempstead: Harvester Wheatsheaf.

Goode, J., Callendar, C. and Lister, R. (1998) *Purse or Wallet? Gender Inequalities and Income Distribution Within Families on Benefits*. London: Policy Studies Institute.

Hills, J. (1998) *Income and Wealth: The Latest Evidence*. York: Joseph Rowntree Foundation.

Holman, R. (1978) *Poverty*. London: Martin Robertson.

Howarth, C., Kenway, P., Palmer, G. and Street, C. (1998) *Monitoring Poverty and Social Exclusion: Labour's Inheritance*. York: Joseph Rowntree Foundation.

Hutton, W. (1995) *The State We're In*. London: Cape.

Kincaid, J. (1973) *Poverty and Equality in Britain*. Harmondsworth: Penguin.

Lister, R. (1998) From equality to social inclusion: New Labour and the welfare state. *Critical Social Policy*, 18(2): 215–25.

McGregor, A. and McConnachie, M. (1995) Social exclusion, urban regeneration and economic reintegration. *Urban Studies*, 32(10): 1587–600.

Murray, C. (1994) The New Victorians and the New Rabble, *Sunday Times*, 29 May.

Natwest Bank (1998) *Natwest Pensions Index*. London: National Westminster Bank.

Novak, T. (1984) *Poverty and Social Security*. London: Pluto.

Office of Fair Trading (1999) *Vulnerable Consumers and Financial Services*. London: The Stationery Office.

Phizacklea, A. and Wolkowitz, C. (1995) *Homeworking Women*. London: Sage.

Smith, R. (1997) Paying the penalty: the impact of the Child Support Act. *Critical Social Policy*, 17(4): 111–20.

Townsend, P. (1979) *Poverty in the UK*. Harmondsworth: Penguin.

Townsend, P. (1998) *Will Poverty Get Worse Under Labour?* Edinburgh: University of Edinburgh.

Vincent, J. (1996) Who's afraid of an ageing population? Nationalism, the free market, and the construction of old age as an issue. *Critical Social Policy*, 16(2): 3–26.

Wilkinson, R. (1996) *Unhealthy Societies: The Afflictions of Inequality*. London: Routledge.

4 EDUCATION AND TRAINING

Fiona Walton

Introduction

Learning 'is a weapon against poverty. It is the route to participation and active citizenship' (Kennedy 1997: 4). For these reasons, among others, education and training have a key role to play in the fight against social exclusion. As the Introduction to this book has shown, social exclusion is a multi-faceted and dynamic process that requires a range of policy interventions. Among these, policies to address inequalities in participation and achievement in education are significant, such is the close relationship between social exclusion, labour market activity and success, and educational achievement. In addition, successful learning can be crucial in developing confidence, motivation and independence.

This chapter begins by establishing the extent to which participation and achievement in education and training is unequal. This is followed by an examination of the extent to which these inequalities impact on the life chances of individuals, thereby contributing to the likelihood of experiencing disadvantage and, consequently, social exclusion. Having established the relationship between education and training and social exclusion, key policy initiatives to address the problem are then discussed. These are considered in terms of the overarching government strategy towards education and training and of specific policies introduced for specific target groups. The chapter focuses on the post-16 agenda and on initiatives aimed at those in their final years of compulsory schooling. Clearly the education strategy for younger school children is also pertinent to the social exclusion agenda, but this is beyond the scope of this chapter.

Inequalities in education and training have occurred as a result of a variety of factors that can be interpreted in a number of ways. There is clearly some debate as to the extent to which barriers to participation and achievement are individual or institutional. Different interpretations of this debate will help to determine what type of intervention is deemed necessary. For example, low levels of participation in education can be perceived to be a result of, among other things:

- personal choice;
- lack of information;
- other limiting factors such as difficulties with access to courses;
- peer pressure;
- a lack of understanding of the value of education;
- previous bad experiences in a learning environment; or
- more fundamental systematic barriers which have evolved through decades of discrimination and inequality.

Responses to these interpretations would range from none at all to large-scale intervention that attempts to address these most fundamental social, cultural and institutional issues. Any analysis is, however, somewhat more complex than this. There is significant interaction between both the institutional and individual causes of inequalities, and these tend to be mutually reinforcing. For example, a relatively high proportion of black males are excluded from schools. This is frequently perceived to be a result of the generally low expectations held of this group. These then (all too often) translate into low aspirations, and consequent disaffection among the individuals themselves. This interaction reflects one of the key characteristics of social exclusion itself – it is a dynamic process that results from a combination of factors including social, cultural and institutional ones, as well as those more closely associated with the individual. As a result, intervention is required at a variety of levels. It can be seen that this is happening in some recent policy initiatives, in particular in responses to disaffected young people in schools which aim to address issues at an institutional, household and personal level.

There has also been some recognition of the extent to which previous policy developments have, in some form, contributed to current problems. For example, the school league tables are seen as a significant contributory factor to the increase in the number of school exclusions, while the introduction of parental choice and the creation of a market culture in compulsory education has contributed to the growth of pockets of disadvantage, in particular within schools at which enrolment is considered unfavourable. As a result, new policy initiatives need to address some of the problems created by previous interventions.

Participation and achievement in education and training

The significance of education and training to the social exclusion agenda is initially established because levels of participation and achievement in education and training are unequal. This inequality has a number of different aspects.

Among young people, despite the notion of compulsory education for all, certain groups are more prone to truancy and school exclusions and less likely to be entered for GCSE exams. These include those from lower socioeconomic backgrounds, those from certain ethnic groups and young people in care. Of those that are entered for GCSEs, 1 in 12 does not achieve any qualifications, while 1 in 3 does not achieve a single pass at Grade C or above (Pearce and Hillman 1998). Low levels of attainment are particularly associated with boys, certain ethnic groups, young people from lower socioeconomic backgrounds, young people in care and young offenders.

In terms of gender, the proportion of boys achieving the required standards at age 7 and 11 in 1998 was significantly below that of girls (by 10 percentage points and 16 percentage points respectively), while only 41 per cent of boys achieved five passes at GSCE compared to 51 per cent of girls. However, while these differences in achievement are significant, differences are less pronounced when examining the failure to obtain *any* qualifications. Approximately 10 per cent of school-leavers do not achieve any level of accredited attainment, with the proportion of boys and girls for whom this is the case being roughly equal. In general, other factors, including socio-economic background, appear to have a greater impact on the likelihood of achievement at school. For example, in 1993, 70 per cent of students with parents employed in the professional occupations achieved five passes in their GCSEs, compared to just 14 per cent of young people from working-class backgrounds (*Economist* 1999).

In post-compulsory education, one in five young people drop out of one-year further education courses before completion, approximately half of those on work-related training courses leave early and many who do complete either their education or training do so without achieving any qualifications (DfEE 1998d). As a result, the potential for disadvantage in later life is established at an early stage.

Low levels of participation and achievement at school are one of the main contributory factors to low levels of participation and achievement as an adult. It is a well-founded argument that the greater the length of initial education, the more an individual will learn in later life (Sargant *et al.* 1997) and that qualifications at age 16 are the key predictor of the likelihood of continuing education (Kennedy 1997): 'The Learning Divide starts early. The longer children can be helped and encouraged to stay on in schooling and full-time education and then to leave it with a liking for learning, the more chance they will have of taking advantage of lifelong learning opportunities' (Sargant *et al.* 1997: 13). Indeed, the National Institute of Adult Continuing Education (NIACE) survey found that 56 per cent of those who left school at 16 had not participated in any learning since completing their full-time education, compared to 38 per cent of those who left education at age 16–17 and only 14 per cent of those who finished their full-time education at 18+.

Although experiences and achievement in foundation learning are key in affecting future learning trends, other factors including class and age can also be seen to impact on the propensity to learn. The NIACE survey of 1997 found that while more than half of the upper and middle classes were current or recent learners, this was the case for only one third of the skilled working class and one quarter of the semi- and unskilled working class. Overall, more than half of the semi- and unskilled working class had not participated in any learning since completing their full-time education (see Table 4.1). These patterns established with current and recent learning were also reflected in intentions to learn in the future.

Table 4.1 Participation in learning by social group (%)

	Upper and middle class	Lower middle class	Skilled working class	Semi- and unskilled working class
Have participated in current/recent learning	53	52	33	26
Have participated in past learning (more than three years ago)	28	21	25	20
Have not participated in learning since leaving full-time education	19	27	42	53

Source: Sargant *et al.* (1997)

Age is a further significant factor that impacts on the likelihood of participation in learning. More than two thirds of those aged 17–24 had participated in current or recent learning, compared to only one third aged 45–54 and one quarter aged 55–64 (Sargant *et al.* 1997). Older workers already tend to be among the least well-qualified in the workplace, and failure to update skills may render them increasingly vulnerable.

Other research into perceptions of learning has resulted in the identification of a number of different categories reflecting the attitudes of adults towards the learning process. In 1996, Market and Opinion Research International (MORI) divided respondents to a survey into four different groups: improvers, strivers, drifters and strugglers. The Campaign for Learning subsequently chose to target 'strivers' and 'drifters' as the key categories from which individuals might be encouraged into learning (Sargant *et al.* 1997). These may, indeed, be the groups that could deliver the highest degree of success should resources be concentrated on them, but an approach such as this is also likely to alienate the 'strugglers' further. In a rather different response to a similar process, Merseyside Training and Enterprise Council (TEC) prioritized the bottom group, termed the 'outsiders', from a survey undertaken by IFF Research (cited in Sargant *et al.* 1997). The characteristics of this group indicated the extent of their disadvantage: they lived in rented property; they were not in the labour market; and they had left school early.

Participation in adult learning is often a work-related activity. However, the provision of training in the workplace is also highly unequal, with certain groups considerably more likely to benefit from investment by their employer than others. Those least likely to receive workplace training include those with few formal qualifications, the low paid, older workers, those in small organizations and those in businesses not represented by trade unions. In particular, using data from the Labour Force Survey, Machin and Wilkinson (1995) concluded that only 5 per cent of those with no qualifications and 7 per cent working in manual occupations were in receipt of work-based training (see Table 4.2). Once again, the clear message is that those who achieved at

Table 4.2 Individuals receiving training

	% receiving training 1993–4
All	16.9
Individual characteristics	
Degree-level qualifications	31.4
Higher intermediate qualifications	19.7
Lower intermediate qualifications	9.7
No qualifications	5.3
Manual	7.3
Non-manual	22.3
Quartile 1 of hourly earnings distribution	12.4
Quartile 2 of hourly earnings distribution	22.8
Quartile 3 of hourly earnings distribution	26.4
Quartile 4 of hourly earnings distribution	27.0
Employer characteristics	
Less than 25 employees	13.3
25 or more employees	20.3
Union member	23.2
Not a union member	13.6

Source: Machin and Wilkinson (1995)

school will continue to learn at work, with the consequence that the divide between the skilled and the unskilled becomes even greater.

There is clearly a link between low levels of participation and low levels of achievement in education and training. Among the adult workforce there are significant differences in attainment levels: 25 per cent have achieved NVQ Level 4 or equivalent; 24 per cent NVQ Level 3; 23 per cent NVQ Level 2; 14 per cent NVQ Level 1; and 14 per cent have no NVQ equivalent qualifications (Labour Force Survey 1998/9). However, an examination of achievement, or not, at NVQ-equivalent levels fails to highlight issues to do with the attainment of basic skills. These are critical in relation to issues of social exclusion as competence in literacy and numeracy is increasingly becoming a prerequisite for participation not only in further education and training and in the labour market, but also in community and everyday activities and in democratic processes.

There is some debate as to the exact extent of literacy and numeracy problems, although recent research has suggested that approximately one in five adults has problems with 'functional literacy' and 'functional numeracy', defined as 'the ability to read, write and speak in English, and to use mathematics at a level necessary to function at work and in society in general' (Moser 1999: 2). Low levels of literacy and numeracy appear to be a particular problem in Britain, as highlighted by the International Adult Literacy and Numeracy Survey, which indicates that only 2 out of the 13 countries surveyed have higher levels of basic skills problems than is the case in this country.

The spatial variation in levels of basic skills is also evident in Britain. For example, work by the Basic Skills Agency (1998) has concluded that approximately 15 per cent of the working-age population has very low or low levels of literacy. This figure is also the same for the Leeds local authority district. However, within Leeds this figure varies from 9 per cent to 26 per cent in different wards, with nine wards recording figures in excess of 20 per cent.

The impact of inequalities on education and training

It is clear that participation and achievement in education and training is highly unequal, and that the propensity to learn and to achieve varies significantly across different groups in society. It is also important to examine the extent to which these inequalities impact on other aspects of life.

The close links between educational attainment and participation and success in the labour market are undeniable and demonstrable. Table 4.3 shows the qualifications profile of individuals according to their labour market activity. At the top end of the qualifications spectrum, the proportion of the economically active and the employed who are qualified to NVQ Level 4 is double that for those either unemployed or inactive. Conversely, the proportion of the unemployed with no qualifications is double that for the employed. There is therefore a clear correlation between low levels of educational attainment and unemployment. It is also the case that those among the unemployed who are the least highly qualified are the least likely to find work and the most likely to remain unemployed long term (Labour Force Survey 1998/9).

Those with poor levels of educational attainment are also becoming increasingly vulnerable and disadvantaged as the labour market and the world of work change due to the pressure of globalization and technological developments. The skill requirements within occupations are increasing, with the move towards an increasingly value-added economy, while demand for the unqualified and unskilled decreases, resulting in heightened competition for jobs at the lower end of the skills spectrum.

Low levels of educational attainment also impact on the earnings potential of those in employment. Work by the Organization for Economic Cooperation and Development (OECD) suggests that the earnings of men with qualifications at or below lower secondary level in the UK are 20 per cent below those with an upper secondary qualification, while the difference for women is 30 per cent (Campbell 1999). Those with no qualifications or low-level qualifications tend to be concentrated in low-skill, low-wage occupations, and,

Table 4.3 Qualifications profile by labour market activity

	NVQ 4+	NVQ 3	NVQ 2	NVQ 1	No qualifications
All 16+	22.3	23.4	22.1	14.6	17.7
Economically active	25.3	24.1	22.7	14.3	13.5
In employment	26.1	24.5	22.5	14.1	12.7
International Labour Organization unemployed	12.9	18.5	24.9	18.2	25.4
Inactive	10.9	20.6	19.7	15.4	33.5

Source: Labour Force Survey (1998/9)

on social excl
olicy framework
iveness agenda,
to theories relat-
er than issues of
obalization and
h of knowledge-
the skills of the
cently, however,
concerns about
icipation in and
and result from,
tiveness agenda
training policy
the justification

red at a number
ork for analysis.
ts which outline
, b). Second, at a
ecific initiat-ives
articularly disaf-
hose who are not
called *status zero*
lts, policies have
ipate in learning;
d those who are
ork environment.
, and particularly
training for all
w.

vide perhaps one
training policy.
ment. Their vision
le value learning
effective contribu-
ual challenge that
nally competitive
promote inclusion
ation. And there is
particular import-
to re-engage indi-
f opportunity and
998a: 5).
roach. First, they
ho were failed by

els of earnings by basic skill levels

Literacy (%)		Numeracy (%)	
Low	High	Low	High
20	11	26	6
29	12	29	10
27	16	22	17
17	20	15	21
7	40	7	46

hong the least likely to receive workplace training. As a
to increase skills, and wages, are relatively limited.
ns can be compounded by a lack of basic skills. Low
numeracy, as we have already seen, are a significant
hey also have a significant impact on earnings. Whereas
with high levels of literacy and 46 per cent with high
rn in excess of £19,200 per annum, this is the case for
se with low levels of literacy and numeracy. Individuals
racy and numeracy are significantly more likely to earn
annum than those with high levels of basic skills (see

l attainment have a significant impact on labour mar-
ngs potential, issues that are both closely connected
agenda. In addition, failure at school and in any sub-
d training can have a wider impact on confidence,
ndence. Research into the lifestyles of 37-year-olds with
cy highlights some of these wider issues. The research
with very low levels of literacy were more likely to
ession than those with average or good skills; that they
tisfied with their life so far than those with good skills;
likely to show a positive attitude towards education
eir children's schooling (Basic Skills Agency 1997).
ipation and achievement in education and training
t on future life chances. There is a clear link between
l attainment and unemployment, with a consequent
exclusion agenda. As such, involvement and achieve-
training is potentially one of the routes out of social

ave been key features of government policy agendas
s, however, been a subtle change in the focus of the
nd training policy since the election of the Labour

government in May 1997, and particularly since their stance
sion has become more prominent. Previously, much of the [
for education and training was associated with the competi
with arguments for improving attainment largely connected
ing to the effectiveness of businesses and the economy, rath
equality and citizenship. It is a well-versed assertion that ʒ
the development of new technologies has resulted in the grov
based industries, with competitiveness therefore hinging or
workforce (see, for example, Reich 1991; Coyle 1999). More r
government policy in this area has begun to demonstrate
issues of inequality. As we have seen, levels of access to, pai
achievement in education are key factors which contribute tc
social exclusion. It follows then, that while the compet
remains important, much that is new in the education an
agenda is aimed at addressing issues of social exclusion, whil
for some existing policies has been refocused.

The education and training policy agenda can be consid
of different levels which provide us with a useful framev
First, the government has published a number of documer
their *strategic approach* to this issue (in particular DfEE 1998
policy level there are a number of target groups at which s
are aimed. In terms of young people, these include those,
fected young people, in education; those in training; and t
engaged in education, training or employment – the so
generation (Mid-Glamorgan TEC 1997). In relation to ad
been developed aimed at those who do not currently parti
those who lack basic skills; those who are unemployed; a
in employment but who are vulnerable in the changing w
In addition, there is increasing pressure on all employer:
those in small- and medium-sized enterprises, to provic
members of their workforce, and not just the privileged fe

Strategy

The DfEE (1998a), in their *Strategic Framework to 2002*, pr
of the clearest signs of the refocusing of education an
References to inclusion are pervasive throughout the docu
demands: 'An *inclusive* and prosperous society where pec
and continuously develop the skills they need to make an
tion' (DfEE 1998a: 1, emphasis added). They identify a c
involves creating an *inclusive* society as well as an internat
economy. Their policy programme includes proposals t
and equality of opportunity and to *increase access and partici*
a particular focus on the socially excluded: 'Learning is o
ance to the socially excluded . . . the challenge for DfEE i
viduals in developing their skills . . . to promote equality
outcome for people across all sections of society' (DfEE 1
Of particular interest are two aspects of the DfEE ap
identify a need to 'encourage young people or adults v

their schools to get back into learning' (DfEE 1998a: 5). This provides clear evidence of a structuralist interpretation of education and training inequalities, laying the blame for low levels of participation and attainment with the institutions responsible for providing education, rather than with the individual. Second, there is a recognition that equality of opportunity does not necessarily equate with equality of outcome. Although equality in levels of attainment is impossible and, in many ways, undesirable, it is recognized that new initiatives must seek to enable individuals to fulfil their potential, and for this to be appropriately accredited in order that individuals can demonstrate their achievements. This, in turn, should have a positive impact on their future life chances.

It is the outcomes of education and training that are of particular importance in relation to the new National Learning Targets, formerly the National Targets for Education and Training. Developed initially by the Confederation for British Industry (CBI), their aim was largely to tackle low levels of workforce skills which were hampering the competitiveness of the economy. Even so, it can be argued (Waring 1996) that improving business competitiveness will also result in improved employment prospects and, therefore, improved standards of living. Thus, the competitiveness and exclusion agendas are inextricably linked. There is, however, a danger in this argument that access to the new jobs is not necessarily equal and that the 'trickle-down' effect of improved competitiveness tends to benefit those most readily able to take up the new opportunities, potentially alienating those who are already vulnerable to an even greater extent.

In many ways, as Kennedy (1997) suggests, the development of the targets was, in itself, divisive, focused as they were on the attainments of the employed workforce, ignoring the educational challenges faced by the unemployed. This has, however, now been rectified with the inclusion of the unemployed in the new National Learning Targets developed in 1998. These specify particular goals for 11-year-olds, 16-year-olds, young people, adults and organizations, the majority of which are far from being achieved. In addition, a new learning participation target has been created (see Figure 4.1). A target relating to key skills has yet to be identified, partly as a result of the difficulties in measuring progress which stem from the lack of an acknowledged and consistent accreditation system for these skills. However, this will be crucial in relation to the social exclusion agenda, for, as we have already seen, lack of these skills (which tends to translate into difficulties in terms of employability) is a particular characteristic of those at risk of social exclusion.

Despite the changes in the targets, critics of the system remain. In particular, Pearce and Hillman (1998) focus on those not expected to achieve the targets – the 50 per cent of adults not expected to achieve NVQ Level 3 and the 50 per cent of 16-year-olds not expected to achieve five higher-grade GCSEs. The question is raised as to whether those deemed unlikely to achieve the attainment levels that the targets require will be ignored in favour of a concentration of resources on those who require the minimum support to reach these levels of achievement. Certainly this is a potential cause for concern, although, as we will see when particular policy interventions are examined, many of the initiatives that the government has proposed in relation to education and training are aimed at those with the greatest difficulty in achieving any level of accreditation.

Targets for 11-year-olds
- 80% of 11-year-olds reaching the expected standard for their age in literacy
- 75% reaching the standard in numeracy

Targets for 16-year-olds
- 50% of 16-year-olds getting five higher grade GCSEs
- 95% getting at least one GCSE

Targets for young people
- 85% of 19-year-olds with a Level 2 qualification
- 60% of 21-year-olds with a Level 3 qualification

Targets for adults
- 50% of adults with a Level 3 qualification
- 28% with a Level 4 qualification
- Learning participation target being developed

Targets for organizations
- 45% of medium-sized or large organizations recognized as investors in people
- 10,000 small organizations recognized as investors in people

Learning participation target
- A 7% reduction in non-learners

Figure 4.1 National Learning Targets for England for 2002
Source: DfEE (1998c)

Government aspirations in relation to education and training, and their proposals for achieving these aspirations, are encompassed in *The Learning Age* Green Paper (DfEE 1998b). This highlights the UK's weak performance in terms of basic and intermediate skills and outlines initiatives aimed at tackling this issue. Once again, learning is linked to the social exclusion agenda – 'learning contributes to social cohesion and fosters a sense of belonging, responsibility and identity' (DfEE 1998b: 11) – as well as to the competitiveness agenda, with the benefits from learning identified for individuals, businesses, communities and the nation. In addition, a key component of the Green Paper is to take the emphasis away from recognizing only formal and traditional methods of training and education: 'we learn in many different ways through formal study, reading, watching television, going on a training course, taking an evening class, at work and from family and friends' (p. 10). This broader definition of learning is particularly pertinent to social exclusion, as non-traditional learners are encouraged back into a learning environment. In many cases, the barriers to traditional education are too great to overcome, but an introduction to learning in a more familiar and comfortable context is regarded as a significant stepping stone to improving skills, motivation, confidence and independence. It is on this foundation that the concept of lifelong learning is built.

New proposals for the coordination of post-16 education (excluding higher education) indicate that new local Learning and Skills Councils will operate within a framework developed by the national Learning and Skills Council (DfEE 1999a). Local learning partnerships will play a key role in providing information, advice and influence at a local level, while the framework will also be aligned with the work of the new regional development agencies.

Policy

Having established that there is a clearly defined strategy aimed at improving levels of participation and attainment in education and training, the specific policy initiatives, most of which are aimed at specific target groups, will now be examined.

Young people and education

In considering education policy, it is largely (although not exclusively) the case that the policies which relate most closely to social exclusion, rather than competitiveness, are aimed at young people. There has been significant recognition that the education system caters inadequately for certain groups of young people who face a variety of barriers (be they institutional, social or cultural) to their attempts to achieve their potential. The consequence is the myriad of initiatives currently being developed or introduced aimed at targeting individuals and schools in order to enable both participation and attainment to be improved. Among these, Education Action Zones, targets for reducing truancy and school exclusions, New Start and issues relating to increasing the flexibility of the curriculum are particularly pertinent. Indeed, although they are distinct and separate initiatives, their aims are closely linked and it is likely that the impact of each will be significantly greater if the synergy to be gained from combining these measures can be captured.

Education Action Zones symbolize much that is proposed by the Labour government in relation to improving attainment within schools. They provide a targeted approach to disadvantage, stipulating the necessity of multi-agency partnership in tackling the issue, but enabling local organizations to identify need and propose appropriate actions to address this (DfEE web site). In some ways, Education Action Zones appear to provide a means by which a number of previously ad hoc initiatives involving a variety of organizations and individuals can be integrated more closely. These include Education Business Partnerships, mentoring by local community groups and the involvement of parents in school activities. With the creation of an action forum within which each of these groups will be represented, a more formal role can be developed for those who have a stake in both the education system and the young people that pass through it.

The concept of Education Action Zones builds on the idea that schools can become the centre not only of educational activity but also of community activity. For example, many of the pilot zone bids included proposals for extended opening hours, family literacy centres, one-stop shops for health and social services and provision for family counselling (Dugdill 1998). Despite the apparent logic in this approach, there has been some criticism of this new emphasis. A report published by the Joseph Rowntree Foundation (cited in Dugdill 1998) indicated that there may be reluctance from parents (particularly those with previously bad experiences in education) as well as pupils to spend an increasing amount of time in school. This may be the case. However, the culture of Education Action Zones should be such that some of the mistrust of schools and education that exists can be overcome; indeed this is one of the most important challenges. In addition, other initiatives which, rather than encouraging individuals into schools, take education out into the community (for example into community centres, sports centres and local libraries) can be used as an alternative approach to attract parents who may not wish to enter traditional education establishments. In particular, Learn Direct (formerly the University for Industry) will aim to stimulate the demand for learning and build upon the new provision of this national network of learning centres.

In attempting to address the problems of educational underperformance in particular localities, the government (DfEE web site) identified potential areas of best practice for Education Action Zones. These included:

- strong leadership;
- shared responsibilities for learning by pupils and their families;
- partnership activity;
- a focus on teaching, with extracurricular activities;
- innovation and flexibility; and
- high and consistent expectations of pupils.

It can be seen that these ideas reflect particular issues associated with (potentially) disaffected young people including lack of direction and motivation; lack of support from home; failure to recognize the relevance of school to the outside world, and particularly the world of work; lack of aspirations, and, consequently low levels of attainment. To this extent, then, attempts to address the problem are being targeted at areas that are recognized at least as being part of the cause.

Within Education Action Zones, initiatives to tackle truancy and school exclusion are likely to be particularly prominent. The publication of the *Truancy and School Exclusion* report (Social Exclusion Unit 1998a) has catapulted this issue to the forefront of the policy agenda. The report highlighted the concerns regarding the 1 million young people that truant annually and the growing number of permanent school exclusions, which reached 12,500 in 1995/6. In particular, the report outlined the disproportionate impact of truancy and exclusions in relation to certain groups of young people. Pupils from lower socioeconomic groups, those who live in social housing and those with lone parents are among the most likely to truant, while the lack of commitment to education among parents was identified as a significant contributory factor. In relation to exclusions, boys, black young people and young people in care are overrepresented. Indeed, young people in care are ten times more likely to be excluded than other pupils. This, once again, highlights the inequalities prevalent within the education system and urgent action is required to address the issue.

The government's proposed target is to reduce both truancy and school exclusions by one third by the year 2002. Initiatives aimed at tackling truancy include home-school agreements, an increasing emphasis on dealing with literacy and numeracy problems at an early age, a truancy crackdown within schools and the development of alternative options to the National Curriculum, particularly including the wider use of work-related training in order to link education more closely to the labour market. These proposals are largely directed at institutional causes of truancy; at improving the school experience in order to encourage pupils to remain in the classroom. The development of home-school agreements does, however, indicate a recognition that addressing the issue only in schools is unlikely to be sufficient. Parents are a key factor in the incidence of truancy and an approach which confronts problems both at school and at home is much more likely to be effective.

In terms of school exclusions, the school league tables and the competitive market culture that has been established within the education system are seen as significant contributors to the problem (Pearce and Hillman 1998). Schools are selective over who they admit in the first place and may be more readily inclined to exclude those who are likely to underachieve in order to maintain good examination results. Thus, previous policy developments have been divisive and have contributed to the current fears about social exclusion. As a result, the government proposes to amend the league tables by adding a 'value added' component which takes into account socioeconomic factors and the extent to which schools have enabled all pupils to improve their potential. However, this proposal has encountered problems of measurement in the past.

In addition to the recommendations of the Social Exclusion Unit, Pearce and Hillman (1998) suggest that schools should be given financial incentives to provide admission to pupils who have been excluded. This may indeed make excluded pupils more attractive to schools, but more specifically it would appear to make them more attractive to schools who are most in need of further financial assistance. This raises the potential for some of the least well-resourced schools to increase their intake of pupils who require the most resource-intensive support. Any movement towards this strategy would, therefore, have to be carefully monitored.

In relation to both truancy and school exclusions, the government will produce statistics and targets at both school and local authority district level. While this has been welcomed by some of the major children's charities, teachers' unions have once again expressed their concern, particularly because targets, as in the past, tend to 'ignore the varying circumstances of schools' (*Labour Research* 1998: 24). Indeed, targets are very much a central component of the proposals, with further goals to be established in relation to the attainment of young people in care. Certainly it is important to monitor progress, but target setting does not, in itself, result in major improvements in achievement, as the National Targets for Education and Training have demonstrated only too well.

Despite some of the misgivings relating to specific aspects of the truancy and exclusion agenda, these proposals provide a significant step towards tackling some of the key issues related to disaffection. Indeed, it has been argued by David Cracknell, Director of Education at Cheshire County Council, that the development of this new agenda 'should counter-balance any tendency to assume that the problem of educational under-performance is tackled simply by raising average levels of attainment without addressing social and economic inequalities' (Cracknell 1998). Keeping as many young people within the education system and using innovative and imaginative methods to ensure that they stay, can provide a starting point for raising attainment for all.

Closely related to issues of truancy and exclusion, the *New Start* strategy aims to re-motivate disaffected young people who have dropped out of learning or who are at risk of doing so (Community Development Foundation 1998). The needs of such young people clearly extend beyond simple solutions based solely around schools and education. It would be too demanding to expect the education system alone to tackle problems which have developed as a result of a combination of social, cultural and educational pressures. As such, following a similar approach to that of Education Action Zones, New Start is built upon the idea that multi-agency involvement is the key to re-engaging young people in education. Partnerships including the careers service, schools, further education colleges, Training and Enterprise Councils, local authorities, the youth service and voluntary organizations (DfEE 1998d) will aim to identify the most effective methods by which young people can be reintegrated in the education system. In doing so, consideration will be given to a variety of areas including:

- advice and guidance;
- peer mentoring and community support;
- developing learning experiences outside school;
- working in the community;
- key skills development; and
- the provision of work opportunities (DfEE 1997b).

The multi-faceted approach that this signifies, whereby young people are given support both inside and beyond the education system, is another important component of strategies to tackle social exclusion. In particular, the Community Development Foundation (1998) highlighted the variety of roles that the community and voluntary sector can perform in helping to re-motivate young people. This may be in the form of mentoring, or providing work experience or simply by acting as an intermediary between school and young people who have dropped out. Building relationships within the community and participating in community activities is identified as a means by which young people can develop confidence and independence, providing a significant stepping-stone to education, training or work. The Foundation does, however, recognize that this approach may not be effective for all young people and this is why the involvement of a range of agencies is so essential. Disaffection does not imply a single, homogeneous entity; young people become disaffected as a result of a wide variety of factors, and routes back into the mainstream are, consequently, different. Support from a community organization; an opportunity provided by an employer; the dedication of a teacher in helping to improve reading and writing; or intensive guidance to enable an individual to make appropriate choices – each (or all) of these could provide the catalyst that re-stimulates a young person, but it will be different for each individual involved.

Integral to education strategy is the issue of *curriculum flexibility*. It is widely recognized that many of the young people who fail to achieve their potential within the education system feel alienated by the structure and content of the National Curriculum. In particular, the relevance of the Curriculum to life after school is unclear. When reviewing the structure of qualifications, Dearing (1996) recommended alternative provision for 14–16-year-olds, particularly involving the use of applied knowledge to link experiences of school and work more closely. The introduction of Stage One GNVQs, which will provide work-related learning for 14–16-year-olds, is one response to this recommendation. Ideas concerning a more vocational route at Key Stage 4 have been echoed in the proposals for Education Action Zones, in the strategy to tackle truancy and exclusion, and in New Start. If these are to be successful, links between schools and employers in particular will need to be strengthened, most specifically through the expansion of the Education Business Partnership initiative.

The proposals outlined above (Education Action Zones, strategies to tackle truancy and exclusion, New Start and curriculum flexibility) are central to the government's approach to education policy. The *Investing in Young People* strategy (DfEE 1998d) also outlines recommendations including a single school-leaving date to ensure that no young person can legally leave school before the GCSE exams; new National Records of Achievement to help young people to plan and manage their own learning; access funds for 16–19-year-olds in education; and a new 'learning gateway' for 16–17-year-olds. The focus of all these policies is clear: they are aimed very strongly towards those who have previously failed to achieve their potential in the education system. Underperformance, disaffection and the lack of motivation, aspirations and interest are the areas that the government has chosen to target in attempts to raise attainment. Attainment, however, is still largely measured by GCSE results for those aged 16, and by A level and GNVQ results for those aged 18. Policies to target those most at risk of underachieving in schools are still failing to address the issue of accreditation, most particularly in relation to vocational options. The consultation document, *Qualifying for Success* (DfEE 1999b) considers issues to do with post-16 qualifications and key skills, particularly looking towards the development of an overarching certificate for advanced-level qualifications, but the outcomes of this have yet to be seen. Until the issue of accreditation is rectified it may be that the lowest achievers remain in school and active in mainstream education, but the difficulties they face after completion will remain unresolved.

Young people and training

The training agenda for young people is less clearly associated with strategies to combat social exclusion than is the case with the education system. Nevertheless, long-running debate about the quality and value of training options and the consequences for those who embark on the programmes means that this is a particularly pertinent area in relation to young people's prospects and their future in the adult labour market.

Training options for young people suffer from a number of problems, relating to the complexity of provision and branding and the image that certain programmes have developed. In particular the quality of youth training and the relatively poor level of positive outcomes in terms of qualifications and jobs have rendered this an option that is, generally, considered to be unfavourable among young people. Indeed, a longitudinal study of schools in Bradford found that 42 per cent of young people agreed that training credits (as they were then termed, and in distinction from modern apprenticeships) were the last option that they would consider (Policy Research Institute 1996). When reporting on the impact of youth credits, Maclagan (1997) quoted a careers officer who suggested that a number of young people remain within the full-time education system simply because of the low status of the training alternative. The significant levels of drop-out from post-compulsory education courses certainly indicate that a number of young people are not making the right choices post-16. These problems have been compounded by systems of funding which encourage competition between post-16 education and training providers, a system which should be overhauled with the development of the new National Learning and Skills Council.

Interestingly, the development of modern apprenticeships, although hailed as a considerable success by employers and apprentices alike, has fuelled the problems of the youth training option. Maclagan (1997) argues that both modern apprenticeships and GNVQs have provided more able young people with a viable alternative to the academic route, thereby alienating those who are forced onto youth training even further. Funding mechanisms, which encourage training providers to 'cream' individuals who are most likely to achieve the outputs required, can mean that the most disadvantaged are unable to access a training place on either scheme, despite the supposed 'guarantee of a training place'.

Frequent changes in the branding of youth training options have also caused confusion. The most recent innovation is the introduction of new *national traineeships*. Unlike many of the previous changes, this has the potential to be more than cosmetic. The aim is to build on the success of modern apprenticeships, but delivering training to NVQ Level 2 rather than Level 3. Perhaps most significantly, unlike youth training, national traineeships will incorporate key skills in the same way that modern apprenticeships do. This is vital. Employers are demanding higher levels of literacy, numeracy and information technology (IT) skills from their recruits, and are also keen that young people possess communication skills and the ability to work in teams. Previously, young trainees outside the modern apprenticeship scheme were being denied the opportunity not only to develop these skills but also to demonstrate that they possessed them. Those graduating from such programmes should now find themselves with greater prospects in terms of employability.

The stigma attached to all aspects of youth training is, however, likely to remain. It is difficult to conceive a time when youth training will be regarded as anything but the poor relation of continuing full-time education. This has particular relevance for the social exclusion agenda as it raises a number of important questions. First, how to develop a work-based route for those who are disenchanted with education at age 16 which will be valued, if not equally with educational achievement, at least as a positive alternative. Second, how to persuade young people that training is valuable and can be the most appropriate choice. Third, how to persuade employers of the benefits of offering training and how to ensure that this is a quality experience. And, fourth, how to establish clear progression routes once training is complete. If these issues could be resolved, young people would be faced with a real choice at age 16 and one that enabled them to approach the adult labour market with confidence.

Young people – status zero
Among the potentially most disadvantaged young people are those who, on completion of compulsory education, find themselves with no clear destination.

This so-called 'status zero' group (meaning that they are not engaged in education, training or employment) are an increasing cause for concern, partly because of their characteristics, and partly because of their prospects for the future. A proportion of this group have been let down by the failure of the guarantee of a training place and, because of the regulations governing the receipt of benefits, 80 per cent of this group do not have any income (Chatrick 1999). Research in South Glamorgan estimated that at any one time between 16 and 23 per cent of 16- and 17-year-olds find themselves in this position (Istance *et al.* 1994), although there are significant problems with accurate measurement simply because these young people have, in effect, 'disappeared'. This group share many of the characteristics of those who are most prone to truancy and exclusion. For example, they include the least qualified school leavers; those from lower socioeconomic groups; social housing residents; those in local authority care; African Caribbeans; and those with learning difficulties (Pearce and Hillman 1998). Inactivity after compulsory education will significantly exacerbate their, already considerable, disadvantage. Indeed, the *Bridging the Gap* report by the Social Exclusion Unit (1999) suggests that young people who are not participating in education, training or work between the ages of 16 and 18 are 'by the age of 21, not only more likely to be unqualified, untrained and unemployed, but are also more likely to earn less if employed, be a parent and experience depression and poor physical health' than their peers.

The problem has been recognized, and this group is one of the main targets of the New Start strategy. In addition, the Social Exclusion Unit (1999) has proposed a number of policy developments in order 'to ensure that young people stay in education, training, or work with a strong education/ training component until they are at least 18'. The four main elements of their approach include:

1 a clear outcome to aim for by 19 – the 'graduation';
2 a variety of pathways to 'graduation' which suit the needs of all young people;
3 building on the education maintenance allowance pilots to engage the most disadvantaged groups, and a youth card to assist with transport and other costs; and
4 a new multi-skill support service, working with all young people, but giving priority to those most at risk of underachievement and disaffection, to support them between the ages of 13 and 19 through education and the transition to adulthood.

One of the greatest difficulties with the status zero group is tracking them down and maintaining contact. Previously, no organization or agency has been responsible for providing support to these individuals, enabling them to 'disappear' with ease. This perhaps altered slightly with the change in focus of the careers service contracts for 1998–9. For the first time there has been an acknowledgement that the disaffected should constitute a priority group for the careers service as they look at how they will work 'to eliminate the wasted resource caused by social exclusion and disaffection' (McManus 1998: 6). There is a realization that all young people do not require equivalent levels of guidance and support from the organization. In particular, a new emphasis has been placed on improving guidance to, among others, those not in education, training or employment (McManus 1998). This may require a significant degree of outreach work as young people are often reluctant to visit the careers office, and it is a resource-intensive task – but a necessary one.

Adults and education

Inequalities in participation and achievement in education among adults, and the consequences of this, have been highlighted earlier in this chapter. While new policy interventions in schools and initiatives targeting young people aim, ultimately, to reduce these inequalities in future generations, there is an immediate need to address issues of disadvantage among adults who are currently marginalized because of their previous educational performance.

The policy agenda for adult education is, perhaps, less coherent than that aimed at young people, partly because adult participation in education is voluntary and partly, it can be assumed, because adults form a much more disparate group, with a wider range of experiences in (and, potentially, barriers to) education. However, the development of the *widening participation strategy* has provided the adult education agenda with an overarching framework from which initiatives can be developed.

The further education sector was the initial target of the widening participation debate. This has, however, been followed by recommendations relating to participation in higher education. In particular, Metcalf (1997) highlighted lack of aspirations and lack of knowledge about higher education as particular barriers to participation for those from lower socioeconomic groups. These were considered to be almost as significant a problem as lack of attainment in school. Clearly, however, where social exclusion and disadvantage are concerned, it is the education provision that can be offered by further education that is likely to be most pertinent.

The Kennedy report, *Learning Works: Widening Participation in FE* (1997), provides a detailed analysis of issues relating to adult education and makes a series of recommendations as to how widening participation can be successfully achieved. The report considers issues of funding, provision, advice and guidance, the involvement of employers and the community, barriers to participation and methods by which participation can be increased. It calls for the development of a Learning Regeneration Fund; for lottery funds to be used to launch a Learning into the New Millennium campaign; for public resources to be redistributed away 'from the gold card of funding for full-time Higher Education . . . to . . . equity of funding for post 16 education' (p. 10); and for there to be a legal duty on television to educate. Overall, the 'irresistible' case for widening participation, for reasons of social cohesion as well as economic well-being, are strongly presented. However, the recommendations are far-reaching and demand a complete overhaul (particularly in terms of funding) of the current system of education, as well as much of the culture of education that is established in the UK. This may, indeed, be necessary but it is unlikely that such significant changes will be made. Rather, movement towards widening participation is likely to be more incremental and to consist of a more *ad hoc* approach which will certainly attract previous non-learners but may not result in the sea change that Kennedy demands.

Rather than embracing the entire Kennedy agenda, it is probably more realistic, if not necessarily more desirable, for approaches to adult education to concentrate on certain areas of recommendation. Overcoming *barriers* to education is key – be they financial, personal or institutional. In addition, there is a significant need to convince non-learners of the value of learning. Removing barriers to education will only be effective if individuals themselves actually want to participate, or are at least aware that participating will benefit them. In many ways education needs to be sold to a significant proportion of the adult population. As such, the national publicity campaign recommended by Kennedy (1997) is key. Learning needs to be promoted as something for everyone and education needs to be demystified. The success of certain campaigns in the past suggest that promotion through all forms of media is an effective method of achieving this. For example, as Kennedy highlights, three 90-second adverts for the Basic Skills Agency's Family Literacy Campaign resulted in 250,000 requests for information and Adult Learners' Week prompted calls from 57,000 individuals. Half of these callers had been unemployed for more than six months (the group had been targeted by the distribution of leaflets advertising a freephone telephone number with their Girocheques), and 40 per cent of callers joined a course within four months (Sargant *et al.* 1997). Television and advertising are key media through which those at particular disadvantage can be contacted and more emphasis should be placed on their role in promoting the lifelong learning agenda.

Perhaps one of the most important target groups for widening participation are those who *lack basic skills*. Levels of literacy and numeracy are particularly poor among a significant proportion of the population and this has a profound impact on their prospects in the labour market and in life in general. Wells (1996) suggests that the problem is exacerbated, not because there are a large number of completely illiterate and innumerate individuals, but because of changing definitions. Rather than being unable to read or add up at all, there are a large number of people who cannot deal with words and numbers at the *level* now required. This relates closely to the changing labour market, in which most jobs require a certain level (at least) of communication skills, along with a certain level of literacy in relation to IT.

The consequences of poor basic skills are severe in terms of both employment and personal development. In establishing an action team to examine skills issues, the Social Exclusion Unit has clearly recognized the problem. In particular, the action team will aim to assess the number of adults in poor neighbourhoods who do not have 'essential employment related and other life skills' and develop action plans with targets to help them to develop these skills (Social Exclusion Unit 1998b: 62). Although the focus is not specifically and exclusively basic skills, it is likely that these will be a significant component of the outcome.

In *The Learning Age* Green Paper (DfEE 1998b) certain of Kennedy's (1997) recommendations in relation to basic skills have been incorporated. In particular, it is proposed that this will become an area of priority for public expenditure and that the provision of basic skills courses will be free. This should certainly help to overcome one of the barriers to participation for adults who are weak in this respect.

Encouraging adults with low levels of basic skills into participating in any type of education is, however, problematic in itself. Perhaps one of the most successful methods of doing this has been developed with the establishment of *family literacy schemes*. These have the dual benefit of attracting adults into education while also developing the foundation skills that young children require in order to benefit fully from school. Family literacy schemes were pioneered by the Basic Skills Agency as part of a strategy to break 'the inter-generational cycle of reading failure' (Tett and St Clair 1996: 369). Evaluation of the schemes has indicated that they lead to an improvement in literacy for both children and parents which remains evident up to nine months later (DfEE web site), and that the schemes have succeeded in encouraging parents into further education and training (DfEE 1997a).

As with young people pursuing alternative routes to the academic one, an additional problem in adult education is the accreditation of the learn-ing that is undertaken, particularly in relation to basic skills. Accreditation symbolizes achievement and this can be critical in empowering adults who were previously more accustomed to failure and can provide them with the confidence and motivation to undertake further learning. As such, issues of accreditation will continue to require careful consideration.

Unemployed adults and training

Training for unemployed adults has differed somewhat from that for young people in that, until the introduction of New Deal, the achievement of quali-fications was not the prime objective. Rather, training programmes were more strongly focused on getting the unemployed back into work. The extent to which these programmes should have demonstrated a greater commitment to education depends on the interpretation of why individuals were struggling to access employment. If low levels of relevant skills and the failure to fulfil employer requirements are significant characteristics of the unemployed, then it is clearly the case that training programmes need to raise skill levels.

Work-based training for adults (formerly training for work, which replaced employment training and employment action) does encourage individuals to work towards a recognized qualification while undergoing a period of work experience. As such, participants should gain access to a larger number of jobs by increasing their skill capabilities and the relevance of these to the current labour market, while at the same time developing relationships with employers (Gardiner 1997). However, between January 1997 and December 1998, just 38 per cent of leavers (and 49 per cent of completers) had gained a full qualification and just half of leavers and completers had achieved a positive outcome. More than 40 per cent had returned to unemployment (Office for National Statistics 1999). For those who were successful in obtain-ing qualifications, a job, or both, these figures do not indicate the extent to which this might have happened without the intervention of training (the deadweight). However, what these figures do suggest is that a significant proportion of training leavers are failing to benefit, in any quantifiable way, from the programmes that they have participated in.

New Deal (discussed in more detail in Chapter 2) re-emphasizes the Labour government's commitment to education and training. All New Deal options include a training element, leading to a recognized qualification, and there is specific provision of a full-time education and training option. Significantly, this option is targeted at those lacking basic skills who do not hold qualifications at NVQ Level 2 or above. This builds upon the provision of pre-vocational courses, introduced to Training for Work, which enable individuals to develop their basic skills before moving into training that is more directly work-related (Donnelly 1997/8). As a result, participants should be better equipped to compete in the labour market.

Employed adults and training

Workplace training is increasingly becoming a factor which can contribute to widening the divide between those who are multi-skilled and will succeed in the labour market, and those who are vulnerable to changes in working practices and the introduction of new technology. There has been a persistent call for employers to increase levels of training for employees over a number of years, largely as a result of economic concerns relating to competitiveness. However, awareness is now growing of the inequalities in workforce training and the potential consequences that this has for both businesses and the employees themselves.

Much of the debate relating to workplace training, and to the adult education agenda more generally, has centred around whose responsibility it is to provide and pay for that training. The previous government promoted their 'individual commitment' approach which has been adopted and modified by the Labour administration, with an acknowledgement that, since individuals, businesses and the nation as a whole benefit from training and education, the responsibility for funding lies with us all. This argument forms the basis on which the new *individual learning accounts* (ILAs) have been built. These involve an investment from an individual, or an individual's employer, which is then topped up by public funds to pay for a course of learning (DfEE 1998b). The accounts are aimed, largely, at those currently in employment with the objective of helping to establish the lifelong learning culture. However, individuals that require particular skills, employees in small firms and people returning to work are being specifically targeted as the scheme is launched. The accounts certainly provide an opportunity for some of the most vulnerable in the workforce to improve their skills, an opportunity which they may not receive from their employer. However, it is well-established that those who have already succeeded in learning tend to continue to learn, while those who have not, do not. As such, the way in which the accounts are promoted will be important in determining whether take-up from traditional non-learners can begin to reverse this trend.

The development of ILAs appears to build on the model established by *employee development schemes* introduced initially by the Ford Motor Group. These provided all employees with the opportunity to undertake some form of learning funded by the company. Significantly, the learning did not have to be work-related, with many employees beginning by participating in a leisure-related course before progressing to areas such as languages and computing. More than half of the workforce took up this opportunity with shop-floor workers as keen to do so as white-collar workers (Tuckett 1996). ILAs follow a similar philosophy, encouraging individuals into any type of learning, in an attempt to increase confidence and motivation. However, it appears unlikely that many employers, particularly those in small- and medium-sized enterprises, will agree to financial support for non-vocational learning, thus leaving the burden of the initial investment, however small, with the individual.

Attempts to encourage employers to provide more training for their work-force are largely symbolized by the Investors in People initiative which TECs have promoted for a number of years. Success, has, however, been relatively limited, with commitments and recognitions way below the goals established by the National Targets for Training and Education. The government remains reluctant to implement compulsion in relation to workforce training, although there has been some debate around issues to do with tax relief. However, when left to make the choice themselves, it appears unlikely that any signific-ant increases in commitment to training among employers will materialize.

Additional funding for the most vulnerable in the workforce is currently available as a result of the European Social Fund *Adapt* and *Objective 4* initiat-ives (to be incorporated into the new Objective 3 under Agenda 2000, the reform of the Structural Funds) which are aimed at those most at risk of redundancy. These fund retraining and skills development appropriate to the needs of the labour market. The initiatives are particularly interesting because they focus on prevention rather than cure. The individuals that they target are still within the employed workforce and the assistance they are given is specifically aimed at ensuring that they remain there. Such an approach should avoid much of the apathy and disillusionment that is characteristic of responses to many initiatives aimed at the unemployed, and may therefore prove significantly more effective.

Conclusion

Recent developments in education and training policy suggest that the gov-ernment is prioritizing those for whom participation and achievement is relatively low. This clearly links closely to the social exclusion agenda as educational attainment has been shown to be a significant factor affecting life chances. The focus on underachievers is certainly to be welcomed and the range of initiatives aimed at both young people and adults, critically, attempt to address many of the identified causes of the problem. However, the development of this policy agenda does entail a number of risks, most specifically in relation to adults.

Providing education and training for young people and for adults are two very different propositions and not simply because education is compulsory for young people aged up to 16. Creating the motivation for participation is essential in relation to all education and training policies and while it is simple to demonstrate that good performance in school is a precursor of good educational and labour market performance in later life, the benefits for underachieving adults to begin the learning process are far less clear. The 'learning pays' argument is well-established, but this relies heavily on the correlation between educational achievement and labour market success or earnings potential. Although it demonstrates that having no qualifications is more likely to result in unemployment or in low-paid jobs, it does not examine sufficiently well the extent to which learning undertaken by the unqualified aged 30 or 40 benefits them in relation to these factors.

There is a danger that the rhetoric of the lifelong learning agenda will overstate what needs to be achieved and what can be achieved. The grandiose claims for a 'learning age' potentially promise too much to those for whom, ultimately, very little may be delivered. There are a number of stages at which the policy can fail, and at which, therefore, policy intervention is most necessary:

- There may be a lack of interest among target groups – they simply do not want to learn. Creating the motivation to learn and stimulating demand, one of the key objectives of Learn Direct, is crucial.
- Increasing participation does not necessarily result in increased attainment, although there may be other benefits including increased confidence, independence and motivation. These (alternative) benefits need to be emphasized in promoting the learning lifestyle. Role models within the community can be useful in this respect.
- There is no consistent and accepted form of accreditation for much of what the disaffected and disadvantaged might achieve. This will impact both on their own feelings of success as well as their capacity to demonstrate their capabilities. Accreditation needs careful consideration – trying to claim equivalent status to academic qualifications is unhelpful; alternative forms of qualification need to be promoted as valuable for their own sake.
- Despite the benefits of self-fulfilment, confidence and motivation that learning and education can bring, for many adult low achievers education is about improving their prospects in the labour market. If they are being encouraged into learning with a message that learning pays, then this has to be borne out. Unfortunately, this is often not the case. There is a significant risk of disillusionment if adults enter learning under the false assumption that this will automatically lead to a stable, well-paid job. It is, indeed, important to encourage individuals into learning, but the messages that they take with them must be carefully thought out. This clearly links to wider labour market issues regarding the availability of jobs, the willingness of employers to recruit from the unemployed and the ability of the unemployed to meet the demands of the labour market. As such, education and training policy needs to be closely aligned with activities in the wider environment.

Despite these issues, prioritizing the disadvantaged in relation to education and training remains critical. Much of the focus on young people should help to alleviate the pressures in future generations, while adults must at least be given the opportunity to enhance their prospects through educational improvement. Events in the wider environment and, most particularly, the economy and the labour market will, in any case, partly determine the success of some of these initiatives. As tools to combat social exclusion, education and training have a significant role to play, but only when combined with other policies to promote inclusion will their full effects be realized.

References

Basic Skills Agency (1997) *Adult Literacy in Britain*. London: HMSO.
Basic Skills Agency (1998) *Adults' Basic Skills*, CD-ROM. London: Basic Skills Agency.

Campbell, M. (1999) *Learning Pays and Learning Works: A Review of the Economic Benefits of Learning.* Leeds: Policy Research Institute.

Chatrick, B. (1999) Learning gateway for 16 and 17 year olds. *Working Brief,* April: 18–19.

Community Development Foundation (1998) *The New Start Strategy: Engaging the Community.* London: CDF.

Coyle, D. (1999) *The Weightless World: Strategies for Managing the Digital Economy.* Oxford: Capstone.

Cracknell, D. (1998) Truancy and social exclusion report. *Anti-Poverty Matters,* 17(summer): 22–4.

Dearing, R. (1996) *Review of Qualifications for 16–19 Year Olds: Full Report.* Middlesex: School Curriculum and Assessment Authority.

DfEE (Department for Education and Employment) (1997a) *Excellence in Schools,* Cm 3681. London: HMSO.

DfEE (Department for Education and Employment) (1997b) *A New Start for Disaffected Young People* (speech by Baroness Blackstone. London: DfEE.

DfEE (Department for Education and Employment) (1998a) *Strategic Framework to 2002.* London: DfEE.

DfEE (Department for Education and Employment) (1998b) *The Learning Age.* London: DfEE.

DfEE (Department for Education and Employment) (1998c) *National Learning Targets for England for 2002.* London: DfEE.

DfEE (Department for Education and Employment) (1998d) *Investing in Young People: Strategy.* London: DfEE.

DfEE (Department for Education and Employment) (1999a) *Learning to Succeed: A New Framework for Post-16 Learning.* London: DfEE.

DfEE (Department for Education and Employment) (1999b) *Qualifying for Success.* London: DfEE.

DfEE (Department for Education and Employment) web site: *http://www.dfee.gov.uk/dfeehome.htm*

Donnelly, C. (1997/8) Training for work needs to focus on meeting education targets. *Working Brief,* December 1997/January 1998: 25–7.

Dugdill, G. (1998) City schools examine partnership benefits. *Urban Environment Today,* 49(9): 8–9.

Gardiner, K. (1997) *Bridges from Benefit to Work: A Review.* York: Joseph Rowntree Foundation.

Istance, D., Rees, G. and Williamson, H. (1994) *Young People Not in Education, Training or Employment in South Glamorgan.* Cardiff: South Glamorgan TEC.

Kennedy, H. (1997) *Learning Works: Widening Participation in FE.* Coventry: Further Education Funding Council.

Labour Research (1998) Absent from the roll call, 87(October): 21–2.

Machin, S. and Wilkinson, D. (1995) *Employee Training: Unequal Access and Economic Performance.* London: Institute for Public Policy Research.

Maclagan, I. (1997) *Out of Credit: A Report on the Impact of Youth Credits.* London: Youthaid.

McManus, J. (1998) New focus for careers service. *Working Brief,* 93(May): 6–7.

Metcalf, H. (1997) *Class and HE: The Participation of Young People from Lower Social Class.* London: CIHE.

Mid-Glamorgan TEC (People and Work Unit) (1997) *Investing in Youth Partnership.* Pontypridd: Mid-Glamorgan TEC.

Moser, C. (1999) *A Fresh Start: Improving Literacy and Numeracy.* Sudbury: DfEE.

Office for National Statistics (1999) *Labour Market Trends,* 107(5): 586.

Pearce, N. and Hillman, J. (1998) *Wasted Youth: Raising Achievement and Tackling Social Exclusion.* London: Institute for Public Policy Research.

Policy Research Institute (1996) *Your Future: Bradford and District Youth Cohort Study. Sweep Two.* Leeds: Policy Research Institute.

Reich, R. (1991) *The Work of Nations: Preparing Ourselves for 21st-century capitalism*. New York: A.A. Knopf.

Sargant, N., Field, J., Francis, H., Schuller, T. and Tuckett, A. (1997) *The Learning Divide: A Study of Participation in Adult Learning in the UK*. Leicester: NIACE.

Social Exclusion Unit (1998a) *Truancy and Social Exclusion*, Cm 3957. London: The Stationery Office.

Social Exclusion Unit (1998b) *Bringing Britain Together: A National Strategy for Neighbourhood Renewal*, Cm 4045. London: The Stationery Office.

Social Exclusion Unit (1999) *Bridging the Gap: New Opportunities for 16–18 Year Olds Not in Education, Employment or Training*. London: The Stationery Office.

Tett, L. and St Clair, R. (1996) Family literacy, the home and the school: a cultural perspective. *Journal of Education Policy*, 11(3): 363–75.

Economist (1999) The trouble with boys, 29 May: 35–6.

Tuckett, A. (1996) Reaching out: barriers to participation in lifelong learning, in Campaign for Learning. *For Life: A Vision for Learning in the 21st Century*. London: RSA.

Waring, M. (1996) Targeting the future: lifelong learning and the national targets for education and training, in Campaign for Learning. *For Life: A Vision for Learning in the 21st Century*. London: RSA.

Wells, A. (1996) Forward to basics: raising literacy and numeracy standards for the next century, in Campaign for Learning. *For Life: A Vision for Learning in the 21st Century*. London: RSA.

5   SOCIAL EXCLUSION AND HEALTH

Ged Moran and Mike Simpkin

Introduction

In policy terms the relationship between health and social exclusion has until recently been, at best, tangential. In fact, until 'joined-up thinking' became a government mantra under New Labour, the split tended to suit both politicians and administrators. Even now that poor health is recognized as a 'key marker for social exclusion' (Social Exclusion Unit 1998, para.1.24), the very phrase betokens an uncertainty about the mechanisms through which the two are linked. This uncertainty raises a number of issues:

- How far is poor health status a consequence of broader patterns of social exclusion – in education, employment, income, housing, etc.?
- How far does poor health status in itself cause or reinforce social exclusion by limiting the capacity of individuals to participate in work, education or social and recreational activities?
- What kinds of social values foster social inclusion and, consequently, are more likely to achieve both improvements in overall health and reductions in health inequalities?
- How readily do these links between health and social exclusion translate into policy interventions likely to be both effective and politically acceptable to New Labour?
- What is the particular contribution of the National Health Service (NHS), as a universal service, in addressing both the structural determinants of ill health and the more specific issues of developing socially inclusive approaches to health care organization and delivery?

⬤ Health, health inequalities and government, 1980–99

Documentation of inequalities: the Black Report and its immediate successors

Much of the debate about health status has been framed in terms of inequality: the extent to which particular individuals and groups fail to achieve and sustain the levels of health (as measured by broad indicators such as life expectancy and incidence of ill health) which are enjoyed by more favoured groups. The Black Report (1980) documented the extent to which substantial health inequalities between social classes had survived over 30 years of the welfare state. It stated that class differences in mortality occur throughout the lifespan, although they are more marked at the start of life and in early adulthood. As a result, by the early 1970s, people in occupational Class V had a two and a half times greater chance of dying before reaching retirement age than those in occupational Class I. This gap appeared to be widening as the steady improvements in mortality rates in the higher occupational classes during the preceding two decades were not matched by improvements in Classes IV and V.

The Black Report offered a structural explanation for these inequalities: namely that the social class gradient largely mirrored the extent to which people had access to the material determinants of health status such as income, housing, education and safe working environments. Because the explanation of health inequalities was multi-factorial, policy interventions needed to be similarly broad-ranging, extending well beyond changes to health care systems to include improvements in areas such as housing, transport, environment, working conditions, social security and other benefits. A follow-up study (Whitehead 1988) concluded that, despite the improving health of the population as a whole, there was convincing evidence of widening inequalities especially among adults, and again emphasized the need for a broad-based strategy to tackle health inequalities.

Although promptly disavowed by the Conservative government, which was only just commencing its second year, the Black Report was in tune with wider developments in thinking about health. The most notable of these was the World Health Organization's (WHO) emerging 'Health for All' (HFA) by the Year 2000 campaign. As the title itself indicates, HFA represented a commitment to an inclusive goal for improvements in health, both nationally and globally. The HFA strategy was based upon a primary care model and underpinned by the explicit identification of key principles, including a commitment to reducing health inequalities, emphasis on community participation in both setting and achieving health goals, and emphasis on the importance of incorporating a range of agencies and sectors in coordinated action to improve health. As such it set an agenda for a new public health which represented a significant challenge to the established bio-medical dominance of health and health care, with its strong focus on high-tech, curative, hospital-based, health care delivery.

The Conservative approach: inequalities as variations

The Conservative government signed up to Health for All in 1985, along with the other governments of the WHO European region, and some recognition of public health issues was achieved in its acceptance of the Acheson Report on *Public Health in England* (Acheson 1988) and in the issuing of *The Health of the Nation* White Paper (DoH 1992). However, the Acheson Report was based on a predominantly medical- and NHS-based view of public health (PHA 1988) and *The Health of the Nation* set its face determinedly against recognition of health inequalities (euphemistically relabelled 'health variations'). The government's main interests in health and health care lay in management and cost control although both the Scottish and Welsh Offices were able to issue health strategies which were slightly more integrated than in England, where health was remarkable by its absence from many government-funded regeneration programmes.

Insofar as the ideas and principles of HFA achieved a toe-hold in the UK during the 1980s and early 1990s, this was due to the commitment and determination of local partners in designated 'healthy cities' (e.g. Liverpool and Glasgow), local agencies (particularly local authorities in cities such as Manchester, Sheffield and Oxford) and those directors of public health (e.g. in Stockport and Sandwell) who were committed to a broader vision. Areas such as these laid the foundations which enabled them to take advantage of the new opportunities offered later by New Labour. More commonly, as it became clear that part of the agenda of 'health alliances' was to shift costs away from the health service, smaller local authorities often found themselves unable to sustain earlier initiatives while those in urban areas, also with reduced budgets, moved away from the health inequalities issue to the more directly economic approach encouraged by regeneration programmes. In the NHS the public health role and expertise became swallowed up in the chaos of commissioning health care within the internal market introduced by the Conservative reforms of 1990.

By the mid-1990s, report after report was documenting social, economic and health inequalities. Phillimore *et al.* (1994) found that for some groups in northern England death rates had actually increased between 1981 and 1991. Senior government representatives participated in a Ditchling Park seminar on *Tackling Inequalities in Health* (Benzeval *et al.* 1995) which restated the importance of addressing health determinants, and the Department of Health itself produced a review, still coyly titled *Variations in Health* (1995). But little tangible emerged in the way of action.

New Labour and health inequalities

Throughout the Conservatives' reign, Labour had used the issue of health inequalities to attack the government on several levels: for economic and social policies which widened inequalities; for rejecting the strategies recommended in the Black Report and subsequent documents; and for both underfunding the NHS and introducing market forces into it in a way which, Labour claimed, exacerbated inequalities in access to health care services. After the May 1997 general election Labour appointed a minister of public health whose early speeches made clear the links between health, poverty and social exclusion. Sir Donald Acheson was invited to chair an independent inquiry into health inequalities and reported in December 1998 (Acheson 1998). Meanwhile new research continued to emphasize links between poor health and social exclusion. For instance, Lewis and Sloggett (1998) under-lined the close links between suicide and unemployment or job insecurity, while Hobcraft (1998) used longitudinal data to establish links between adult outcomes such as malaise and early parenthood with broader socioeconomic and demographic factors. The long-running debate triggered by the Black Report finally appeared to be becoming a major influence on government policy.

The Acheson inquiry on health inequalities

The Acheson inquiry (Acheson 1998) found that although death rates had fallen among both men and women in the years since the Black Report, the difference in rates between those at the top and the bottom of the social scale had widened. For example, in the late 1970s death rates were 53 per cent higher among men in Classes IV and V compared with those in Classes I and II; by the late 1980s they were 68 per cent higher among men, while among women the differential had increased from 50 per cent to 55 per cent. This reflected a difference in life expectancy between the top and bottom of the social scale of five years for men and three years for women (Acheson 1998: 11).

Like the Black Report (1980) and Whitehead (1988), the Acheson inquiry (Acheson 1998) endorsed a socioeconomic model to explain health inequal-ities. The main determinants of health are seen as layers of influence from the individual lifestyle factors through social and community networks to wider influences such as living and working conditions. Overall there are the economic, cultural and environmental conditions prevalent in society as a whole. The report emphasizes that the interactions between these layers are crucial for an understanding of patterns of health and inequality – individuals do not exist in a vacuum:

> socio-economic inequalities in health reflect differential exposure – from before birth and across the life-span – to risks associated with socio-economic position. These differential exposures are also important in explaining health inequalities which exist by ethnicity and gender.
>
> (Acheson 1998: 6)

The implications of the socioeconomic model are that a 'broad front approach' is necessary if interventions are to be effective:

> We have therefore recommended both 'upstream' and 'downstream' policies – those which deal with wider influences on health inequalities such as income distribution, education, public safety, housing, work employment, social networks, transport and pollution, as well as those which have narrower impacts, such as on healthy behaviours.
>
> (Acheson 1998: 8)

Apart from its specific proposals in these policy areas, the Report emphas-izes the importance of incorporating a health inequalities dimension into all relevant policy decisions, arguing both that the impacts on health inequal-ities need to be explicitly evaluated and that the policies themselves should be formulated to reduce these inequalities by favouring the less well off.

The overall spread of Acheson's recommendations is impressive, ranging from insulation and heating systems (Recommendation 12.1) to reform of the European Union (EU) common agricultural policy (Recommendation 19). Issues of implementation are less clear.

Political Implications for New Labour

Despite Labour's apparent enthusiasm for addressing the health inequalities agenda, the political rhetoric sat uncomfortably with the fact that the party's own ideological shift substantially affected the potential scope and nature of any intended action to reduce health inequalities. Labour's early reluctance to adopt any explicit objective of narrowing income differentials, and its espousal of the importance of 'wealth creation rather than distribution' (albeit tempered by a degree of 'redistribution by stealth' in successive budgets) does not bode well for a concerted attack on the root causes of inequalities. By emphasizing economic competitiveness and individual opportunity, reshaping the welfare state to emphasize personal responsibility, and accepting the pre-existing Conservative public spending plans for its first two years in office, Labour quite explicitly signalled a break with many of the redistributive assumptions and policy mechanisms which had underpinned its social demo-cratic past. Since these assumptions and policy approaches were fundamental to earlier strategies for reducing health inequalities, it was unclear exactly how Labour's rhetoric around the health inequalities debate was to be con-verted into meaningful policy interventions. Indeed, Wainwright (1996) has argued that such rhetoric served precisely to placate traditional Labour activ-ists in the health field and disguise the extent to which the broader ideological retreat undermines any possibility of effective action on the issue.

'The New NHS' and 'our healthier nation'

The demands of the New Labour health ministers created a massive change in atmosphere to which both the NHS Executive and health authorities had to adjust. Suddenly the word 'inequalities' infiltrated into national and local NHS reports. A White Paper, *The New NHS: Modern, Dependable* (DoH 1997), which concentrated on a better integrated health service, was closely followed by *Our Healthier Nation* (DoH 1998a), a complementary and consultative Green Paper on wider health issues. The Green Paper addressed issues of the physical and social environment – neighbourhoods, community safety, trans-port, access to high-quality health and social services. Poverty, employment and social exclusion were identified as specific socioeconomic factors affect-ing health. Participation in society and helping people improve their own economic and social circumstances were seen as key contributions to improv-ing health. True to communitarian values, *Our Healthier Nation* proposed a national contract between government, local agencies, communities and individuals, each with their own role to play in improving the health of the population as a whole, while also improving the health of the worst-off at a faster pace so as to narrow the health gap.

Success in improving health was, in part, predicated on the success of other government measures to address exclusion – in other words, on the implementation of healthy public policy. Finding ways in which the Department of Health could directly contribute to the agenda was more difficult. Although the Green Paper was broadly welcomed, the principal criticisms focused on an apparent retreat from the inequalities agenda which it claimed to espouse, back towards a disease approach (selecting coronary heart disease, cancers, accidents and mental health as priority areas), not dissimilar to *The Health of the Nation* (DoH 1992). The proposed 'contracts' appeared quite heavily weighted towards local obligations. And in relation to social exclusion, the use of a 'healthy settings' approach focusing on schools, workplaces and neighbourhoods as vehicles for health improvement seemed itself to be socially exclusive (APH, HEA, King's Fund 1998: 3.31).

There was a marked contrast in the pace with which the two agendas were developed. The most fundamental structural change in *The New NHS* (DoH 1997) was the introduction of primary care groups (PCGs) intended as mechanisms which could wind up the general practitioner (GP) fundholding scheme and bring the commissioning of health services closer to health need. In fact the introduction of PCGs proceeded so fast that they were effectively implemented in April 1999 before the Health Bill had passed through Parliament. Similarly, health improvement programmes (with a specific focus on health inequalities) were to be constructed as a partnership commitment for every health authority area and the first version also ran from April 1999. The NHS direct telephone scheme, which aims to make primary care advice more accessible was rolled out through England. Free eye tests for people over 60 were reintroduced. A series of national service frameworks was commenced to set and monitor national standards. Two new institutions, the National Institute of Clinical Excellence (NICE) and the Commission for Health Improvement, were set up, though their impact on social exclusion seemed likely to be limited. Evidence criteria for the success of drugs and procedures did not, at least in initial briefs, go beyond bio-medical factors to include issues of culture and the treatment environment. Nor did they appear to offer any real guarantee against the persistence of publicly invisible rationing criteria applied on a local basis.

The White Paper, *Saving Lives: Our Healthier Nation* (DoH 1999a) did not appear until July 1999, a year or so after the date originally anticipated. An accompanying paper (DoH 1999b) gave a coherent if rather anodyne and self-congratulatory account of government policies relevant to the Acheson (1998) recommendations on reducing health inequalities. Some of the delay reflected genuine development in thinking especially in relation to social exclusion. However Whitehall infighting played its part, both over the wider political and economic implications of the 'joined-up' approach to public health and over specific polices such as the fluoridation of drinking water. The general implications of the White Paper (including the introduction of more ambitious disease prevention targets) are beyond the scope of this chapter but it is worth noting some subtle changes.

Saving Lives: Our Healthier Nation (DoH 1999a) made explicit connections with New Labour ideology: 'Striking a new balance – a third way – linking individual and wider action is at the heart of our new approach' (para. 1.27). Active citizenship (developed in part through a new Healthy Citizens initiative including 'health skills' and 'expert patients' programmes) was at the heart of the new notional national contract spelt out in the phrases 'People can . . . Local players and communities can . . . National players and government can . . .' The language was optimistic and the content laid out a wide range of opportunities, particularly for an 'empowered health service', whose leading position was symbolized by the addition of *Saving Lives* to the *Our Healthier Nation* title. Clear encouragement for local policy initiatives and programmes was backed by a commitment to spread awareness of best practice. The settings approach was maintained, but less explicitly, being woven into the chapters on individuals and communities. Further attention to social exclusion and health was promised in future urban and rural White Papers and the development of multi-disciplinary public health was to be more comprehensively resourced than ever before. The Health Education Authority became the Health Development Agency whose remit included health inequalities.

The attention to access and standards at the heart of this reorientation of the NHS was complemented by a zonal approach to health and disadvantage which mirrored the way in which social exclusion was being addressed in other fields such as regeneration, employment and education. Although the history of geographically-targeted social policy initiatives has been problematic, evidence suggests that location does make a specific contribution to health inequalities independently of the effects of poverty and deprivation (Curtis and Rees Jones 1998; Macintyre 1998; but cf. Sloggett and Joshi 1994).

The concept of Health Action Zones (HAZs) had been floated before the election without anyone having a particularly clear idea of what they might entail. By March 1999, 26 HAZs had been selected by ministers, ranging from Luton (population 180,000) to Merseyside (population 1,400,000) with the objective of pioneering creative partnerships to modernize services, targeting health inequalities and responding to social exclusion. The duty of PCGs to engage with local communities was enshrined in their terms of reference. Healthy living centres (funded through the National Lottery) were promoted as core networks to enable healthy living in disadvantaged areas and to address wider health determinants. Ministers lost no opportunity to stress the importance of involving local communities and bringing in front-line staff to influence policy development (showing that employees are also regarded as active citizens). HAZs were also expected to address the health and health chances of excluded communities which are not based around neighbourhoods, including people with disabilities and chronic illness.

⬤ Material interventions, health inequalities and social exclusion

The difference between health improvement and social exclusion

The acceptance across Europe of the need to address social exclusion by governments of the centre right as well as the centre left suggests that targets and policies based on social exclusion are likely to be less radical (though sometimes more coherent) than those which arise more directly from an inequalities agenda.

While the evidence summarized above strongly supports the connections between poor health, poverty and social exclusion, health improvement is a complex phenomenon. A marginal improvement in material circumstances may not improve health (for example by exposure to greater risk). Economic regeneration undertaken without assessing health consequences may worsen health for at least some. Similarly, social inclusion may have deleterious consequences, illustrated at a global level by the way in which world free trade agreements have legitimated the intrusion of multinational food and chemical companies into self-sustaining local agricultural economies. Narrowly materialist interventions do not necessarily reduce social exclusion, however important (and potentially politically difficult) such measures may be.

Other significant factors also come into play, including the degree of inequality within a society and its effects not just on health status but on conscious and unconscious perceptions of health. The psychosocial dimensions of health produce opportunities within the social exclusion agenda but also some potentially damaging consequences.

Policy implications

A first problem for policy makers is that, despite a concentration of poor health at the bottom of the social scale, poor health status is not exclusively concentrated in a single identifiable group; rather, it is a gradient from the top to the bottom. Thus, while highly targeted strategies aimed at improving the position of the worst-off may have some benefits, they will not eliminate health inequalities.

A second, more fundamental problem is that even wide-ranging and more politically controversial redistributive strategies rest on the assumption that material differences in control over resources are in themselves the primary explanation for differences in health status. This assumption needs major qualification. Wilkinson (1996) and others suggest that, for developed countries, once a threshold of material wealth is achieved there is only a limited connection between further increases in absolute wealth (as measured by per capita gross national product) and subsequent improvements in health status. Within individual societies, it is changes in *relative* income which over time have a greater impact both on the overall health status of the population and on health inequalities, rather than improvements in the absolute income levels of the worst-off. Thus countries such as the USA and UK, in which income inequalities are wide, also experience the widest health inequalities. Conversely, countries such as Sweden and Japan which enjoy more equal wealth distribution also enjoy longer life expectancy and more equal health status between social classes. In Scotland, the Grampian and Border regions share the lowest mortality rates, while being at opposite ends of the average income levels – Grampian being the richer. Part of the explanation may be that both regions have narrower ranges of income distribution than the other mainland regions (McCormick and Leicester 1998). In effect, the creation or elimination of health inequalities has to be seen as a dynamic, psychosocial process, embedded in the relationships between social groups and the psychological stresses suffered by those of relatively low social and economic status, rather than simply relating to the behaviour or lack of skills or material resources of those who are most health disadvantaged.

This analysis raises some difficult questions for policy makers. First, it suggests that economic policies which are based on the assumption that some of the benefits of economic growth will necessarily 'trickle down' to the worst-off and thereby reduce inequalities in health status are ill-founded. Unless the narrowing of income inequalities is pursued as a specific policy objective, health inequalities will remain or even widen. Second, it demands considera-tion of the psychosocial pressures through which the experience of relative poverty translates into poor health status – and of alternative approaches which might alleviate these pressures.

Social cohesion as a possible factor for good health

On the face of it, this psychosocial dimension is exactly what the concept of social inclusion is intended to address. While Wilkinson's (1996) emphasis on redistribution may be unwelcome, two other strands of his argument (one social, the other bio-medical), dovetail more readily with Labour's approach. First he uses evidence from a number of anthropological and other studies to argue that part of the reason why more egalitarian societies are healthier is that they tend to be more socially cohesive. He suggests that 'what may be important is a sense of camaraderie, or something approaching a community of values capable of ensuring that public space is social space and the extent to which people trust each other' (1997: 132). Similarly 'the public sphere of life remains a more social sphere than it does elsewhere . . . People come together to pursue and contribute to broader, shared social purposes; that is the social cohesion' (p. 136).

The second bio-medical analysis draws on the physiology of stress, first discussed by Wilkinson mainly in relation to animal studies. Stress and inequality are harder to document for humans and the most relevant work has been in the field of occupational health. Despite concern in the early 1980s about the links between executive stress and coronary heart disease, it is well documented that workers on lower grades suffer much worse health than their superiors (for instance, the famous studies by Marmot *et al.* 1991 of the British civil service). Karasek and Theorell (1990) developed an explanat-ory model suggesting that this risk was linked with jobs characterized by high demand, low control over decisions and low social support. Wilkinson is now working with Marmot to develop our knowledge of the physiological implications of the consequent stress (Marmot and Wilkinson 1999). Although these studies are initially set in the working environment, the model is more widely extendible to the stress of poverty (both of paid work and of caring). Potential remedies lie both in developing a greater awareness of how to control stress (many community projects find that complementary therapies which offer forms of relaxation are in high demand) and, more radically, in develop-ing empowerment not just as part of citizenship but for its physiological benefits as well.

Although some critics consider Wilkinson's (1996) choice of evidence to be selective (West 1997), the tracing of links between social organization and health go back to Durkheim and beyond. Wilkinson uses Putnam's (1995:

664–5) definition of social capital ('features of social life – networks, norms and trust – that enable participants to act together more effectively to pursue shared objectives') to present social cohesion as both supportive and enabling. In studying the effectiveness of Italian regional governments, Putnam (1993) concluded that effective government was closely related to the strength or weakness of the civic community, as measured by indicators such as voter turnout, newspaper readership and membership of voluntary, sporting and cultural organizations. Strong civic community is linked to high levels of social capital. Gillies (1997: 15) suggests that 'communities with a high level of social capital are characterised by high levels of trust, positive social norms and many overlapping and diverse horizontal networks for communication and exchange of information, ideas and practical help'. Putnam noted only in passing that there was a significant link between strong civic community and both narrower income distribution and lower infant mortality rates, but a number of subsequent studies have sought to link health outcomes with social capital and social cohesion more closely (e.g. Kawachi *et al.* 1997; Campbell *et al.* 1999). Elstad (1998: 611) summarizes this approach: 'the underlying hypothesis is that the degree of social inequalities is highly influential on the formation or deformation of social capital, which is, in its turn, significant for peoples health'.

At a policy level, recognition of the importance of social cohesion and social capital links the health agenda to a wider, rights-based agenda for challenging social exclusion. If values such as trust, mutual respect and tolerance are to be fostered, the case for legislative and other strategies to counter different forms of discrimination is further strengthened by the acknowledgement that such approaches can contribute to overall improvements in health and the reduction of health inequalities. Such strategies can extend to cover not only the broad areas of race, gender or sexuality, but also the discrimination and social exclusion faced by groups with more specifically health-related problems, such as the stigma suffered by people with mental health problems, the physical and social exclusion of those with physical disabilities and the isolation suffered by many carers. Furthermore, a concern to build social capital necessitates consideration of process as well as content: 'democratic participatory styles in social organisations, from the family to the political system, ensure self-respect and feelings of being appreciated by one's surroundings, and have therefore additional health-enhancing effects' (Elstad 1998: 610; cf. also Bosma *et al.* 1999).

Social regulation: the counterpoint to social cohesion

Labour's initial period in office included some positive responses to these challenges, such as legislation on the homosexual age of consent, and the introduction of the Carers' National Strategy (albeit modestly funded) in 1999 (DoH 1999c). The impact of the Stephen Lawrence Inquiry may also strengthen the impetus to tackle institutional racism, especially in the public sector. For example, the NHS Executive issued a major new strategy document, *Tackling Racial Harassment in the NHS: A Plan for Action* in December 1998 (NHS Executive 1998) which explicitly acknowledged that past efforts on this issue had been woefully inadequate. Despite the government's reputation for excessive central control, improving opportunities for active participation in policy making by individuals and communities has been a theme of both constitutional reforms such as devolution and policy initiatives such as New Deal for communities and HAZs.

Yet at the same time, just as socially inclusive Europe can also be seen as fortress Europe, rejecting outsiders, other policy initiatives seem to reflect much less inclusive values. The initial draft Immigration and Asylum Bill imposed severe restrictions on the civil rights, financial support and, consequently, health of extremely vulnerable populations, which were only partially modified after vociferous parliamentary opposition from within the Labour Party.

Public safety has been a major driver for policy reform and its importance can be backed by the frequency with which crime and the fear of crime have featured in community health surveys. There is no doubt that violence is also a public health issue (Stanistreet *et al.* 1998). Health authorities have been drawn into new statutory community safety partnerships. The subtitle of the White Paper *Modernising Mental Health Services* (DoH 1998b) was *Safe, Sound and Supportive*, and the accompanying national framework gave a similar prominence to safety and security. The populist rhetoric of health ministers about the 'failure of community care' (DoH 1998b), whatever its qualifications, risks reinforcing prejudice and stigma towards a much wider group of people with mental health problems whose behaviour presents no danger to the community. Subsequent proposals to detain people with personality disorders who have not committed any crime further underlined the primacy of public safety issues in mental health policy making. The hard-won recognition of some mental illness as, in part, an expression of legitimate social deviance has disappeared.

Clearly it would be premature to assess the health impacts of Labour's approach, not least because the measurable health benefits of broader policies will take many years to flow through. But the apparent tensions in existing policy making illustrate that the pursuit of social cohesion is open to a range of interpretations and links particularly easily to the communitarian elements of Labour philosophy, which emphasize reciprocal rights and obligations. Dwyer (1998) suggests this introduces a form of 'conditional citizenship', citing a 1996 lecture by Tony Blair tellingly entitled 'The rights we enjoy reflect the duties we owe'. In the absence of a coherent strategy to address the broader determinants of social inequality – notably income distribution – there is a danger that the pursuit of social cohesion may come to be based not on acknowledging and respecting diversity, but on an increasingly regulated moral order which places particular emphasis on the centrality of paid work and the need to eliminate particular behaviours which are seen as deviant.

Levitas (1996) points out that much of the rhetoric of the social exclusion debate focuses heavily on participation in the labour market as the key marker of inclusion. This emphasis can certainly be identified in Labour's approach, where paid employment is presented simultaneously as a moral imperative, a badge of social inclusion and the key mechanism for poverty alleviation (especially when reinforced by changes in welfare benefits). From a health perspective, while employment can potentially offer significant benefits, this emphasis on work is problematic. First, it often assumes that paid work is by definition desirable, asking few questions about the nature of the jobs which are likely to be available, despite growing evidence of the creation of significant new occupational health hazards through monotony and lack of control at work (Bosma *et al.* 1997), insecurity and casualization. Second, the positive potential of minimum wage legislation as a mechanism for reducing poverty and inequality has been limited by the relatively low initial figure set. Finally, in the absence of a much stronger commitment to anti-discriminatory legislation and provision of appropriate support services, the emphasis on paid work risks stigmatizing and further excluding those whose poor health status or responsibility for dependants limits the possibility of taking up employment.

Similar tensions may surface in a number of the specific health-related policy interventions which Labour has prioritized, such as drug abuse, parenting, teenage pregnancies and smoking. In each case the individual and social costs are sufficiently high to legitimize the issue as a policy concern, and the government's initial approach seeks to be broad-ranging and inclusive rather than merely punitive (for example, in trying to shift the focus of drugs policy more towards education and treatment rather than narrow law enforcement; in extending the role of health visitors in family support; and in linking teenage pregnancies to issues such as educational and economic opportunities for girls and the availability of good sex education and contraceptive services). There is also some recognition that these are issues which need long-term strategies rather than 'quick fixes'. However, the Social Exclusion Unit's policies on teenage sexual health counterbalance a welcome challenge to British reticence about sex education in schools with a highly moralistic approach to teenagers who do not heed the call to reduce pregnancies (Social Exclusion Unit 1999). Similarly the role of health visitors in government proposals on *Supporting Families* (Home Office 1998) can be interpreted as suggesting a case-based and individualistic support role for troubled families rather than a broader approach to general public health nursing for children. It should also be remembered that the past role of public health in regulating personal behaviour has not always embodied values of inclusiveness and social justice. For example, belief in eugenics as a mechanism for controlling perceived deviance captured the imagination of many progressive political activists and public health professionals both in the UK and elsewhere, and survived in impeccably social democratic Sweden until the 1960s. While the context for Labour's policy initiatives is clearly different, the nature of the issues prioritized for action makes them potentially vulnerable to a return to more victim-blaming and stigmatizing approaches if the current strategies are not seen to be producing results within an acceptable timescale.

Social inclusion and universalism in the NHS

The previous section suggested that health presents a problem in terms of the social exclusion agenda first because overall health status within a society is not easily addressed just by targeting a specific group or groups and second because there may be unintended consequences for health of an agenda based on social inclusion and social regulation. While there are plenty of signs that the government recognizes such difficulties, they are likely to be downplayed because of the centrality of inclusive moral values to its political programme. This section explores the implications for the NHS as a facility which is intended to be universal and is specifically valued as such. Does the availability of a universal service automatically have a universal effect (an idea we refer to as 'simple universalism')? If not, does implementing a more genuine universality offer an alternative approach which is free of some of the moral strictures of the social inclusion approach?

Universalism in the NHS

The NHS was established in 1948 as an explicitly universalist and inclusive service – comprehensive, available to all and free at the point of use. Equal access was enshrined as a key theme, and health was to be promoted by an expansion of health centres. It was expected that other aspects of the welfare state would contribute to the health improvement of disadvantaged people. The ideal of the NHS reflected an ideological, even a moral commitment to equity (Bevan 1952), backed by a pragmatic judgement that if the middle classes saw themselves as benefiting from the service they would defend it, whereas a separate state-funded service reserved for the poor would become a second-class residual service.

To a significant extent this judgement has been vindicated by events: although some activities such as dentistry and optical services have to a large degree been privatized except for the very poor, and 14 per cent of the population now has some form of private health insurance, the NHS retains an enduring political appeal. However, the socially inclusive ideal of the NHS has always been endangered first by the continually threatened erosion of universalism itself, and second by the extent to which a universal service has ever been achieved in practice.

Threats to universalism

Right from the start, the ideal of the NHS faced restrictions, most of which have appeared in different guises ever since – necessary concessions to the medical and professional lobbies; restraints imposed by the post-war economy; costs of meeting previously hidden need, rising expectations and drug costs; and the manoeuvring of political interest groups including Conservative governments of the 1950s (Webster 1994). There was little early capital investment and when building commenced it was of hospitals rather than health centres. The growing complexities of health care administration led to the NHS becoming organized as a predominantly curative and sometimes, in the case of mental illness, incarceratory service. Early intentions to promote health within the NHS were gradually lost on the way.

Even with significant increases in NHS resources, the gap between what is medically possible and what is deemed politically affordable is likely to widen. The Conservative government's 1991 NHS reforms legitimized so-called 'post-code rationing' (sometimes open, sometimes concealed) of access to particular services at the local level. Gradually this rationing affected not only perceived minority services such as infertility treatment and gender reassignment, but also new drugs to combat cancer and, even more fundamentally, the availability of NHS funding for continuing care (residential or home-based nursing services following discharge from hospital). This represented the most unambiguous move to shift costs either to local government, or, more worryingly, to patients themselves. This dynamic is not just a feature of the NHS. A survey of primary care systems in selected European cities recently concluded that the structure of health care systems 'has become so complicated, diverse and fragmented that it is almost impossible for consumers to find their way through the system . . . with those in greatest need often having the greatest difficulty' (Birmingham Health Authority 1998: para. 5.2).

New Labour has reasserted the importance of national standards and is introducing a variety of national agencies and frameworks to guide and monitor their implementation. However, it has already had to face high-profile rationing decisions at national level, such as restrictions on the prescribing of Viagra. The government has also deferred consideration of the findings of its own Royal Commission on Care for the Elderly, which supported continuing NHS (and therefore free) provision of nursing services. If this trend continues, a de jure universal service may drift towards a de facto two-tier service, with the more affluent groups increasingly resorting to private health care. Such a drift, however gradual, would inevitably have long-term implications for the range and quality of NHS services offered to those who continued to rely upon it.

Politically, it seems highly unlikely that a Labour government (even one increasingly attracted to selectivism and targeting in other areas of social policy) would explicitly abandon the historic commitment to universalism. Nevertheless, the growing resource pressures of an ageing population and the need for radical improvements in crucial (and expensive) aspects of health care such as cancer treatment pose continuing challenges to the philosophy of universalism and comprehensiveness in NHS provision.

The failure of simple universalism to achieve equity

A key component of social exclusion is unequal access to services. The apparent provision of universal health care meant that it was politically convenient to take for granted the achievement of equal access. This had two related consequences. First, difficult issues around the social and economic determinants of health need not occupy centre stage, since the NHS was available to pick up the results. Second, the NHS could be left to concentrate on illness and disease. It took time for the limitations of these assumptions to become apparent.

Titmuss (1968) drew attention to research which showed that higher income groups got more advantage out of the NHS than those most in need, a situation encapsulated by Tudor Hart in the so-called 'inverse care law' (Tudor Hart 1971). The Black Report (1980: ch. 4) highlighted access as a partial but important contributor to health inequalities, pointing out that poorer people faced not only more illness but a lower level and poorer quality of provision. For many people unevenness in provision was symbolized by inner-city areas with a ramshackle primary care system, staffed by single-handed general practitioner (GP) practices often of dubious quality, but containing large technologically advanced teaching hospitals, treating patients from a much wider area.

Whitehead (1988) asked whether anything approaching social justice in health existed in the UK. To the three equity issues identified in the Black Report (equal access to available care, equal treatment for equal cases and equal quality of care), she added equal access for equal need (p. 267). Despite some imaginative schemes throughout the country, there was insufficient evidence to suggest that the aim of equal access was being addressed in any coherent and effective way. Similar conclusions could be drawn for the 1990s. The lack of consistent progress was underlined by Acheson's (1998) Recommendation 37 that the provision of equitable access to effective care, in relation to need, should be a governing principle of all policies in the NHS. The Inquiry also drew attention to the 'inverse law of prevention' whereby those most at risk experienced the least satisfactory access to preventive services (Acheson 1998: 112).

Another form of universalism: the population approach to public health

A side-shoot of universalism is the desire to avoid interventions based on 'victim blaming'. The ideal of a universal service dovetails into the resurgence of the 'population approach' to preventive medicine, most clearly expounded by Rose (1992). Ill health is seen as arising from the behaviour and circumstances of society as a whole, and the population approach seeks to move the whole distribution of particular risk factors (including their extremes) in a favourable direction. Thus the incidence of heavy drinking, for example, with its concomitant risks to health and public order, can be shown to be related to mean levels of drinking. Marmot (1998) uses Rose's theory to focus preventive medicine away from individual risk factors to those which can be found in the social environment and to suggest that more health gain may be achievable by broader interventions. This broader sweep for interventions links both with the development of the concept of social capital already discussed and with growing attention to the potential of 'healthy settings' (see below). Both Rose and Marmot are open about the ethical dilemmas of such a social engineering approach, but there can be no doubt about its potential appeal to those already associated with communitarianism.

Limits of universalism

Both a universally available health service and a broader socially-oriented understanding of health are essential to avoid the institutionalization of social exclusion in health issues. However, the conclusions drawn by Acheson (1998) and his predecessors show clearly that defending the NHS as a universal service is not a sufficient strategy for addressing the health impacts of social exclusion. If the NHS is to play a full part in this challenge, it needs both a systematic attempt to assess how it can influence the wider structural determinants of health status and also a cultural change in the way it provides health care, especially to many socially disadvantaged or excluded groups.

Despite (or perhaps because of) the English *The Health of the Nation* strategy (DoH 1992), there was little evidence before 1997 of substantial NHS engagement with wider issues. Some health authorities took on nominal links at strategic level through representation on City Challenge, Single Regeneration Budget and other partnerships concerned with economic and social regeneration. However, they were rarely key players except on health care issues (with occasional honourable exceptions). At community level again there were some examples of experiments or even a commitment to community development initiatives, especially under the 'healthy city' banner (Baker 1998), but these were patchy, insecurely funded and often marginal. A formal evaluation of the *The Health of the Nation* strategy found that it had had only limited impact, particularly on resource allocation at a local level (DoH 1998c).

The Acheson Inquiry on health inequalities (Acheson 1998), quoted above, recommended both 'upstream' and 'downstream' interventions. But, as Hilary Graham (1999: 4) succinctly observes, getting the balance right is far from simple:

> Reductions in health inequalities represent downstream solutions which require strategies which target upstream influences. How to equalise access to the determinants of good health is likely to be a question framed by disagreements about the evidence, both on causal pathways and on effective solutions.

A further problem for policy is that if health improvement is regarded as dependent on advances elsewhere, history suggests that health issues will be secondary to other priorities – including costs. However, downstream interventions in the health sector itself are unlikely to produce quick wins unless they are related to NHS activity figures – which may not necessarily indicate health improvement.

Cultural change

Little has been done to address the inverse law of care since it was first propounded, and the Acheson inquiry confirms the pattern (Acheson 1998). Indeed some reforms, like the introduction of GP fundholders in 1992 tended to reinforce the process, since the GP practices who were in the best position to take advantage of fundholding were rarely in highly disadvantaged areas. Efficiency indexes and performance standards (including Patients' Charters) had little to do with equity and could be easily subverted. While there were some significant service improvements, assessments which might indicate a need to redistribute resources were unlikely to be commissioned. Health commissioners and providers were forced to some extent to consider issues of women's health, services for disabled people and specific health needs of black and minority ethnic groups. But these rarely affected mainstream activity and issues of race and racism, if addressed at all, were often considered more in the context of the NHS as employer rather than as service provider. An equity audit commissioned by North Cheshire Health Authority (Johnstone *et al.* 1996) found that better-off parts of the area had significantly more elective surgery for coronary heart disease and for hip or knee joint replacements despite the need for both being much greater elsewhere. Poorer parts of the district with the highest proportion of people over 65 had the lowest proportion of district nurses. Similar findings exist elsewhere and point to the need for major adjustments in resource allocation, service priorities and methods of service delivery.

The future of universalism in the NHS: The Labour response

Despite flaws in the original commitments to universalism and equity, these principles remain the basis of public loyalty to the NHS. But their survival in the future may depend on the outcome of two issues:

- Whether it is possible to resist the process evident in other areas of the welfare state, whereby resource pressures result in de facto residualism, thus institutionalizing social exclusion in health care as the better-off increasingly vote with their feet.
- Whether the political will and institutional capacity exists within the NHS to address the broader determinants of health.

Labour's proclaimed intention in the White Papers outlined above was to address these issues head-on. Despite a pledge to avoid massive NHS restructuring, the need for a reshaping of organizational culture and priorities could not be gainsaid. 'Improved access' would have to mean more than just a few telephone advice services. Success would depend on a genuine commitment to a stronger focus on promoting the public health and on primary/community care; a challenge to narrow professional dominance; the development of more participative democratic structures; and the adoption of a genuine universalism which recognized and respected diversity rather than one which assumed or even demanded uniformity from those who were most disadvantaged or discriminated against. Could the NHS deliver?

There is no doubt that the first wave of Labour health ministers were genuinely committed to (and staked a great deal on) being able to revive the NHS as part of creating a healthier society. In some ways the broad consensus over the need to address social exclusion was safer territory than the implementation of public health commitments at a macro level (for example over tobacco policy and food safety), where health becomes just one of several competing priorities. The general tenor of policy was met with enthusiasm on the ground (despite degrees of reservation). Successes could reasonably be claimed for a range of progressive developments which could act as symbolic flagships, beacons or trail-blazers without being subject to the difficulty of fluctuating quantitative targets such as hospital waiting lists.

However, there was very real difficulty in creating specific new health initiatives which effectively addressed the health issues of social exclusion. In relation to HAZs, the leader of the formal evaluation team, Ken Judge (1999: 20), considered that:

> there is no lack of ambition or commitment to address the problems that all of the HAZs have identified. But far too often it proves to be profoundly difficult to link well-specified interventions or activities to

credible consequences or targets that have some logical association with strategic objectives.

Judge concluded that this *was* possible (and instanced a programme on housing and health) but at this stage the 'beneficial outcomes' remain uncertain. Nor will simply using the HAZs as distribution points for funding necessarily mean that health inequalities are addressed. For example, the majority of adult smokers are in lower income groups and often under stress because of caring responsibilities (Graham 1993; DoH 1999a: 6.6). Yet the £10 million smoking cessation programme for HAZs to implement during 1999/2000 (DoH 1999a: 6.13; NHS Executive 1999) seemed to have been designed without any real thought of how to make it a realistic opportunity for people who are disadvantaged, apart from offering one week's free nicotine patches for those on benefit.

Universalism has been advanced in this chapter as a key element for addressing social exclusion. On the broader issue of equitable access the New Labour government seemed after two years to have made more advance, especially in primary care (other than dentistry). NHS Direct appeared in mid-1999 to be becoming a popular service, despite the qualms of some professional bodies. However, there was less evidence on the ground that health authorities were prepared to take seriously the issues of equitable access to hospital treatment. Equity audits still seemed to exist more on government wish lists than in local business plans, although the inclusion of equity measures in the National Performance Indicators could be expected to have some effect. Equity in employment and opportunities for social investment by the NHS were other areas for expansion.

Some delays were due to practical difficulties of readjustment in an environment where all the priorities are changing. Most health authorities had been preoccupied with the organizational consequences for themselves and others of setting up PCGs. Few had had real contacts with the local voluntary and community sectors, while rapid deadlines for responding to complex issues severely limited opportunities (at any rate in the first year) to involve either local communities or front-line staff. Despite the encouragement for public health in *Saving Lives: Our Healthier Nation* (DoH 1999a), the position of the discipline (and that of health promotion) in the NHS structure remained uncertain. The brave rhetoric could not on its own prove that the NHS had a real capacity to achieve any real redirection of resources towards the greatest health needs. Nevertheless, in mid-1999 the development of local partnerships was still at a very early stage and anecdotal evidence suggested some real though variable beneficial impact on relationships between GPs and other professions and agencies at the PCG level. Even relatively isolated sections of the NHS such as the central Estates Department were initiating dialogue about rethinking the assumptions on which NHS property is designed and developed – a potentially major contribution to social inclusion if the inherent barriers of conventional design could really be shaken off.

As in other policy areas, the government's overriding commitment has been the promotion of social cohesion, and, at the more local level, of social capital. The population approach to, and the association between, levels of ill health and relative inequality offer linked rationales for this policy direction. *Saving Lives: Our Healthier Nation* made a specific link between social cohesion and the prevention of coronary heart disease. It also suggested that new local health structures should encourage active lifestyles around sport and art which could play key roles in supporting urban regeneration and environmental action to create social cohesion and healthy neighbourhoods (DoH 1999a: 6.20, 4.34–40).

Gowman (1999) sets out some of the strengths and weaknesses of the healthy neighbourhood concept and believes it could form the basis of a comprehensive, effective and practical programme to improving public health. The introduction of healthy living centres as community-focused facilities could be expected to provide a concrete focus to such endeavour and con-siderable care was taken to build flexibility into the bidding system. However, the early models were all built on long-standing community initiatives and more ambitious projects such as the Neptune Health Park in Sandwell (directly addressing health and regeneration themes) were based on tested partnerships. If political priorities dictate a need for 'quick wins', the fragile process of community development may prove impossible to sustain; while issues of maintaining neighbourhood involvement over a series of life cycles will be shelved. Success will depend on the willingness of authorities at central and local level to take mechanisms of consultation and participation seriously rather than using them for purposes of ad hoc legitimation.

There is also the question of how far it is realistic to expect those who have been marginalized to become 'involved'. As researchers into primary care and health promotion have pointed out:

> Institutions . . . often lose touch with, ignore, or are prevented from find-ing significant numbers of people who are effectively disenfranchised. They form an 'unknown or hidden society' often in opposition to prevail-ing values, standards and norms. To that extent, conventional social policy initiatives are unlikely to have a significant effect on those groups who may well value their exclusion.
>
> (Birmingham Health Authority 1998: 6.5)

Such cautions apply not only to self-proclaimed deviant groups such as substance abusers or young people who have dropped out of all the New Deal arrangements, but also to groups which have a distinct cultural identity. These barriers do not mean that inclusion policies are doomed to failure: even in disadvantaged areas there is significant social capital in the form of informal networks providing mutual help and support (Campbell et al. 1999; Forrest and Kearns 1999). In some cases relatively simple innovations which treat the needs of marginalized groups seriously (such as the issuing of per-sonal health records to travelling families in the 1980s) can have significant and positive effects. However, the difficulties do warn against treating the neighbourhood approach as a panacea.

Conclusion

Labour has chosen to give a high profile to issues of poverty and social exclusion, including commitments to abolish child poverty and reduce health inequalities. Despite Wainwright's (1996) scepticism, it seems unlikely that such high-profile hostages to fortune would be offered unless there was some belief that effective action could and would be taken in a range of policy areas. The key questions remain whether or not Labour's approach to social exclusion is based on a flawed analysis of what can be achieved in practice, and whether any perceived failures will result either in growing neglect of the issue or in increasingly punitive approaches.

The prospects for many policy areas with significant implications for health are dealt with in other chapters. Government action within the health field itself contains major positive features. The importance of issues of health inequality and social exclusion is clearly recognized, together with a proactive role for government in responding to the challenges. In particular, the emphasis on 'joined-up government' is especially appropriate for a multi-faceted issue such as health. Ministers have created and encouraged a variety of opportunities to experiment with new approaches such as HAZs, and have launched specific initiatives such as the Carers' National Strategy which, despite their modest beginnings, have considerable potential for future development. But the problems remain formidable. Not only is the knowledge base for effective intervention very limited, but government is having to deal with pre-existing organizational structures and cultures which are inappropriate for the task in hand and undergoing very considerable organizational upheaval. There are signs that Labour's New NHS could become the foundation for significant changes in current resource distribution and organizational priorities, but success will depend on real commitments at a local level. It remains to be seen whether this approach is persuasive enough to enthuse not just key agencies but also the socially excluded themselves to become involved in the process of long-term change.

More broadly, Labour's refusal to give an explicit commitment to redistribution limits the extent to which specifically material causes of ill health can be ameliorated through state intervention. Even redistribution by sleight of hand does little to improve perception or self-worth among those in need. To the extent that Labour's overall economic policies risk widening existing inequalities rather than creating a constituency for greater equality, it will become even more difficult to create the conditions for increasing social capital and social cohesion. This broader context imposes severe constraints on pursuing the lofty objectives of *Saving Lives* (DoH 1999a). Although the White Paper clearly acknowledged the importance of Wilkinson's (1996) arguments about relative inequalities, as well as highlighting more specific health hazards such as occupational stress and job insecurity, there is little evidence so far that these health arguments have had much impact on wider policies – a sharp reminder of the limitations of 'joined-up government' when health priorities conflict with others.

Despite these limitations, advocates of the 'new public health' have to recognize that Labour's agenda represents the nearest potential implementation of the ideals of healthy public policy that is likely to occur in the UK in the immediate future. Any high-profile failure could easily mean a reversion to far more traditional approaches. In such a complex enterprise it will be crucial that the benefits of placing health inequalities in the context of a social, environmental and economic approach to health do not founder by becoming tied to moral or even false expectations derived from the communitarian agenda.

Finally, it must be remembered that while other government systems (such as state benefits) can penalize those who do not conform, the universalized health service has to remain open to all. It is perhaps for this reason that the preservation of a real universalism, which is capable of encompassing many forms of diversity, remains an essential element of any strategy for responding to the health problems which are linked to social exclusion.

References

Acheson, Sir D. (1988) *Public Health in England: The Report of the Committee of Inquiry into the Future Development of the Public Health Function*, Cm 289. London: The Stationery Office.

Acheson, Sir D. (1998) *Independent Inquiry into Inequalities in Health: Report*. London: The Stationery Office.

APH, HEA, King's Fund (1998) *Our Healthier Nation: A Response to the Public Health Green Paper*. London: APH, HEA, King's Fund.

Baker, P. (1998) A healthy new development. *Healthlines*, 57: 8–10.

Benzeval, M., Judge, K. and Whitehead, M. (eds) (1995) *Tackling Inequalities in Health*. London: King's Fund.

Bevan, A. (1952) *In Place of Fear*. London: Heinemann.

Birmingham Health Authority (1998) *Primary Care Audits: Social Exclusion and User Participation in Health Promotion in Rotterdam and Birmingham (UK)*. Birmingham: Birmingham Health Authority.

Black Report (1980) *Inequalities in Health: Report of a Research Working Group*, in N. Davidson and P. Townsend (eds) (1988) *Inequalities in Health*. London: Penguin.

Bosma, H., Marmot, M., Hemingway, H. *et al.* (1997) Low job control and risk of coronary heart disease in Whitehall II (prospective cohort) study. *British Medical Journal*, 314: 558–65.

Bosma, H., van de Mheen, H.D. and Mackenbach, J.P. (1999) Social class in childhood and general health in adulthood: questionnaire study of psychological attributes. *British Medical Journal*, 318: 18–22.

Campbell, C., Wood, R. and Kelly, M. (1999) *Social Capital and Health*. London: Health Education Authority.

Curtis, S. and Rees Jones, I. (1998) Is there a place for geography in the analysis of health inequality? *Sociology of Health and Illness*, 20(5): 645–72.

DoH (Department of Health) (1992) *The Health of the Nation: A Strategy for Health in England*, Cm 1986. London: HMSO.

DoH (Department of Health) (1995) *Variations in Health: What Can the Department of Health and the NHS Do?* London: HMSO.

DoH (Department of Health) (1997) *The New NHS: Modern, Dependable*, Cm 3807. London: HMSO.

DoH (Department of Health) (1998a) *Our Healthier Nation*, Cm 3852. London: The Stationery Office.

DoH (Department of Health) (1998b) *Modernising Mental Health Services: Safe, Sound and Supportive*. London: The Stationery Office.

DoH (Department of Health) (1998c) *Health of the Nation: A Policy Assessed*. London: The Stationery Office.

DoH (Department of Health) (1999a) *Saving Lives: Our Healthier Nation*, Cm 4386. London: The Stationery Office.

DoH (Department of Health) (1999b) *Reducing Health Inequalities: An Action Report*, Cm 4386. London: Department of Health.

DoH (Department of Health) (1999c) *Caring about Carers: A National Strategy for Carers.* London: The Stationery Office.

Dwyer, P. (1998) Conditional citizens: welfare rights and responsibilities in the late 1990s. *Critical Social Policy*, 18(4): 493–517.

Elstad, J. (1998) The psycho-social perspective on social inequalities in health. *Sociology of Health and Illness*, 20(5): 598–618.

Forrest, R. and Kearns, A. (1999) *Joined-up Places? Social Cohesion and Neighbourhood Regeneration.* York: Joseph Rowntree Foundation.

Gillies, P. (1997) Social capital: recognising the value of society. *Healthlines*, 45: 15–17.

Gowman, N. (1999) *Healthy Neighbourhoods.* London: King's Fund.

Graham, H. (1993) *When Life's a Drag: Women, Smoking and Disadvantage.* London: Department of Health.

Graham, H. (1999) Inquiry into inequalities in health. *Health Variations*, 3: 2–4.

Hobcraft, J. (1998) *Intergenerational and Life-Course Transmission of Social Exclusion: Influences of Childhood Poverty, Family Disruption, and Contact with the Police*, CASE Paper 15. London: London School of Economics.

Home Office (1998) *Supporting Families: A Consultative Document.* London: The Stationery Office.

Johnstone, F., Lucy, J., Scott-Samuel, A. and Whitehead, M. (1996) *Deprivation and Health in North Cheshire: An Equity Audit of Health Services.* Liverpool: Equity in Health Research and Development Unit, Liverpool Public Health Observatory.

Judge, K. (1999) National evaluation of Health Action Zones, *PSSRU Bulletin*, 11: 18–20.

Karasek, R. and Theorell, T. (1990) *Health, Work, Stress, Productivity and the Reconstruction of Working Life.* New York: Basic Books.

Kawachi, I., Kennedy, B.P. and Lochner, K. (1997) Social capital, income inequality and mortality. *American Journal of Public Health*, 87(9): 1491–8.

Levitas, R. (1996) The concept of social exclusion and the new Durkheimian hegemony. *Critical Social Policy*, 16(1): 5–20.

Lewis, G. and Sloggett, A. (1998) Suicide, deprivation and unemployment: record linkage study. *British Medical Journal*, 317: 1283–6.

McCormick, J. and Leicester, G. (1998) *Scottish Council Foundation Response to the Social Exclusion in Scotland Consultation Paper.* Edinburgh: Scottish Councils Federation.

Macintyre, S. (1998) The importance of place. *Healthlines*, 55: 8–9.

Marmot, M.G. (1998) Improvement of social environment to improve health. *The Lancet*, 351: 57–60.

Marmot, M.G. and Wilkinson, R. (1999) *The Social Determinants of Health.* Oxford: Oxford University Press.

Marmot, M.G., Davey Smith, G.D., Stansfeld, S. *et al.* (1991) Health inequalities among British civil servants: the Whitehall II study. *The Lancet*, 337(8750): 1387–93.

NHS Executive (1998) *Tackling Racial Harassment in the NHS: A Plan for Action.* London: Department of Health.

NHS Executive (1999) *New NHS Smoking Cessation Services*, Health Service Circular HSC 1999/087. London: Department of Health.

PHA (Public Health Alliance) (1988) *Beyond Acheson: An Agenda for the New Public Health.* Birmingham: Public Health Alliance.

Phillimore, P., Beattie, A. and Townsend, P. (1994) Widening inequality of health in northern England 1981–1991. *British Medical Journal*, 308: 1125–8.

Putnam, R.D. (1993) *Making Democracy Work: Civic Traditions in Modern Italy.* Princeton, NJ: Princeton University Press.

Putnam, R.D. (1995) Tuning in, tuning out: the strange disappearance of social capital in America. *Political Science and Politics*, December: 664–83.

Rose, G. (1992) *The Strategy of Preventive Medicine.* Oxford: Oxford University Press.

Sloggett, A. and Joshi, H. (1994) Higher mortality in deprived areas: community or personal disadvantage. *British Medical Journal*, 109: 1470–4.

Social Exclusion Unit (1998) *Bringing Britain Together: A National Strategy for Neighbourhood Renewal*, Cm 4045. London: The Stationery Office.

Social Exclusion Unit (1999) *Teenage Pregnancy*, Cm 4342. London: The Stationery Office.

Stanistreet, D., Jeffrey, V. and Bellis, M. (1998) *Violence and Public Health: Developing a Policy Agenda*. Liverpool: Department of Public Health, University of Liverpool.

Titmuss, R.M. (1968) *Commitment to Welfare*. London: Allen & Unwin.

Tudor Hart, J. (1971) The inverse care law. *The Lancet*, 27 February 1971: 405–12.

Wainwright, D. (1996) The political transformation of the health inequalities debate. *Critical Social Policy*, 16(4): 67–82.

Webster, C. (1994) Conservatives and consensus: the politics of the National Health Service 1951–64, in A. Oakley and A.S. Williams (eds) *The Politics of the Welfare State*. London: UCL Press.

West, P. (1997) Review of R.G. Wilkinson, *Unhealthy societies: the afflictions of inequality*, in *Sociology of Health and Illness*, 19(5): 668–70.

Whitehead (1988) The health divide, in N. Davidson and P. Townsend (eds) *Inequalities in Health*. London: Penguin.

Wilkinson, R.G. (1996) *Unhealthy Societies*. London and New York: Routledge.

Wilkinson, R.G. (1997) What health tells us about society, *Soundings Special: The Next Ten Years*. London: Lawrence & Wishart.

6   HOUSING AND SOCIAL EXCLUSION

Murray Hawtin and Jane Kettle

> Housing is relevant to social exclusion because of the connection with education, employment prospects and health. Children brought up in damp, overcrowded or noisy conditions will find it difficult to study. Those living in estates which have a poor reputation may find themselves disadvantaged when making job applications. Poor housing can also impact on health, particularly that of children and thus have an effect on school attendance. It can also have a substantial effect on the morale and mental health of parents who have to cope with problems such as dampness day after day.
>
> (Scottish Office 1999a: ch. 2.8)

Introduction

Desirable housing policy outcomes have been characterized by different post-war governments in terms of a separate house for every family that wishes to have one in 1945, a decent home for every family at a price within their means in 1971, and a decent home within the reach of every family in 1995 (Holmans 1995). The current government is no exception and has made similar statements of intent. However, speaking at the 1999 annual convention of Leicestershire Housing Associations, David Butler, the chief executive of the Chartered Institute of Housing, predicted that the key drivers of housing policy in the next millennium would be social exclusion, health inequality and crime (Butler 1999: 10). Does this indicate, therefore, that attempts to achieve a well-housed, inclusive society have failed? And how do such broader issues of social exclusion, health inequality and crime relate to housing?

Debates about the relationship between housing policy and social exclusion have tended to focus on the 'extent to which the processes operating within the housing sector contribute to the generation of deprivation' (Lee and Murie 1997: 4). Bad housing, and the problems that come with it are, of course, associated closely with poverty; the poor are usually ill-housed. Housing from this perspective is seen as an economic problem. Adequate housing is crudely explained as a simple function of the distribution of income; there would not be a 'housing problem' if everyone had sufficient income. A more sophisticated approach admits that there are inefficiencies within the housing market although these are seen as particular problems within an overall system that generally functions well. Other housing commentators have approached housing issues from the perspective of particular groups that are ill-housed. According to this view, housing issues are the aggregated problems of specific groups within an otherwise well-functioning housing system. At worst this approach blames the victim (the elderly, single parent households, ethnic minorities) and at best it ignores the underlying systematic housing issues.

Disagreement as to the causes of housing problems is further complicated by the lack of an agreed definition as to what the term 'housing' encompasses. It certainly includes shelter, but must go beyond that to include home and the community as well. 'For a house to be a home, and so promote good health, it needs to be affordable; in good repair; safe; secure; of adequate size and design; with appropriate support for the activities of daily living for people unable to look after themselves; and situated in a suitable environment' (National Housing Federation, undated: 3). A home is therefore important not only for survival, but is also one of the central foundations for a fulfilling personal life. If a resident feels safe, secure and able to afford their home, and if they feel proud living there and want to invest time and money in it, they are more likely to feel included in their community and society more generally. Conversely, poor housing both relates to and contributes to problems of social disadvantage. Researchers and policy makers are becoming increasingly aware of the ways in which living in impoverished environments contributes to exclusionary processes, and the fact that investment in housing yields wider economic and social benefits including improved heath and reduced crime.

Housing has become a major commodity for the majority of people. As a commodity it is primarily produced for profit: those who cannot afford market prices will not get decent accommodation. However, housing differs from other commodities: it is one of the basic necessities of life; it is the most durable of consumer goods; and it involves the largest amount of personal investment. But more significantly in this context, housing is central to a person's identity and contributes to the structuring of social relationships:

> housing processes can be understood as types of processes which either promote social inclusion or contribute to social exclusion. Social exclusion through housing happens if the effect of housing processes is to deny certain social groups control over their daily lives, or to impair enjoyment of wider citizenship rights.
>
> (Somerville 1998: 772)

Somerville's definition of social exclusion through housing goes beyond simply identifying poor housing as an inevitable outcome of the profit-driven housing market. It includes other aspects which relate to (or are consequences of) poor housing, including constrained opportunities and lack of participation in decision making. The *provision* of inadequate housing, therefore, may not in itself be exclusionary; as important may be the way in which it is provided and managed.

Tenure policy and social exclusion in housing

After World War II, successive governments turned to local authorities to provide the much-needed accommodation for households from diverse social backgrounds. Good quality housing with low rents was seen as a key plank in the development of the welfare state. By the mid-1970s the housing circumstances of the majority of British citizens had improved considerably and the problems faced by those in housing need had changed. The problems of overcrowding, shortage, unfitness and disrepair, and exploitative landlordism had been largely eradicated by an expansion in council housing, massive slum clearance programmes and the introduction of rent controls in the private sector. The policy processes driving these measures are well documented (Merrett 1979; Nuttgens 1989; Balchin 1995; Williams 1997).

By 1971, 50 per cent of householders in England and Wales were owner-occupiers; 30 per cent rented their home from the local authority or, in very small numbers, from housing associations; and 20 per cent were the tenants of private landlords (Whitehead 1997). The contemporary situation represents a considerable shift, with 68 per cent of householders now owner-occupiers, 18 per cent living in council tenancies, 4 per cent in housing association accommodation and 10 per cent in the private rented sector (CIH/JRF/CML 1999).

This rapid and extreme shift in tenure distribution highlights the importance that has been attached to the house as a vehicle for expanding personal wealth – the promotion of owner-occupation has underpinned and informed policy throughout the second half of the century. Once the post-war housing shortages had been addressed, British housing policy became increasingly linked to individual consumption. Owning one's own home was equated with greater life choices and a freedom from either the restrictions of 'bad' landlords or the over-paternalistic state. Although it has been shown that the process of commodification was well-established before the 1980s (Forrest and Murie 1988), it could be argued that between 1979 and 1997, and more especially since 1988, housing policy was, in fact, *tenure* policy with most initiatives aimed at promoting home ownership over all other forms of tenure. Between 1979 and 1997 there were 18 major pieces of housing legislation, many of which were designed to diminish the role of municipal landlords (Holder *et al.* 1998) and increase the stigma of council housing. These included measures to enhance the power and choice of tenants to exit the council sector (either through the opportunity to purchase or to chose a new landlord); to reduce capital resources available to local authority landlords thereby preventing them from constructing new homes and resulting in the developmental role being passed to housing associations; and to revive private renting. Inevitably the overall impact of these changes has been felt most keenly within the social housing sector (that is, housing owned, let and managed by local authorities and registered social landlords (RSLs) who now may be housing associations, local housing companies, Housing Action Trusts, etc). Some 30 per cent of tenants have exercised the Right to Buy which, along with related polices, has resulted in over 2 million dwellings being sold.

The growth in house purchase has made Britain truly a 'nation of home-owners'. This process of state subsidized individualism (Forrest and Murie 1988) has, furthermore, been encouraged through a mortgage taxation relief system that is finally being terminated according to proposals presented in the 1999 Budget. However, since the mid-1990s council tenants have been effectively penalized. In 1999 the Treasury will make £700 million from council tenants and in the following year around £850 million. Since the Thatcher government changed the housing finance system the government has been reducing subsidies to local housing authorities, resulting in council tenants who are not on housing benefit subsidizing those who are:

> A system where the nation collectively supports the housing costs of people on low incomes in the private sector, including housing associ-ations, but where almost a third of costs of supporting the same housing costs of people in the public sector is paid for by tenants themselves is a public scandal.
>
> (Challis 1999)

Although the current government is proposing to remove this rent rebate subsidy from the housing revenue account to redress this inequality, some have argued that the introduction of resource accounting (a new system of measuring budgets) will leave tenants in the same position although less conspicuously so. The total amount of government money spent on council housing appears set to remain static under the new system, principally due to pressure from the Treasury.

Another policy used in the privatization of welfare housing has been the overall drive from 'bricks and mortar' subsidies to means-tested subsidies, although with unintended consequences. The subsidy regime of the 1980s meant that local authority rent rises were driven firmly by central govern-ment and housing association rents. The strongly upward trend reflected both the deregulation of rents and the higher cost of private finance as a proportion of capital costs (Ginsberg 1997). This imposition on the social rented sector of a drive to make rents reflect market levels has inevitably led to a massive increase in spending on housing benefit. In 1999, housing benefit payments accounted for over 10 per cent of total welfare spending and cost £12 million. It was noted by the chancellor of the exchequer in the 1999 Budget statement that the system is complex to administer and vulnerable to fraud. Current government proposals include replacing hous-ing benefit for low-income tenants with a tax credit system. This radical pro-posal appears to acknowledge, finally, that housing benefit acts as a disincentive to work for many tenants because of its massive contribution to the so-called poverty trap. Under current regulations, many people who are unemployed and in receipt of housing benefit face a marginal tax rate of 95 per cent if they take jobs.

Effect of tenure policy on social housing

Overall investment in social housing has declined significantly since 1980, resulting in dramatically fewer properties being built and a decline in the condition of existing ones. Over 30 per cent of newly-built RSL homes fail the National Housing Federation affordability test (MacLennan and Pryce 1998); over £2 billion is required to carry out essential repairs and mainten-ance to council housing stock, and 1 in 13 council homes were unfit for occupation (DoE 1996). Although estimates of the amount of money needed to invest in council housing ranges from £10 billion to £20 billion it is unlikely that significantly more resources will be provided. Currently there is only £500 million available each year to clear the backlog of investment. According to the most optimistic estimates, without considerably more invest-ment it would take 20 years to clear this backlog. The overall housing invest-ment is going to work out at £3.5 billion less over the term of the Labour government than the last term of the Conservatives. Hilary Armstrong, then minister for local government and housing, told Shelter that 'we acknow-ledge that there is a £10 billion backlog in social housing repairs, we know that the £5 billion pounds over this parliament (from the capital receipt initiative) won't solve all the problems. But it is a major injection of new funding into the system, and we want to see it work' (Birch 1998). Social inclusion through choice of tenure is the rhetoric of this, and previous, govern-ments. However there is little choice available to those who cannot afford to change tenure or who wish to stay in the public sector provided that their houses are improved and there is no stigma attached to council housing.

The reduction in new-build, along with the Right to Buy, has resulted in substantially less affordable housing now being available; there is an estim-ated shortfall nationally of over half a million affordable homes for rent. Availability of socially rented housing, however, is geographically determined, being most plentiful in areas where there has been a loss of employment and where demand for labour is low (Lee and Murie 1997). One of the most problematic overall effects of the general lack of social accommodation has been to make access to social housing almost solely dependent on *need*. In 1997, over 110,000 households were accommodated in the sector because they were homeless. In addition, as more affluent tenants have bought their homes, the social base of the sector has narrowed with a higher proportion of low-income households and those dependent on welfare benefit (two thirds of social tenants are either wholly or partly dependent on state benefits). It has also become a tenure of young households and older people, with the traditional role of council housing for housing two parent families with children becoming less evident. The boundaries between this residual housing sector and owner-occupation have become more stark and have exacerbated social divisions.

These conditions have contributed to the phenomenon previously known as 'difficult to let' or 'problem estates', characterized by residents who are highly vulnerable and living in poverty and where child densities, crime levels and empty and abandoned properties are high. In these areas, typically, few people are in employment, and a downward spiral develops as the economic-ally active tenants leave the area. It has been estimated that over 3 million

Britons are living in what are described as the worst 1300 social housing estates (DETR 1997). In September 1997, Peter Mandelson, former minister without portfolio in the Labour government, declared that the social exclusion facing the residents of Britain's worst estates was the 'greatest social crisis of our time' (*Housing Today* 1997: 1). It is important to recognize that 'worst' is here defined in terms of crime rates rather than disrepair or lack of demand for the properties in the area.

A more recently acknowledged phenomenon, although not a new one, is that neighbourhood dissatisfaction on some estates has become so high that abandoned and boarded-up properties are the norm. One of the major underlying factors influencing low demand is the continuing flow of population from older industrial areas, exacerbated by increasing residential mobility within low demand areas. Many people want to live in the inner urban areas of London and the South where house and land prices are spiralling out of the reach of local people and affordable housing providers.

The Social Exclusion Unit report (1998b) devotes a considerable part of its housing section to low demand and suggests that there are two broad policy responses. The first is to endorse abandonment. This strategy is being considered in some detail by the Housing Corporation but is a very costly option especially for the public sector. The other option is to reverse what has been described as the decentralization of employment and population (Webster 1999). One of the major implications of this would be to change the rent structure within the RSL sector to halt the haemorrhage of tenants to the private sector. Improving regional economies would thus help to stem the flow, giving a clear role for regional development agencies. Other policies may need to be implemented such as redrawing city boundaries, creating new urban green-field sites or creating business areas within existing urban regions.

Although the general pattern of deprivation and low demand applies both nationally and at a local level, it varies considerably geographically. Lee and Murie (1997) suggest that deprived groups are concentrated in different patterns within different cities. They argue that although deprivation remains concentrated in many inner-city areas, evidence also shows that it exists in more dispersed or peripheral areas. Furthermore, the most deprived areas of cities are not exclusively areas of council housing; many are areas of mixed tenure, reflecting the growing differentiation of other housing tenures including home ownership. Some of the poorest sections of the community live in owner-occupied homes. For example, black and ethnic minority households which are economically disadvantaged and those who have long-term illnesses are not heavily concentrated in council housing. Characteristically their exclusion is individually experienced and less likely to manifest itself in the form of the deteriorating environment that is so often associated with council estates, although some homeowners and privately renting households do live in what they perceive to be highly problematic neighbourhoods (Burrows and Rhodes 1998).

Furthermore, although people who rent from RSLs and local authority housing landlords are more likely to have a lower income, and most new entrants to social housing are cash poor, it is not the case that all consumers of social housing are excluded. Research has shown that people living in areas often described as problem housing estates do not necessarily become segregated from the rest of society, and people generally defined as being in poverty tend not to see themselves as socially excluded but share 'professional' aspirations such as having a good job (Dean and Taylor-Gooby 1992; Jordan 1992). Indeed the participation and involvement mechanisms of many landlords may foster a sense of inclusion that may be denied to more affluent households in other tenures. It is not the provision of inadequate housing that is necessarily exclusionary but rather its location and the means by which it is provided. The north-south divide in terms of property prices has a substantial impact on job mobility and may contribute to exclusionary processes. The standard construction types promoted by many construction companies and standard house types used by RSLs effectively denies access to people with particular disabilities or cultural needs. Notions of neighbourhood safety and values exclude entry to people who are 'other'; witness the 'Nimbyism' displayed where care in the community schemes or developments by black and minority ethnic housing associations are proposed in areas where community mobilization is well-planned and powerful. These exclusionary processes are largely independent of tenure grouping.

Estate-based policies

Where tenure has become an indicator of deprivation, solutions include breaking up the monopoly tenure of social housing and focusing programmes on the worst estates. Two of the principal means of challenging exclusion in areas of concentrated social housing are, first, encouraging a mix of tenure within estates and, second, using regeneration as a vehicle for social improvement.

Mixed tenure

Commentators have argued that within areas of high deprivation the higher concentrations of poor people tend to exacerbate the problems. Wilson (1987, 1996) argues that this fosters an economically and socially damaging set of norms tending to suppress ambition and self-confidence. Lack of appropriate networks (Perri 6 1997) and role models (Atkinson and Kintrea 1998) have also been said to exacerbate the deprivation spiral. Years of targeting the public housing sector on the poorest households in America has created similar issues of residualization. A former secretary of the US Housing and Urban Development Department (HUD), Henry Cisneros, called it 'warehousing the poor' (Page 1999). HUD are now attempting to attract moderate income households into the sector through freezing rents and giving preference to working families. Recent legislation also requires every public housing project to have a broad income mix with 40 per cent of accommodation reserved for the lowest income groups and the rest for higher earners. Page (1999: 7) argues that this is the way forward for Britain: 'Regeneration has three elements – physical, economic and social. Social regeneration is the hardest of these to tackle, but may be the missing ingredient . . . which makes poor areas better places to live and ensures that once a regeneration area is fixed, it stays fixed'.

'Balanced communities' are considered to be those which contain people who are in work and those who are not; single people and those with children; people with special needs and those without; and all age groups. They entail having a mix of tenures, rented and owner-occupied. 'Mixed tenure' has been adopted politically as a way of creating stable communities in estates dominated by social housing. However, this approach alone appears not to result in truly mixed social communities, but rather in areas polarized crudely between rich and poor. Indeed, Jupp, a researcher at DEMOS, recently found that on mixed tenure estates contact between owners and renters was below the national average; nearly two thirds of owners did not know the name of their tenant neighbours (Jupp 1999). The research also found that, generally, owner-occupiers were happy to move into mixed tenure estates. However, on such estates the overall satisfaction relating to factors such as graffiti, noise and friendliness was below the national average for social housing. For such mixed estates to work the social housing element should not be seen as the tenure of the socially excluded. Considerable investment is needed if not a significant change in policy direction as well as culture. London's South Bank in Greenwich was to be the site of the first 'millennium village'. The estate was to be of mixed tenure. However, there were accusations that the developer put the affordable housing in the least attractive part of the site. The architect resigned and the developer terminated the arrangements.

Despite this, the government appears set to follow the example in America and attempt to engineer the correct balance of the population on estates to ensure stability. Under new codes of practice for allocating council housing, possibly to be included in the forthcoming housing Green Paper, local author- ities are being urged to balance their role as social landlords in meeting immediate housing need with their responsibilities for management and maintenance. This includes ensuring that vulnerable or homeless people are not concentrated in less popular areas while complying with their statutory homelessness duties and ensuring quality and fairness in allocations. This is particularly problematic in areas suffering from a shortage of supply of accommodation and high levels of deprivation, but it is also an issue in areas where there is little demand regardless of tenure. Local authorities will be asked to address these issues of sustainable and balanced communities with little additional resources for housing.

Regeneration schemes

In addition to mixed tenure estates the other principal estate-based solution put forward by the government to address social exclusion is regeneration schemes. When discussing the Social Exclusion Unit's report (1998b) on neighbourhood renewal and the New Deal for communities 'pathfinders', the minister for local government and housing, Hilary Armstrong, asserted that the national strategy will in particular 'look at what more we can do to maximise the role of housing' (*Housing Today* 1998: 13). That the government proposes to spend more than £3 billion under the New Deal for regeneration programme highlights their concern (Prescott 1998). The timescale they have set for the 18 action teams covers the next 10 to 20 years. Within this programme around £800 million will go to the New Deal for communities to tackle around 20 of what the Social Exclusion Unit calls 'the country's worst estates'. Regeneration and housing programmes will be brought together locally to enhance economic and employment opportunities. This three-year programme includes the housing element of the government's commitment to tackling social exclusion. Local authorities will be able to use the money to transfer stock, but only if this meets the objective of tackling social exclusion.

The Social Exclusion Unit (1998b) see the day-to-day management and maintenance of properties as being a key element in processes of inclusion, together with encouraging and facilitating participation and community initiatives. They also recognize that the role of housing in social exclusion may vary in different parts of the country and that local responses and flexibility are needed. However, the implications of the wide range of patterns of deprivation regionally and locally for national policies are significant. In an attempt to develop primary legislation which may be applied consistently in all areas without limiting the flexibility of local authorities, the Urban Task Force produced a report on urban renewal in July 1999 in which they made 105 recommendations dealing with a range of issues. One recommendation was to create designated urban priority areas, enabling local authorities and their regeneration partners (including local people) to apply for special packages of housing and incentives to assist neighbourhood renewal. The report also recommended that urban regeneration companies should be established to coordinate or deliver area regeneration projects by ensuring that local authorities, RSLS and regional development agencies have sufficient powers to participate fully as partners. In addition the report recommended that housing regeneration companies should be established to undertake regeneration in areas where there is badly deteriorated and vacant housing stock. The Urban Task Force recommends RSLs as the lead agency for these companies.

Focusing on these worst social housing estates may have the effect of 'ghettoizing' social exclusion, of packaging up the socially excluded into identifiable enclaves to which remedial policies can then be applied. So while social housing is the sector in which policy initiatives can be most expediently delivered, a significant number of households who, using the Department of the Environment, Transport and the Regions (DETR) analysis of local conditions, live in squalid or excluded neighbourhoods, will be unaffected. There is a danger in assuming that targeting resources on mass council estates will tackle the issues of deprivation in cities as a whole. Whereas this may be appropriate in some cities, such targeting would seriously neglect the problems of deprivation which exist in large areas of other tenancies in other cities.

The current policy focusing on large-scale, predominantly social rented estates is far from being a new idea. The Priority Estate Project was established under a Labour government in 1979 and throughout the Thatcher years developed 'ways of improving living conditions on run-down council estates which are difficult to let' (DoE 1982: 1). Since then considerable knowledge and experience has been gained in relation to effective forms of housing interventions and investment in such areas, together with ways of addressing wider economic and environmental issues through regeneration projects. However, there has been less research on the impact of policy initiatives aimed at developing empowerment, capacity building and citizenship. As a consequence many of the current housing-based regeneration schemes only pay lip-service to such issues which we later argue should be at the heart of solutions to social inclusion.

Much of the work of the government in terms of neighbourhood strategies and innovative projects focuses on the symptoms of social exclusion rather than its underlying structural causes. As such they have been accused of overemphasizing the role of certain elements within the community. Punitive policies, focusing on issues of antisocial behaviour, lone parents and crime, risk blaming the poor for their predicament. Housing organizations are at the centre of the powerful new measures contained within the Crime and Disorder Act 1998. RSLs now have the power to request magistrates to implement antisocial behaviour orders restraining persistent offenders. The policies of community safety orders and probationary tenancies, both pioneered by New Labour, are 'behind two of the most draconian measures yet pioneered to monitor and control how local residents behave on council estates' (Cooper and Hawtin 1997: 274).

Exclusion and access to social housing

Owner-occupation, as a commodified tenure, could be perceived as being *more* exclusionary than social housing in terms of access, being dependent on the ability to pay. However, the introduction of the concept of need and managerial control into social housing has also had an impact on the degree of exclusion within social housing (Harloe 1995). There appear to be emerging two classes of 'housing excluded' people: the deserving and the undeserving. Communities understandably seek the ejection of those tenants who they regard as responsible for antisocial behaviour and problems such as crime and vandalism, drug abuse and prostitution. However, many of these antisocial tenants have dependent children and have to live somewhere. Addressing social exclusion by 'clearing' the problems from estates has wider implications for society which need to be considered.

Research funded by Shelter (Butler 1998) found that almost 33,000 households, many of whom were vulnerable and in housing need, had been excluded or suspended from the housing registers of 44 local authorities between 1996/7 and 1997/8. If applied to all English local authorities, almost 200,000 households would have been excluded. This represented a fourfold increase between 1996/7 and 1997/8. The survey found that only 3 per cent of recorded exclusions were as a result of antisocial behaviour; the vast majority were for rent arrears. One authority had excluded more than 3000 households for rent arrears in one year alone. Some authorities were found to exclude people for very low levels of arrears – of less than £100 (a figure not incompatible with a delay in housing benefit). Households that get into arrears are characteristically those in greatest poverty, or least able to manage their circumstances for other reasons. Exclusion policies are also being applied to non-housing debt or rent arrears arising in the private sector. In many cases the intention of policies was clearly to exclude households, not only from social housing, including RSLs, but also from private rented accommodation, often leaving people with nowhere to go in the area. Furthermore, Butler found that, despite the increasing numbers of exclusions and suspensions, local authorities are generally not monitoring this and are therefore unaware of the effects and implications for themselves or those households excluded, or whether such policies can be justified in terms of achieving their aims. Butler concluded that exclusion through housing management is therefore not an appropriate tool for dealing with complex social problems.

Denying people access to social housing marginalizes them, removing their contact with services such as health and education, and moving them into insecure, possibly unsuitable or dangerous housing. Homeless young people, for example, are twice as likely to suffer from psychiatric disorders as young people who are not homeless (Craig et al. 1996). Homelessness, therefore, is not just a symptom of social exclusion but also a major cause. Homeless people, unable or unwilling to fit into society due to physical, economic or psychological reasons, are alienated from their local community. They lack the security to participate or obtain employment and many experience ill health. This exclusion may be further perpetuated as children of families that are homeless are disadvantaged at school and fall behind in their education.

During 1997 a total of 165,790 households were officially recognized as homeless by local authorities, and more than 8500 asylum seeker households were eligible for benefit. Street homelessness presents the most visible and acute problems. Of course rough sleeping is not the only form of homelessness. 'Unofficial' homelessness – that is, single people living in squats or short-term housing – is estimated in London alone at 50,000 people, with many more forced to lodge with friends or relatives. Under the 1996 Housing Act, local authorities have a duty to provide temporary accommodation for homeless households for two years, but only if they are satisfied there is no other accommodation available. The Act contains no provision for a duty to provide a permanent home to homeless families, and there are fears that, as this two-year duty expires, many families will face yet more uncertainty.

Butler's (1998) research found that, after rent arrears, age was the second most common reason for local authorities to exclude people. The definition of 'vulnerability' within the statutory obligations to house homeless people for local authorities does not include homeless care leavers under the age of 21. Age restrictions can mean that young people, referred by social services or other agencies, may be denied access to social housing. Furthermore, the restrictions on housing benefit for those under 25 have been blamed for contributing to the exclusion of this group. Housing issues are key to young people in poor neighbourhoods. Many do not have sufficient income, experience or knowledge of network skills to obtain and maintain an adequate home.

The Social Exclusion Unit (1998a) is focusing not only on those trapped within the worst housing estates but also on the problems of the homeless. It is adopting two policy approaches: prevention and helping homeless people into permanent housing and, once there, helping them avoid becoming homeless again. There has been an emphasis on all relevant agencies working together to address the range of issues affecting homeless people. The government has recently introduced the Homeless Action Programme to run in tandem with the objective for each local authority to have a single homelessness strategy, which provides opportunities to integrate work with homeless people within mainstream local and regional policies. The principal initiative in assisting them to gain access to housing is the Rough Sleepers Initiative. £145 million is being invested to help local authority-led partnerships develop various initiatives to tackle the problem in London, and £35 million outside London. The government has resolved to reduce rough sleeping by two thirds in England through the Rough Sleepers Initiative by the year 2002. The aims of the Initiative were outlined by Tony Blair in his introduction to the report, *Rough Sleeping*:

> It is bad for those who do it, as they are intensely vulnerable to crime, drugs and alcohol, and at high risk of serious illness, and premature death. And rough sleeping is bad for the rest of society. The presence of some rough sleepers on the streets will attract others – often young and vulnerable – to join them. Many people feel intimidated by rough sleepers, beggars and street drinkers, and rough sleeping can blight areas and damage business and tourism.
>
> (Social Exclusion Unit 1998a: 2)

In wishing to 'deliver clear streets' the report hints at coercing homeless people into hostels: 'If new powers are needed to ensure places are taken up, the government will reconsider the matter', and although it states that a 'zero tolerance' policing approach would not achieve anything, this is qualified by 'while there is nowhere suitable for many rough sleepers to go' (Social Exclusion Unit 1998a).

Housing allocation policies are also crucial in enabling access to housing by those who are excluded. A proposed housing Green Paper in 2000 is expected to address the allocation of council homes. A new code is likely to increase the emphasis on a broader, strategic role for local authorities in relation to housing need and homelessness within the context of other welfare policy objectives. The development of inter-agency working, additional preventative measures and homelessness strategies will be encouraged, and authorities required to move beyond a narrow interpretation of need, particularly as it applies to young people, single homeless and domestic violence cases. Less clear is how the government intends to overcome the issues of competing priorities for limited resources between departments such as housing and social services. Such issues underline the differing definitions of need between such departments and often serve to undermine collaboration (Arblaster *et al.* 1996). Another issue which is unlikely to be addressed is the availability of appropriate accommodation in many areas.

Excluded groups and housing

Race

A greater proportion of black and ethnic minority young people are becoming homeless compared to the rest of the population (Davies *et al.* 1996). Of the young women who entered Centrepoint between 1996 and 1997 there was an overrepresentation of black females in the 16 to 17 age range (Centrepoint 1997). Homelessness is, however, only an extreme of poverty and it is well documented that people from black and ethnic minorities are overrepresented among the poorly paid and unemployed generally. The Social Exclusion Unit have highlighted that in areas of high concentrations of deprivation residents are four times as likely to be from black and ethnic minority backgrounds (Social Exclusion Unit 1998b). Such poverty leads to poor housing circumstances – for example, 30 per cent of Pakistani households and 47 per cent of Bangladeshi households are living in overcrowded conditions, compared with 2 per cent of white households (*Housing Today* 1999: 1).

However, not only are black and ethnic minority people at an economic disadvantage alongside poor white people, but they suffer the additional disadvantages of institutional racism, discrimination and racial harassment. For example, research has shown that local authority allocation processes have been a factor in imposing mobility constraints on black and ethnic minority tenants (Henderson and Karn 1987); housing agencies have failed to respond appropriately to the needs of black and ethnic minority tenants (Skellington 1996); and finance institutions apply more stringent criteria for assessing the status of black people applying for private housing loans (Ginsburg 1992). Issues such as these have led to black and ethnic minority groups feeling excluded from many residential locations. Although the causes of integration and segregation of black and ethnic minority people are complex and multi-faceted, decisions about housing location tend to be less related to economic grounds than based on a perception of the external environment where fear of either rejection or harassment may impair mobility.

Lee and Murie (1997) discovered in their study that although the highest levels of deprivation were found in the local authority sector, the link between poverty and council housing was significantly weaker among the black and ethnic minority population, who constituted proportionally fewer tenants in that sector. They concluded that the implications of this were that targeting council housing is less likely to be effective in reaching deprived black and ethnic minority groups than deprived groups within the white population.

Black and ethnic minority people are also underrepresented in relation to participation in housing management. Cooper (1991: 4) comments that this lack of involvement:

> is not a result of apathy amongst black tenants but is due mainly to the exclusion of black households from participation. Exclusion takes the form of blatant refusal to allow black tenants to use community facilities or to gain access to other available resources such as funding, the non existence of black workers on tenants' federations, activities organised from the perception of white tenants which had little appeal to black tenants, and the absence of issues of importance to black households on tenants associations' agendas.

Similarly, public participation within planning exercises has traditionally been characterized as undertaken by middle-class, middle-aged, able-bodied white men (Croft and Beresford 1996).

Recent research suggests that issues of race remain at the margins of the urban policy framework and that the specific needs of black and ethnic minority groups have not been considered explicitly in regeneration policies (Brownill and Darke 1998).

Gender

Housing policies and changes also affect women. Women-headed households (mainly lone mothers) form a disproportionately large group of tenants within the council housing sector as compared to male-headed ones. Although council housing accommodates only 18 per cent of all households, it accounts for 30 per cent of all female-headed households. This higher proportion of female households in council housing is partly due to council allocation policies based on need, and also reflects the problems women face in trying to access other forms of housing. Therefore, reductions in social rented housing, and other policies adversely affecting the sector, disproportionately affect women, increasing the risk of official and hidden homelessness and forcing them into unsuitable accommodation.

The *General Household Survey, 1996–97* shows that nearly three quarters of all households headed by men, and only half of those headed by females, are owner-occupied (ONS 1997). Although most women are housed in owner-occupied accommodation this is primarily as part of a married couple; access to home ownership by women is therefore most likely to be achieved if they are married. Home ownership through the mortgage system is geared towards those in better-paid, secure, full-time employment – in other words, male rather than female patterns of employment. Women's position in both the labour market and the family, therefore, places them at a disadvantage in obtaining (and sustaining) access to housing.

Lone parents, especially those headed by a woman, are highly reliant on the social rented sector, partly due to allocation based on need and partly because of financial restrictions preventing access to owner-occupation (they are half as likely to be owner-occupiers as other families with dependent children). However, such households are also found in other tenures, and this pattern varies between cities (Lee and Murie 1997). As with black and ethnic minority groups, national policies targeted at council housing estates do not necessarily reach those in most need. The DETR have estimated that 80 per cent of the 4.4 million additional households expected by 2016 will be single person households (DETR 1998) – therefore, policies to address this area of housing need are urgently required.

Disability

Disabled people suffer exclusion in many spheres including education, employment, income and housing, and much of the reason for their physical, social and political marginalization is related less to their individual impairment than to the housing and environment in which they live (Barton 1996). It is estimated that there are 4.25 million people with mobility problems in Britain, and that more than three quarters of a million physically disabled people are inadequately housed. However, there are only around 80,000 homes accessible to them (Barnes 1996). Mainstream properties are principally designed for people who are male, fit and aged between 18 and 40. What little provision there is for people with disabilities has usually been designed under the label 'special needs housing' within the social rented sector (Cooper and Walton 1995). The problem is exacerbated in areas where there is a lack of accessible transport and accessibility to other buildings (shops, public houses, meeting places and so on). Housing which is not up to mobility standards also means disabled people are unable to visit friends and relatives in mainstream housing, factors which severely limit opportunities for social interaction and inclusion.

Because of their lack of economic power, people who are disabled find it more difficult to sustain a place in the housing market. This is aggravated by grants for adaptations to private dwellings having been reduced over the last few years. An estimated 50 per cent of households with people with a disability live in the social rented sector (considerably higher than the average), largely because local authorities have had a statutory responsibility since the Chronically Sick and Disabled Persons Act, 1970 for the special needs of people with disabilities (Morris 1990). Consequently, the declining investment in social housing and new-build programmes, and the residualization of that sector, has particularly affected disabled people by restricting their choice of suitable accommodation. In addition, higher concentrations of vulnerable people in social housing would suggest a need for higher standards of stock maintenance and repair, and higher quality, responsive and sensitive housing management. Reduced revenue budgets, however, make this difficult, adding to the marginalization and exclusion of many tenants forced to live in this sector.

Closely allied to the process of exclusion is the concept of dependency, since being independent is the primary requirement for social inclusion. However, as Cooper and Hawtin (1997: 263) argue:

> people with disabilities have largely been treated as incapable of making their own decisions, a process founded on the traditional 'medical model' of disability. Individualising service provision, and targeting resources is based on this traditional view of disability which sees people's problems as arising from their personal impairment and 'treatment' is needed to restore 'normality'.

Such styles of working patronize and demean users, making unacceptable assumptions about their needs. Services are provided in ways that stifle development of confidence and creativity in those who need it most. This view has, however, been challenged by the rise of the 'social model' of disability which focuses on the way people can be disabled by society rather than on an individual's functional limitations. Housing exclusion for disabled people, may, for example, be imposed by the design of buildings, and the impact of marginalizing policies which overemphasize 'special needs accommodation'.

Some of the most vulnerable and potentially excluded groups in society are those covered by community care strategies. Commentators have argued that the housing sector is in a key position to play a lead role in helping to integrate this group into mainstream society (Arblaster et al. 1998). Initiatives helping people to stay in their own homes include Care and Repair, Staying Put, floating wardens, alarm systems and well-designed housing, such as 'lifetime homes' or forms of adaptable housing. Although general housing plays a very important role in the normalization process for disabled people and social care users, they have often been excluded from living such a 'normal' life. Housing for people with health or social care needs is often distinctive (if not stigmatizing) in character and although placed geographic-ally 'within' a community it may not necessarily be *part* of it. Normalization requires disabled people and community care users to have an 'ordinary' home while maximizing their ability to control decisions about their everyday life. The focus is on living independently with the role of 'tenant' rather than of 'client'. The development of an 'ordinary' housing policy, however, cannot work without a reallocation of resources towards domiciliary support, adaptations, day care and home nursing and there is little evidence of govern-ment support for this.

Housing inclusion through participation

Individualism and personalizing social problems were seen by many as key characteristics of the 1990s, epitomized by Margaret Thatcher's famous comment that 'there is no such thing as society'. The concept of social exclusion, however, is based on the notion that societies and individuals can only achieve their potential when living and working together, an import-ant aspect of which is the extent to which citizens take an active part in shaping their own lives. Successful inclusionary policies, therefore, are not possible unless residents not only feel safe, secure and comfortable but also feel that they belong, have ownership of what is going on, feel proud of where they live, do not feel oppressed and feel able to control their living environment. 'Social inclusion' is a term that may be used to describe a wide range of processes, and therefore involves concepts such as stakeholding, citizenship, partnership participation and empowerment. The implications of these concepts for policy and its implementation within housing have focused around issues of tenant participation (Cooper and Hawtin 1997, 1998).

Tenant participation is a flexible concept encompassing a wide spectrum of meanings, values and conditions. It can therefore be embraced by organ-izations adopting very different ideologies and cultures for very different purposes. To many organizations, the benefits of tenant participation are solely concerned with improving the service delivery, the image of the organ-ization and their relationship with the tenants. Improving tenants' aware-ness of the service providers' constraints is seen as an important step towards minimizing conflict. Others, however, recognize that participation can lead to people having an opportunity to take part in decision making, and even help to develop a sense of an inclusive community. On a personal level parti-cipation may bring independence, self-esteem, dignity, experience of working together and community belonging.

Participation can be developed using a range of methods designed for different purposes. Mechanisms include informing users about the service, consulting them individually or collectively about particular proposals through, for example, surveys, and inviting them to open meetings. *Service perspective* approaches such as these are typically organized by professionals, and are usually designed to benefit the provider more than the tenant; involvement often feels 'top-down' and inaccessible to users. Alternatively, *user perspective* approaches may be adopted, where tenants are enabled to organize themselves collectively, identify their own issues for consultation, have a real influence on policy, take an active part in its implementation and are even encouraged to campaign for change. This 'grass-roots' approach challenges the values and needs of the agency (whether professional or bureaucratic) and puts the needs of tenants, individually or collectively, at the centre of the service. Tenants' organizations, however, need to be adequately resourced, informed and supported.

A third approach is that of *tenant control*. Tenants may be enabled to take over all or part of the management and maintenance of their properties through an agreement with their landlord. Although 'tenant management cooperatives' have existed since the late 1970s, larger 'estate management boards' have been encouraged by successive governments since 1989. Although the majority of tenants do not wish to take on the full responsibility for running their estate, such potential powers certainly represent a significant change in tenant/landlord relationships (Hawtin 1998).

However, as with social inclusion more generally, there are many factors which may inhibit individuals from participating, including: relative states of poverty; physical and mental disability; personal feelings of discrimination; disempowerment or oppression; and lack of confidence or skills based on poor education and other experiences. Often lack of participation (or apathy as it is usually and wrongly labelled) is the consequence of the landlords' attitude and historic culture based on a 'feudal' landlord/tenant relationship. Fear of losing power is one reason for the continuance of the traditional culture, although empowerment of tenants need not mean that providers lose their share of 'power'. What is needed is a change of relationships, involving tenants on an equal basis.

Another concern many agencies express is that tenants may not fully 'represent' their constituency. Questioning their representativeness, and therefore their validity and legitimacy, may further undermine tenants' confidence. (The 'representativeness' of elected council and RSL board members is rarely as vociferously challenged.) As highlighted earlier, one of the weakest elements of tenant participation has been contesting the exclusion of marginalized groups and has even 'mirrored rather than challenged broader oppressions and discriminations' (Croft and Beresford 1996: 187).

Despite these misgivings, tenant participation has become an important facet of social housing over recent years. Under the Conservative governments of the late 1980s and 1990s it became part of the consumerist approach to welfare, making social landlords more directly accountable to their 'customers' and giving tenants a choice to 'opt out' of the sector (Lusk 1997) The New Labour government also stated as soon as it came into office that it wanted 'tenants to be consulted and fully involved in the decision-making process' (Armstrong 1997). Since then evidence of tenant participation has been included in the requirements for Housing Investment Programme submissions for government housing subsidies, and all English housing authorities are required to develop 'tenant compacts' with their tenants by April 2000.

These developments, however, need to be seen in the light of New Labour's overall policy on social exclusion. This strategy appears to be founded on an interpretation of citizenship which expects individuals and families to take greater responsibility for their own welfare. It shifts the focus and responsibility away from structural causes and onto the poor and excluded themselves. The New Labour view of inclusion into a community has been described as 'part of a strategy aimed at restoring social cohesion through fostering conformity and criminalising dissent' (Cooper and Hawtin 1998: 75). As Foucault (1982) pointed out, individuals are 'subjectified' and oppressed by the state and its professionals through a process whereby power-holders identify and label sections of society (e.g. as 'antisocial tenants' or 'socially excluded') and are thereby able to subject them to prescribed forms of treatment and social control. Indeed the process of citizen participation has been attacked from various sources as being tokenistic and a means of controlling, placating, treating, manipulating, and/or incorporating discontented groups while achieving the legitimation of the state (Arnstein 1969; Croft and Beresford 1990; Dowson 1990; Cooper and Hawtin 1997, 1998).

However, despite such criticisms, there are also strong arguments for supporting the notion that participatory methods may, if accompanied by certain values and beliefs, also be a tool for real inclusion and empowerment. They have the potential to achieve greater accountability and democracy. Such an approach, based on community development, has been called *resident involvement* by Cooper and Hawtin (1998). It is based on the belief that whole communities can develop solutions to their problems by setting their own agendas, developing community initiatives and even delivering services which are managed by the community to meet the community's specific needs. The focus is less on treating the 'problems' of individuals or even 'deprived areas' and more on understanding and addressing the structural causes of those problems. It involves challenging oppression from below using 'liberating education' to enable people to take charge of their total environment (Friere 1972). A starting point for agencies, in addition to establishing participative structures and supporting the tenants' movement and tenants' management where requested, is to change their own cultural stereotypes and avoid oppressive language such as 'problem families', 'antisocial tenants', 'deprived estate' and even 'social exclusion'. Negative assumptions about people living on council estates, those who are homeless, those who obtain housing through community care, lone parents, etc. must be challenged. It is important to understand and listen to people's own experiences and 'hold on to the principle that users are entitled to a decent quality of service and to housing which is appropriate to their needs as they see them' (Stewart 1998: 56).

Conclusions

Solutions to housing exclusion are necessarily complex and based on interpretations of the underlying causes. They may include a re-examination of tenure, estate-based solutions, addressing issues of access to housing and the involvement of tenants themselves in finding solutions.

Although policies over the last few decades have assumed that the principal answer to housing exclusion is to encourage owner-occupation as the 'norm' to aspire to, it is important to note that being an owner-occupier does *not* guarantee a sense of social inclusion. We have suggested that while home ownership has been seen as an escape from the oppression of a private or state landlord, it also serves the interests of the state, increasing economic profitability and consumption as well as increasing political stability and dividing the traditional working classes. In addition, owner-occupation can be oppressive by potentially inhibiting protest by giving owner-occupiers a stake in the system, impeding mobility and forcing people into other stereo-typical roles and relationships. Furthermore, in recent years, affordability within the tenure has become an issue, and while entry to home ownership is not generally a problem for all but the poorest, with the range of finan-cial institutions willing to lend, exit from the sector has been problematic for marginalized owners, whether because of negative equity, difficulties in selling their property, or changes in circumstances such as unemployment or relationship breakdown.

Housing exclusion affects people in all tenures; it also affects people from specific groups. Some writers have argued that disabled people and women are excluded from the rights of citizenship through their 'status of depend-ency' which undermines their ability to recognize and exercise rights (Barbalet 1993). Others have found that welfare provision is unresponsive and stig-matizing rather than becoming a tool of inclusion. The provision of a more privatized form of welfare through quasi-market systems, introduced during the 1980s and 1990s has also been widely criticized for personalizing problems. There is therefore a growing demand for state provision to become responsive and flexible to the different needs of disadvantaged groups while simultan-eously ensuring collective rights, responsibilities and social justice. The nature of exclusion is, however, different for different groups. Brownill and Darke found, for example, that women may be excluded through a range of factors including lack of confidence, domestic responsibilities and ethnic discrimina-tion. Ethnic minorities, they found, especially have to face attitudes which stereotype them, as well as barriers due to language or custom (Brownill and Darke 1998).

The Social Exclusion Unit, and its Scottish equivalent, have adopted a model of deprivation according to which there are multi-faceted causes and symp-toms: 'since social exclusion is a multi-dimensional problem, the government believes that it requires a multi-dimensional response' (Scottish Office 1999a: ch. 3.3). Since the nineteenth century, utopian solutions to social problems have been developed including philanthropic housing developments, garden cities, housing cooperatives, self-build solutions and the squatters movement. The recent Scottish housing Green Paper (Scottish Office 1999b) clearly sees 'community ownership' as the great panacea to tackle social inclusion and promote community empowerment as well as to save Scotland's poor-quality housing stock from total disrepair. (However, the Green Paper failed to adequately address the problem of what would happen if the new commun-ity landlords fail to allocate housing to people in genuine housing need.)

In addition to mixed tenure estates other current policy solutions are based on the principles of partnership, collaboration and 'joined-up working'. Since the Page Reports (Page 1993, 1994), which addressed the broader aspects of housing, housing management has encompassed a wide range of other initi-atives within the community including those centred on children and youth, credit unions and LETS (local exchange trading system). Within RSLs such initiatives are known as 'Housing Plus'. Housing finance policy interven-tions driven by this more holistic vision for the future of RSLs may have an inclusionary impact. Current proposals for a new framework for the Housing

Corporation's Approved Development Programme (ADP) are likely to be designed to create a more flexible and responsive regime which reflects and responds to local needs with greater sensitivity (Housing Corporation 1999). The proposed production of regional housing statements should constitute a clear example of 'joined-up thinking'. The product of close liaison between regional key players, they should describe local housing circumstances within the context of the local economy, regional planning strategies, predicted demographic changes and the need for housing investment. RSLs and local authorities will be able to develop more effective and certain strategies in a context where longer-term planning assumes primacy over previous formulaic assessments of housing need, which, anyway, omit many aspects of disadvantage and exclusion. RSLs are recognized as key partners in providing new social housing in areas of high demand, contributing to regeneration schemes and taking over stock from local authorities. Local authorities are being encouraged to look at both the public and private sectors to get the best housing for local people.

This holistic view is a welcome approach after the anti-society policies of previous governments. However, underlying much of the rhetoric appears to be the vision of a homogeneous, classless society which scarcely tolerates difference, such as travellers or some homeless people who choose to exclude themselves. If real exclusion is to be addressed, the underlying structural issues of poverty and poor housing have to be faced. Current housing in all sectors needs to be brought up to an adequate standard; housing needs to be suitable for vulnerable and disabled people; and sufficient quantities of affordable housing has to be provided in areas where people require it. In addition, the stigma of social housing has to be systematically challenged. In providing and managing social housing there has to be a non-judgemental and liberating approach. This means listening to people as individuals, not as consumer units, and enabling them to collectively organize and, if necessary, take control.

References

Arblaster, L., Conway, J., Foreman, A. and Hawtin, M. (1996) *Asking the Impossible? A Study of Interagency Working to Address the Housing, Health and Social Care Needs of People in General Needs Housing*. Bristol: Policy Press.

Arblaster, L., Conway, J., Foreman, A. and Hawtin, M. (1998) *Achieving the Impossible: Interagency Collaboration to Address the Housing, Health and Social Care Needs of People Able to Live in Ordinary Housing*. Bristol: Policy Press.

Armstrong, H. (1997) Speech to Shelter, 22 May.

Arnstein, S. (1969) A ladder of citizen participation. *Journal of the American Institute of Planners*, XXXV (4 July): 216–24.

Atkinson, R. and Kintrea, K. (1998) *Reconnecting Excluded Communities: The Neighbour Impacts of Owner Occupation*. Edinburgh: Scottish Homes.

Balchin, P. (1995) *Housing Policy: An Introduction*, 3rd edn. London: Routledge.

Barbalet, J.M. (1993) Citizenship, class inequality and resentment, in B. Turner (ed.) *Citizenship and Social Theory*. London: Sage.

Barnes, C. (1996) Institutional discrimination against people with disabilities and the campaign for anti-discrimination legislation, in D. Taylor (ed.) *Critical Social Policy: A Reader*. London: Sage.

Barton, L. (ed.) (1996) *Disability and Society: Emerging Issues and Insights*. Harlow: Longman.

Birch, J. (1998) Question time. *Roof*, Sept/Oct: 19–21.

Brownill, S. and Darke, J. (1998) *'Rich Mix': Inclusive Strategies for Urban Regeneration*. Bristol: The Policy Press and Joseph Rowntree Foundation.

Burrows, R. and Rhodes, D. (1998) *Unpopular Places? Area Disadvantage and the Geography of Misery in England*. York: Joseph Rowntree Foundation/The Policy Press.

Butler, D. (1999) Plan for demand. *Housing Today*, 119.

Butler, S. (1998) *Access Denied: The Exclusion of People in Need from Social Housing*. London: Shelter.

Centrepoint (1997) http://www.centrepoint.org.uk/policy.htm.

Challis, P. (1999) Rich pickings, *Guardian*, 24 March.

CIH/JRF/CML (Chartered Institute of Housing/Joseph Rowntree Foundation/Council of Mortgage Lenders) (1999) *Housing Finance Review*. Coventry: CIH.

Cooper, C. (1991) Tenant participation in the 1990s. *Black Housing*, 7(11): 4–5.

Cooper, C. and Hawtin, M. (eds) (1997) *Housing, Community and Conflict: Understanding Resident Involvement*. Aldershot: Arena.

Cooper, C. and Hawtin, M. (eds) (1998) *Resident Involvement and Community Action: Theory to Practice*. Coventry: CIH and HAS.

Cooper, C. and Walton, M. (1995) *Once in a Lifetime: An Evaluation of Lifetime Homes in Hull*, Occasional Papers no. 3. Hull: Policy Studies Research Centre, University of Lincolnshire and Humberside.

Craig, T.K.J., Hodson, S., Woodward, S. and Richardson, S. (1996) *Off to a Bad Start: A Longtitudinal Study of Homeless Young People in London*. London: The Mental Health Foundation.

Croft, S. and Beresford, P. (1990) *From Paternalism to Participation: Involving People in Social Services*. London: Open Services Project/Joseph Rowntree Foundation.

Croft, S. and Beresford, P. (1996) The politics of participation, in D. Taylor (ed.) *Critical Social Policy: A Reader*. London: Sage.

Davies, J. and Lyle, S. with Deacon, A., Law, I., Julienne, L. and Kay, H. (1996) *Discounted Voices*. Leeds: University of Leeds.

Dean, H. and Taylor-Gooby, P. (1992) *Dependency Culture: The Explosion of a Myth*. Hemel Hempstead: Harvester Wheatsheaf.

DETR (Department of the Environment, Transport and the Regions) (1997) *Mapping Local Authority Estates*. London: HMSO.

DETR (Department of the Environment, Transport and the Regions) (1998) *Planning for the Communities of the Future*. London: The Stationery Office.

DoE (Department of the Environment) (1982) *Priority Estates Project: Improving Problems on Council Estates – A Summary of Aims and Progress*. London: HMSO.

DoE (Department of the Environment) (1996) *English House Condition Survey*. London: HMSO.

Dowson, S. (1990) *Keeping it Safe: Self-advocacy by People with Learning Difficulties and the Professional Response*. London: Values into Action.

Forrest, R. and Murie, A. (1988) *Selling the Welfare State: The Privatisation of Public Housing*. London: Routledge.

Foucault, M. (1982) The subject and power. *Critical Inquiry*, 8(summer): 777–95.

Friere, P. (1972) *Pedagogy of the Oppressed*. Harmondsworth: Penguin.

Ginsberg, N. (1992) Racism and housing: concepts and reality, in P. Braham, A. Rahansi and R. Skellington (eds) *Racism and Anti-racism: Inequalities, Opportunities and Policies*. London: Sage.

Ginsberg, N. (1997) Housing, in A. Walker and C. Walker (eds) *Britain Divided: The Growth of Social Exclusion in the 1980s and 1990s*. London: CPAG.

Harloe, M. (1995) *The People's Home: Social Rented Housing in Europe and America*. Oxford: Blackwell.

Hawtin, M. (1998) Estate management boards: their development and significance, in C. Cooper and M. Hawtin (eds) (1998) *Resident Involvement and Community Action: Theory to Practice*. Coventry: CIH and HAS.

Henderson, J. and Karn, V. (1987) *Race, Class and State Housing: Inequality and the Allocation of Public Housing in Britain*. Aldershot: Gower.

Holder, A., McQuillan, W., Fitzgorge-Butler, A. and Williams, P. (1998) *Surviving or Thriving? Managing Change in Housing Organisations*. Coventry: Chartered Institute of Housing.

Holmans, E. (1995) *Housing Demand and Need in England, 1991–2011*. York: Joseph Rowntree Foundation.

Housing Corporation (1999) *Developing the Approved Development Programme: A Consultation Paper*. London: Housing Corporation.

Housing Today (1997) 18 September.

Housing Today (1998) 14 May.

Housing Today (1999) 25 February.

Jordan, B. (1992) *Trapped in Poverty? Labour Market Discussions in Low Income Households*. London: Routledge.

Jupp, B. (1999) *Living Together: Community Life on Mixed Tenure Estates*. London: DEMOS.

Lee, P. and Murie, A. (1997) *Poverty, Housing Tenure and Social Exclusion*. Bristol: The Policy Press.

Lusk, P. (1997) Tenants' choice and tenant management: who owns and who controls social housing?, in C. Cooper and M. Hawtin (eds) (1997) *Housing, Community and Conflict: Understanding Resident Involvement*. Aldershot: Arena.

MacLennan, D. and Pryce, G. (1998) *Missing Links: The Economy, Cities and Housing*. London: Housing Corporation/NHF.

Merrett, S. (1979) *State Housing in Britain*. London: Routledge & Kegan Paul.

Morris, J. (1990) *Our Homes, Our Rights: Housing, Independent Living and Disabled People*. London: Shelter.

National Housing Federation (undated) *Housing For Health*. London: National Housing Federation.

Nuttgens, P. (1989) *The Home Front*. London: BBC Publications.

ONS (1997) *General Household Survey, 1996–97*. London: HMSO.

Page, D. (1993) *Building for Communities*. York: Joseph Rowntree Foundation.

Page, D. (1994) *Developing Communities*. York: Joseph Rowntree Foundation.

Page, D. (1999) From over there to over here: US regeneration lessons. *London Housing News*, 78(May–June): 5–7.

Perri 6 (1997) *Escaping Poverty: From Safety Nets to Networks of Opportunity*. London: DEMOS.

Prescott, J. (1998) *Housing and Regeneration Policy: A Statement by the Deputy Prime Minister*, 22 July. http://www.regeneration.detr.gov.uk/hrp/index.htm.

Scottish Office (1999a) *Social Exclusion: The Strategic Framework*. http://www.scotland.gov.uk/inclusion/ssin10anx2.htm.

Scottish Office (1999b) *Investing in Modernisation: An Agenda for Scotland's Housing*, Cm 4272. Edinburgh: Scottish Office.

Skellington, R. (with Morris, P.) (1996) *'Race' in Britain Today*. London: Sage/The Open University.

Social Exclusion Unit (1998a) *Rough Sleeping: Report by the Social Exclusion Unit*. London: The Stationery Office.

Social Exclusion Unit (1998b) *Bringing Britain Together: A National Strategy for Neighbourhood Renewal*, Cm 4045. London: The Stationery Office.

Somerville, P. (1998) Explanations of social exclusion: where does housing fit in? *Housing Studies*, 13(6): 761–80.

Stewart, G. (1998) Housing poverty and social exclusion, in I. Shaw, S. Lambert and D. Clapham (eds) *Social Care and Housing*. London: Jessica Kingsley.

Urban Task Force (1999) *Towards an Urban Renaissance: The Final Report of the Urban Task Force*. London: E & FN Spon.

Webster, D. (1999) Employment change housing demand and sustainable development, in S. Lowe (ed.) *Housing Abandonment in Britain: Studies in the Causes and Effects of Low Housing Demand*. York: University of York.

Whitehead, C. (1997) Changing needs, changing incentives: trends in the UK housing system, in P. Williams (ed.) *Directions in Housing Policy: Towards Sustainable Housing Policies for the UK*. London: Paul Chapman.

Williams, P. (ed.) (1997) *Directions in Housing Policy: Towards Sustainable Housing Policies for the UK*. London: Paul Chapman.

Wilson, W. (1987) *The Truly Disadvantaged: The Inner City, the Underclass and Public Policy*. Chicago: University of Chicago Press.

Wilson, W. (1996) *When Work Disappears: The World of the New York Poor*. New York: Knoph.

7 ACCESS TO SERVICES

Ian Sanderson

Introduction

As economic and social trends over the past quarter century have exacerbated inequalities and produced an increasingly polarized society, concerns about the condition of urban life have grown (Healey *et al*. 1995), as has the recognition of the degree of poverty and social exclusion experienced by rural communities (Cloke 1993; Chapman *et al*. 1998). Although there has been a tendency for research to focus on the role of economic restructuring in producing these trends, greater attention is now being given to the 'arena of consumption' and particularly the role of access to services, provided by both private and public sectors, in processes of social exclusion. In particular, many local authorities have developed anti-poverty strategies in which an important place is given to the objective of improving access to, and take-up of, their services by disadvantaged groups in the community.

This focus raises issues around the potential role of improved access to services in promoting social inclusion. This chapter considers these issues with a particular emphasis on the scope for action at the local level. The next section seeks to establish the importance of access to key services to social capital and how factors operating in localities can erode or prevent access, thus contributing to social exclusion. This is followed by a brief analysis of how the increasing penetration of market principles into the organization and delivery of public services has resulted in changes which disadvantage poor and vulnerable groups. Some evidence of the extent of inequalities in the benefits secured from public services is then reviewed and there is a brief discussion of the situation facing rural areas. The final section considers the potential for action at the local level to address social exclusion by improving access to services with particular reference to local authorities' work on anti-poverty strategies.

Place, access to services and social exclusion

In an increasingly diverse and fragmented society there is growing concern about the implications of social polarization and a realization of the complexity of the factors which contribute to 'disadvantage' as experienced by groups and individuals in their communities. It is clear that 'place' can be a factor of considerable importance – as Dorling and Woodward (1996: 73) argue, 'polarisation happens to groups of people over space and through time. It's a dynamic process and can produce quite clear geographical patterns to society'. Moreover, Van Kempen (1997: 434) argues that there is a specifically spatial or 'locality' effect constituted by 'social patterns and behaviour that can only be explained by the specific characteristics and social structure of the local environment in which they evolve'. The complex set of factors which are mediated through 'place' are captured in the concept of social exclusion as defined by Madanipour (1998: 76): 'an institutionalised form of controlling access: to places, to activities, to resources and to information'.

For Healey, place constitutes a 'locus of access to relational resources' which provide opportunities and constraints; therefore, the lack of opportunities in particular places to achieve the means for 'human flourishing' contributes to social exclusion (Healey 1998: 58–60). The composition of 'relational resources' is important in that it comprises material, social, cultural and symbolic elements. Madanipour (1998) and Van Kempen (1997) argue that space or 'locality' has a strong influence on the degree to which individuals or groups can gain access to these 'relational resources' which affect their 'life chances'. A key element of Van Kempen's analysis is the emphasis on the role of public welfare services in this process. Thus, she argues that in areas of concentrated poverty, or 'poverty pockets', public services experience 'crowding effects' which result in queuing, lower quality of service, 'creaming' of more promising clients and lowered expectations on the part of both officials and clients. Moreover, people are disempowered by negative perceptions of, and feelings about, the locality, by stigmatization processes, and by lack of cultural and social capital which places them at a disadvantage in encounters with officials who control access to provision.

The importance of the concepts of social and cultural capital in the analysis of the role of public services in relation to processes of social exclusion is emphasized by Wacquant (1998). Wacquant's analysis indicates how 'social disinvestment' – the withdrawal of public services – can create a vicious cycle of decline in social capital. He distinguishes between *informal social capital*, consisting of 'resourceful social ties based on interpersonal networks of exchange, trust, and obligations' and *formal social capital*, 'the set of resources and values that individuals may draw upon by virtue of membership in, or connection to, formal organizations' (p. 28). Wacquant argues that the deterioration in public services in America's inner cities has proceeded to the point where 'public institutions operate as *negative social capital* that maintain ghetto residents in a marginal and dependent position' (p. 29). Thus, not only do they fail to provide adequate levels of welfare support, but they can be provided in a punitive and disruptive manner:

> The erratic and arbitrary nature of procedures and decisions, the organizational culture of contempt for 'clients' (who are routinely made to

feel that they are expendable, interchangeable, and a burden to all; that their time, knowledge, and efforts at survival are worthless), the lack of coordination between agencies, the inconsistencies and conflicts between the bureaucratic requirements of various branches and programs which often work at cross-purposes, all lead to tense and adversarial relations between social service personnel and recipients.

(Wacquant 1998: 31)

Moreover, the withdrawal of public services from inner cities has contributed to the development of an alternative underground economy, in which drug-dealing plays a major role, and to the 'depacification of everyday life' further eroding social capital, isolating, stigmatizing and excluding inner-city residents (Wacquant 1998: 34–5).

The process of 'organizational desertification' (Wacquant 1998: 34) has proceeded further in North American inner cities than in Britain but, as indicated above, many commentators have expressed concern about the effects of the restructuring of public services during the 1980s and early 1990s in this country under the influence of 'New Right' ideology. Pitts and Hope (1997) provide an analysis of how the withdrawal of public services from socially deprived neighbourhoods in Britain is undermining social capital and exacerbating social exclusion. They argue that social capital depends, at least in part, on investment in 'cultural capital' delivered 'through agencies providing resources and services to local communities – in education and training, housing, health and other forms of social and recreational service' (p. 41). However, increased central government control and the introduction of quasi-market processes and 'managerialism' in local public services since the early 1980s have eroded their capacity to deliver cultural capital and combat 'social dislocation' in deprived neighbourhoods (pp. 50–3).

Therefore, a 'social capital' perspective highlights the importance of access to a range of 'relational resources' and the role of disinvestment by private and public institutions in socially deprived localities in undermining the capacity of communities to combat processes of social exclusion. Such localities easily slide into a 'vicious cycle' of decline in which processes 'fuse together in dragging particular "poor places" ever deeper into the snares of poverty' (Philo *et al.* 1995: 179–80). The next section reviews briefly some recent evidence of how policies of deregulation and marketization in relation to certain important services have impacted upon these processes.

The market and services for the poor

We will examine three types of services which play an important role in sustaining people's 'life chances' and which have experienced, in different ways, increasing penetration of market principles into their organization and delivery. First, financial services have experienced deregulation and significantly increased competition and 'are changing in ways which are having important implications for the level of access millions of people have to finance and credit' (Leyshon and Thrift 1996: 1150). Second, the key utility networks – water, waste, gas, electricity and telecommunications – have been privatized with the result that 'access to networks and quality of provision is becoming increasingly differentiated between places and among companies and households' (Healey 1995: 147). Third, in key public services, such as education, housing, health and transport, 'quasi-markets' have been introduced, involving a separation of purchaser and provider roles and an element of user choice between providers, again with implications for access to these services by different groups (LeGrand and Bartlett 1993; Roberts *et al.* 1998).

Processes of restructuring in the financial services sector have attracted considerable attention as increased competition and a 'flight to quality' have heightened inequalities in access to banking, insurance and mortgage facilities resulting in the phenomenon of 'financial exclusion' which disproportionately affects poorer and more disadvantaged groups (Ford and Rowlingson 1996; Leyshon and Thrift 1996). Recent research by Kempson and Whyley (1999) indicates that 7 per cent of households in Britain do not use financial services and a further 20 per cent use just one or two. Those at greatest risk of financial exclusion are women, the young, the elderly, the unemployed and members of certain minority ethnic groups (especially Pakistani and Bangladeshi). Moreover, there is an important spatial dimension to financial exclusion since poorer communities have borne the brunt of the closure of bank branches, and access to insurance and mortgage services is affected by location of residence (McCormick and Philo 1995; Ford and Rowlingson 1996).

However, Ford and Rowlingson (1996) argue that in analysing processes of financial exclusion it is also important to examine 'informal' and 'non-regulated' financial institutions and services such as hire purchase, local shop credit, mail order, pawnbrokers and moneylenders. People with low incomes may resort to such services not only as a result of exclusion from the 'formal' sector but also due to a conscious preference for 'cash transactions, for a weekly budgeting cycle, and for processes that were informal and non-bureaucratic', conditioned by 'cultural tradition, custom and practice' (Ford and Rowlingson 1996: 1347, 1354). Mail order and moneylending services tend to operate through locally-based agents, often women, and access to them can be informal and rapid, heavily conditioned by social relationships and networks. However, exclusionary criteria also operate in these services including 'some combination of unemployment, extreme poverty, lone parents, residents of high-rise flats, areas characterised by high rates of crime or physical deprivation, and individuals or households with poor payments records' (Ford and Rowlingson 1996: 1358). Ford and Rowlingson's work has highlighted how the pattern of provision of financial services is embedded in the 'social relations of the community', thus constituting a potentially important aspect of social capital.

The privatization of the utilities was an important element in the programmes of Conservative governments during the 1980s and early 1990s affecting the gas, electricity, water and telecommunications industries. It was argued that privatization would increase efficiency and that competition would develop, reducing prices and improving responsiveness and quality of service for customers (Kempson 1997; Marvin *et al.* 1999). The effect has been to replace standardized, integrated homogeneous networks and service provision by a 'patchwork' of regulated privatized companies 'developing their infrastructures and services with an extremely complex 'layering' of spatial dynamics' (Graham and Marvin 1995: 178). As a result there is considerable concern about the resulting spatial and social inequalities as the privatized utilities pursue 'cherry picking' and 'social dumping' in the pursuit of profit. Thus, in spite of regulation, the most lucrative social and spatial segments of the market are the focus for growth of competition and investment at the expense of 'marginalized' areas and lower income households:

> There is increasing evidence that utility privatisation has radically altered the relationship between utility companies and their domestic customers. Competition creates winners and losers. The corollary of a competitive strategy is the social dumping of unprofitable and marginal consumers and the withdrawal from zones of little commercial opportunity.
>
> (Marvin *et al.* 1999: 117–18)

These developments have potentially important implications for social exclusion. On the one hand, they have a direct impact on the experience of poverty for those who have difficulty paying bills who are increasingly being transferred to pre-payment meters resulting in a growth of rationed use and self-disconnection from fuel and water supplies (Kempson 1997: 211; Marvin *et al.* 1999: 118–21). Such difficulties can exacerbate the trends towards financial exclusion discussed above. Moreover, low levels of telephone connectivity among poorer households erode the capability to maintain social relationships for support and information on opportunities, and to maintain contact with social and welfare services (Marvin *et al.* 1999: 121).

There are also a number of potential indirect impacts which will arise to the extent that the privatized utility companies 'disinvest from declining or peripheral localities, so withdrawing or at least damaging the vital infrastructural support systems for development within those places' (Graham and Marvin 1995: 180). This would further weaken the local economies of such localities and promote 'uncoupling' from the mainstream economy (see McCormick and Philo 1995: 11) thus exacerbating social exclusion in the economic arena. Moreover, there are also potential impacts in the political arena since the privatization of the utilities has placed control over basic infrastructure networks beyond local democratic influence, and this can be seen as contributing to the broader process of institutional fragmentation at the local level which has eroded people's influence over decision making in relation to key services which affect their 'life chances'.

The third area of policy change which illustrates how market forces impact upon processes of social exclusion is the development of 'quasi-markets' in various public services – notably education, health, community care and social housing. The aim of these reforms by Conservative governments was to increase efficiency, choice and responsiveness to needs by introducing competition in the provision of services but with the role of purchaser, on behalf of 'consumers', vested in the state agency and managers or professionals therein (LeGrand and Bartlett 1993). Evaluations of the impact of quasi-market reforms have indicated concerns about equity implications due to 'cream skimming' and 'adverse selection' (LeGrand and Bartlett 1993; Bartlett *et al.* 1998). An illustration of these implications can be provided by a brief look at changes in school education.

The Education Acts of 1988 and 1992 introduced reforms which were designed to increase parental choice of schools, based upon improved public information and accountability, and enhance school autonomy by devolving budgetary and management responsibilities from local education authorities and providing opportunities for schools to develop independently of local education authorities (Ranson 1995; Whitty *et al.* 1998). These reforms were intended to lead to increased diversity of provision, better and more efficient management of schools, and enhanced professionalism and school effectiveness. However, fewer schools than anticipated left their local education authorities so the changes introduced under the local management of schools have constituted a major element in the impact of the reforms (Whitty *et al.* 1998). Although there is some evidence of improved efficiency and responsiveness to some 'consumers', strong concerns have been expressed about equity implications. First, a policy of parental choice benefits better educated and higher social class families 'who are more alert to educational rights, problems and opportunities' (Gorard 1998: 6) thus increasing the socioeconomic segregation of schools. Second, there is evidence that greater powers of choice by schools leads to 'cream skimming' to the disadvantage of children from working-class families, children of African Caribbean descent and children with special educational needs (Gorard 1998: 6; Whitty *et al.* 1998: 102–3).

Therefore the evidence on the effect of educational reforms is that competition reinforces unequal access to education. As Ranson (1995: 121) argues: 'It is a zero-sum "game" in which if there are to be winners there are sadly always going to be losers'. Again, there is an important spatial dimension since it is the schools and families in the more affluent neighbourhoods which tend to be winners at the expense of those in inner-city areas (Smith *et al.* 1997; Whitty *et al.* 1998: 103). Given the importance of education as a basis for gaining access to economic, social and cultural opportunities, there are strong grounds for concern about the contribution of school education reform to the problem of social exclusion in socially deprived neighbourhoods.

The case of educational reform also highlights the adverse impact of market-driven reforms on rural areas. Thus, Ribchester and Edwards (1999) indicate that over many years educational provision in rural areas has been progressively withdrawn from smaller settlements and concentrated in larger centres. Conservative government reforms created an even more unsympathetic educational and economic environment for smaller schools. The rationalization of provision in rural areas has reduced choice; as Gorard (1998: 7) argues: 'Low population density and travel restrictions mean that many families in rural areas effectively have no choice at all'. Ribchester and Edwards (1999: 60) conclude that the case of educational provision confirms Cloke's (1993: 118) argument that 'rural areas are not particularly good areas for market competition'. Thus, Cloke argues that reforms in education and health have made smaller rural service outlets vulnerable while reforms in housing and transport and the privatization of the utilities have had adverse effects on lower income groups. In relation to the latter, he argues as follows: 'As rural areas can generally be regarded as expensive to service, any move towards charging the *real* costs of providing infrastructural services *without* cross-subsidy will inevitably lead to increases in the cost of rural living and to further disadvantage for lower income groups living in the countryside' (p. 118).

The deregulation of local bus transport further illustrates this point as the 1985 Transport Act introduced competition and required privatization of bus undertakings, thus undermining the potential for cross-subsidy within comprehensive local public transport networks (Simpson 1996; White 1997). The effect has been increased competition on 'profitable' routes/times but reduced services on 'marginal' routes/times. Within a context of reduced passenger numbers and increased fares, services at evenings and weekends and in sparser rural areas have suffered as local authorities have found it increasingly difficult to allocate resources for subsidies. The adverse consequences for those who are dependent upon public transport have been exacerbated by 'service instability, poor passenger information, and losses of through-ticketing and comprehensive off-vehicle travelcard facilities' (White 1997: 43). It can be argued, therefore, that the deregulation of local bus transport has contributed to social exclusion by eroding accessibility to services. The situation is particularly acute in many rural areas with some three quarters of rural settlements having no daily bus service (Boardman 1998).

It is evident that due to the extension of market principles in their organization and delivery, services which play an important role in maintaining 'formal' social capital have changed in ways which have adversely affected the 'life chances' of disadvantaged groups and areas. Such changes have curtailed access to 'relational resources' of an economic, social, cultural and symbolic nature, thereby contributing to processes of social exclusion.

Moreover, as the state has withdrawn from the provision of welfare, new modes of organization of local public services and supporting discourses have developed which have more subtle effects on social exclusion beyond the 'formal gaze' of democratic accountability. Thus, in relation to public health and policing, Fischer and Poland (1998) argue that poor people are increasingly excluded by modes of service provision and discourses which are presented as self-evidently desirable and uncontentious. For example, the state monopoly over policing is being eroded by a 'multitude of private, civil and commercial institutions and agencies providing "private" policing, safety and security' (Fischer and Poland 1998: 188). One manifestation of this process is the increasing 'privatization of public space' in, for example, shopping malls, entertainment complexes and housing complexes, 'policed' by private security companies, and from which 'undesirable' people are excluded (primarily groups of youths and the homeless) (Fischer and Poland 1998: 191; see also Madanipour 1998). Fischer and Poland also argue that the 'unobjectionable' discourses of 'community safety' and 'community policing' support 'subterranean' processes of coercion and control through the targeting of 'problem' groups and neighbourhoods for removal and exclusion.

Inequalities in benefits from public services

In this section we consider briefly some evidence on the extent of inequalities in the benefits secured from public services, access to which is so important to sustaining social capital. An analysis of the local distribution of public spending was recently undertaken for the Department of the Environment, Transport and the Regions (DETR) by Bramley *et al.* (1998) using administrative data and various modelling methods to estimate spending per head at local authority ward level and relating this to the DETR's index of deprivation.

They found that there is generally a positive relationship between expenditure per head and degree of deprivation but with significant variation indicating that deprivation is far from being the only influence on expenditure levels.
Indeed, they found that the relationship between spending and deprivation
at ward level is non-linear, rising mainly at higher levels of deprivation,
indicating that over quite a wide range of deprivation levels spending is
relatively invariant. This suggests that in all but the most deprived areas,
spending tends not to rise proportionately with increasing deprivation.

The study found that different services displayed differing degrees of relationship with deprivation. A first group of services are strongly or moderately
skewed towards deprived, low-income areas. This group comprises means-
tested social security benefits, personal social services for children and mental
illness, school meals, housing and environmental capital spending, and targeted programmes such as Single Regeneration Budget (which are all strongly
skewed). Major social security benefits related to disability and ill health,
personal social services for older people and other adult groups, primary and
special needs education and bus subsidies are more moderately skewed towards
poorer areas.

A second group of services display little correlation with deprivation. This
group includes secondary education, training, some social security benefits
(e.g. child benefit), health services and most local environmental services
such as sports and leisure, refuse collection and street cleaning. Finally, a
third group of public expenditure clearly gives more benefit to more affluent
areas. This group includes higher education, road and rail subsidies, retirement pensions, and certain local environmental services such as parks.
The authors conclude that this research (which excludes the effect of taxation) calls into question the assumption that public spending is heavily
redistributive:

> The increment in per-capita spending associated with higher levels of
> deprivation is moderate rather than dramatic in scale. Non-deprived
> areas in our case study cities still receive substantial amounts of spend-
> ing, close to the national average for the programmes analysed. Several
> major spending programmes provide patterns which are relatively flat
> across the bands of deprivation.
>
> (Bramley *et al*. 1998: 178-9)

An important conclusion from this research is that 'services managed by
local government target resources more strongly on deprived areas' and that
local authorities are closer and more responsive to 'the problems of deprivation and their consequences on the ground' (Bramley *et al*. 1998: 182).
However, patterns of spending are limited as a measure of the effect of
differential provision of, and access to, public services; expenditure inputs
can only be a proxy for usage and benefits. Evidence on the latter is limited
at the local level but research by Bramley and LeGrand (1992) in Cheshire
found a pro-middle-class bias in the provision and usage of county services,
the picture being dominated by education (although the relationship to
income was neutral). Other research on usage patterns from MORI surveys
has confirmed this picture, while research on the usage of sports and leisure
facilities 'tends to show that the better off and middle classes make more use

of them' (Bramley and LeGrand 1992: 10). On the basis of the available evidence, Bramley and LeGrand conclude that 'local government cannot be seen as a powerful engine of progressive redistribution' (p. 27).

The above two studies therefore do not provide grounds for optimism about the benefits secured from public services by poorer people and localities – although local authorities are better at targeting resources on deprived areas than central government, they do not achieve significant redistribution. The pessimistic stance is taken by Geddes (1997: 215–17) who argues that 'the extent and form of public provision in deprived neighbourhoods is often very deficient' and that initiatives at the local level to address social exclusion 'are mostly constrained by limited resources and power over crucial determinants of poverty and deprivation'.

Erosion of services in rural areas

Much of the work which has been done on inequalities in provision of public services has tended to focus on the problem of urban deprivation. However, in recent years there has been a growth of concern about the incidence of poverty and deprivation, and the erosion of public service provision, in rural areas. The Rural Development Commission has been active in commissioning research into the problem and a recent study (Hale and Capaldi 1997) examined the level of spending on, and provision of, various local government services in rural areas relative to more urban areas. The underlying problem derives from the lower standard spending assessments (SSAs) for rural areas which result in lower levels of government grant aid. The study examined four areas of activity: personal social services, concessionary bus travel, continuing education, and sport and recreation. In relation to social services for the elderly, adult education and leisure provision, the research found lower levels of provision for residents in rural areas than in more urban areas and lower take-up of concessionary travel passes due to the poorer levels of public transport provision. Moreover, it was concluded that access to services is a key factor; low population density means that people have to travel relatively long distances to facilities but it is often difficult to make these journeys by public transport. In another study for rural local authorities, Hale (1998: 9) concludes:

> The people who live in rural areas receive fewer services than their urban counterparts; those services are often provided to a lower standard than in urban areas; because public transport is generally poor in rural areas they are more likely to need to travel by car in order to use the facilities; and that in turn means that they will usually face higher travel costs than people living in urban areas if they need to use local authority services.

Other research into social exclusion in rural areas has highlighted problems of access to services which, as previously discussed, has been exacerbated by the effects of privatization and 'marketization'. Although up to a quarter of rural households are estimated to be living in or on the margins of poverty, the scale of rural poverty tends to be hidden in official statistics because it exists in small pockets (Chapman *et al.* 1998; NREC 1998; Shucksmith and Chapman 1998). Nevertheless, Cloke *et al.* (1995) and Chapman *et al.* (1998) argue that poverty and social exclusion are severe problems in most rural areas and difficulties of access to public services contribute to these problems. As argued above, the decline of public transport has been particularly problematic since it has hit vulnerable groups such as the unemployed, the elderly, women and young people and has resulted in a 'forced' increase in car ownership out of sheer necessity which represents 'a major drain on a low-income family's resources' (NREC 1998: 2).

Policy responses

So, what is the potential for action at the local level to address social exclusion by improving access to services? Recent policy responses have been formulated within a new 'paradigm' of urban governance. This emphasizes the need for local government to develop a 'community leadership' role, fostering the development of 'partnership' between key local economic and political actors in private, public, voluntary and community sectors, building 'social networks' within which the role of the state is increasingly seen as 'enabling', 'building capacity' and 'levering in' resources rather than directly providing services (Healey *et al.* 1995; Stewart and Stoker 1995; Clarence and Painter 1998). This paradigm is evident in Blair's (1998: 13) vision of local government:

> It is in partnership with others that local government's future lies. Local authorities will still deliver some services but their distinctive leadership role will be to weave and knit together the contribution of the various local stakeholders. To ensure that the shared vision is delivered by bringing cohesion and co-ordination to the current fragmented scene. They will mobilise investment, bid for funds, champion the needs of the area and harness the energies of local people and community organisations.

This 'Third Way' model of local governance is evident in a range of policies: Single Regeneration Budget, the Health, Education and Employment Action Zones and the 'modernization agenda' for local government (DETR 1998a). However, it is possible to question the extent to which this provides an effective policy response which is capable of addressing the 'structural factors' behind social exclusion (Goodwin 1995; Lovering 1995). First, local action per se can have only limited impact given the importance of wider economic and social processes which cause social exclusion and the limits to the scope of decision making at the local level in relation to broader welfare policies which are important in addressing it. Second, the effectiveness of local action is, in any case, undermined by the fragmentation of powers and responsibilities within localities, by problems in achieving coordination across services and agencies and specifically by the erosion of the powers and responsibilities of democratically elected local government. From this perspective, caution must be exercised in assessing the effectiveness of local authorities' initiatives to address poverty and social exclusion, and indeed such caution has been widely acknowledged (see Bramley and LeGrand 1992; Philo *et al.* 1995; Geddes 1997; Donnison 1998). Indeed, in a study of local authorities' anti-poverty strategies, Alcock *et al.* (1995) provide little evidence of the effectiveness of local strategies in addressing and alleviating poverty and social exclusion. Moreover, they found significant problems with corporate (cross-service) and partnership (multi-agency) working and they emphasize that:

> it is important to recognise the constraints within which the challenge to local poverty must be made. However great their commitment, local authorities cannot promise to be able to remove or prevent local poverty, for this is inevitably the consequence of national or even international economic and political trends, over which local politicians and officers have no control.
>
> (Alcock *et al.* 1995: 96)

Critics of 'localism' will question whether local authority anti-poverty strategies fulfil as much a legitimatory as a practical purpose, helping to give the appearance that the apparatus of urban governance is indeed tackling the key economic and social problems in localities (see Lovering 1995). From this perspective, local action is essentially marginal to the problem, merely 'sticking plasters on an ever-deepening wound' (Goodwin 1995: 80). Only national policy action to 'challenge the systems we live under and the power structures which sustain them' (Donnison 1998: 138) can be effective in addressing poverty and social exclusion.

However, while it is clearly the case that national government policies in relation to key areas of welfare provision have the greatest role to play, concerted action at the local level can play an important part in improving people's access to job opportunities, to services (both private and public, upon which they rely as essential means to 'normal' living), to cultural and recreational opportunities which enhance quality of life, and to social networks which provide support and interaction with others. These are the 'relational resources', access to which underpins 'inclusionary' processes, which are experienced by people within their localities.

The priority for local authorities, then, is to maximize their potential impact through concerted strategic approaches which are able to harness all the available resources and energies and focus them, through effective planning, organization and management, on the needs of those experiencing social exclusion. Many have called for a strengthening of the powers and capacities of local government as the basis for an effective anti-poverty policy. Donnison (1998: 207), for example, argues that local authorities should have 'powers to do anything that is not forbidden by the laws of the land, and sufficient financial freedom to make those powers effective'. As indicated above, Bramley *et al.* (1998) argue that the fact that local government has the capacity to target resources more effectively on deprived areas than central government provides grounds for increasing local government's powers and financial freedom. Bramley *et al.* also advocate the review of existing formulae for the allocation of central government grants to local authorities.

Despite the hopes and expectations of local government raised by the Labour government's 'modernization agenda' (DETR 1998a), it would appear that a cautious policy is to be adopted in relation to the powers and financial freedoms of local authorities. Although a new duty to promote the social, economic and environmental well-being of localities is likely to be conferred, it is clear that only when authorities have demonstrated their capacity for effective management, for continuous improvement in the efficiency and quality of services, and for improved responsiveness and accountability to local people will they be allowed enhanced powers and financial freedoms – and even then it is likely to be on a selective basis. Therefore, the key challenge for local government over the coming years in relation to the development of strategies and action to promote social inclusion is to maximize the effectiveness of such action within the scope of existing powers and responsibilities. A number of key aspects can be highlighted.

First, it is vital to ensure that social inclusion strategies adopt a long-term perspective underpinned by political commitment, and embody a strong corporate approach which can ensure the commitment of departments and services to changing their policies and practices. Such strategies should be integrated with other corporate strategies and with the plans of service departments. Moreover, to ensure they are properly resourced, they should be linked with authorities' financial strategies.

Second, such strategies must seek to engage the commitment of all relevant local agencies, either through joint working or partnership arrangements or by seeking to influence the way they deliver services so as to promote social inclusion. Agencies such as health authorities, employment services and benefits agencies in the statutory sector and various voluntary sector organizations will be amenable to partnership relations and efforts can be made to influence the utilities and local financial institutions.

Third, strategies must be developed with full and meaningful participation by the local people who are experiencing social exclusion. This presents a real challenge to local authorities since one aspect of the exclusion experienced by such people relates to processes of local decision making, so they are often characterized as 'hard to reach' in consultation exercises. However, a concerted effort to involve such people (and build their capacity to become involved) in the development of strategies and, indeed, in their subsequent implementation and monitoring, is essential to the effectiveness of such strategies and, moreover, can play an important role in helping to promote 'inclusion' for those involved in the process.

Fourth, in order to be effective in achieving benefits for the poorest and most vulnerable people and groups, strategies must be needs-led. The argument for 'needs-driven' public policy as the basis for promoting distributive justice has been made elsewhere (Sanderson 1996). Bramley and LeGrand (1992: 27) found that 'where services are allocated on a needs basis they are generally pro-poor'. A needs-based approach implies a commitment to researching the causes of social exclusion and the attributes of 'need' which can be addressed by local action. It implies a commitment to opening up and democratizing decision-making processes and giving local communities a voice in negotiating the definition of their needs and the desired outcomes from strategies and plans. It implies a commitment to evaluation as the basis for assessing the effectiveness and impact of strategies and policies and for learning how to improve such effectiveness (Sanderson 1996).

Increasing priority has been given by local authorities in recent years to the development of 'anti-poverty' strategies – both in response to heightened recognition of the growing problem of poverty and social exclusion (in particular as it affects certain groups and areas) and as a result of authorities' increasing awareness of the need for a corporate approach to address broader economic and social objectives in the context of the emerging 'paradigm' of urban governance discussed above. In May 1999, 140 authorities had such strategies in place (LGA 1999). Alcock *et al.* (1995: 77–89) identify a number of common themes in approaches to developing such strategies. These include:

- targeting of action on both groups and areas identified as experiencing acute poverty and deprivation;
- decentralization of services to promote access for local people and, in some cases, to devolve decision-making power;
- increasing concern to integrate the promotion of economic and community regeneration and develop 'self-help' initiatives such as credit unions and local exchange trading systems;
- strong emphasis on efforts to maximize or maintain the incomes of poor people through welfare rights and benefit take-up campaigns, advice on debt and managing money and reorganization of council tax and housing benefit administration to encourage take-up;
- modification of charging policies to provide reduced cost or free services for particular target groups.

The concern to improve access to essential services figures prominently in such local strategies. A good illustration is provided by Birmingham City Council's (undated) strategy which includes three aims in this respect. First, to ensure equity of access to services by raising awareness of service departments to prevent inadvertent exclusion, and taking account of the needs of low-income people in planning services. Second, to ensure services are promoted among people on low incomes and involve service users in developing methods to encourage take-up. Third, to develop mechanisms to deliver services locally through decentralized arrangements.

In seeking to improve access to public services, there are a number of barriers which 'social inclusion strategies' should address. First, lack of *information* may be a significant barrier to take-up of services. Analysis is required of where take-up is low relative to need, and the causes of such low take-up, as the basis for targeted action to improve information on service availability and eligibility and to address other obstacles (e.g. reluctance to undergo means testing). The second important barrier to access is *financial* and much can be done to help poorer people through selective action to reduce (or waive) user charges for groups such as the unemployed, pensioners and disabled people. A broader approach to the financial dimension could include action to promote take-up of all welfare benefits, to encourage the take-up of 'mainstream' financial services, and to promote the development of alternative financial services (such as credit unions and local exchange trading systems) for poor people in areas forsaken by the mainstream services. Increasingly, local authorities are recognizing the potential role of the voluntary sector in this area of anti-poverty work (LGA 1998).

The third barrier to access is *physical* or *spatial*. Many local authorities are addressing this aspect by decentralizing service provision through neighbourhood offices, often providing a 'one-stop shop' approach with a single office dealing with all (or many) council services and, in some cases, other agencies' services also (Burns *et al.* 1994). A good example is provided by the network of 'council centres' in Cumbria which provide access to the services of all three tiers of local government – i.e. county, district and parish/town (LGA 1998: 34). Increasingly, the potential role of information and communication technologies is being investigated as a means of overcoming problems of spatial access, and these can have special applicability in rural areas (NREC 1998).

The role of public transport in promoting access for poorer people to spatially distributed opportunities and, again, in helping to address social exclusion in rural areas, is widely acknowledged and has received an impetus with the Labour government's *A New Deal for Transport* White Paper (DETR 1998b; Enoch 1999). 'A fairer, more integrated society' is one of the stated aims of an integrated approach. Five-year local transport plans, which local authorities will be required to produce, must include 'measures to reduce social exclusion and address the needs of different groups in society' (DETR 1998b: 111). The Rural Bus Partnership Fund will provide £150 million over the period to 2002 to support socially necessary services, and a 'rural bus challenge' is designed to promote innovative schemes – for example, using the vehicles of other public service providers and the voluntary sector. The Rural Transport Partnership Scheme specifically aims to improve access to jobs and services to reduce social exclusion through better coordination of voluntary, local authority and commercial services, and improved integration of rural bus, rail and taxi services (DETR 1999).

Finally, there is an important *cultural* barrier to access as emphasized by Van Kempen (1997), who argues that public services in 'poverty pockets' are subject to negative stigma and the behaviour and attitudes of front-line officials can have an adverse effect on the expectations of poor people and on their access to services. This aspect is recognized by Donnison (1998) who argues that there is a need to change the culture of public services and to 'treat poor people with greater courtesy and kindness' (p. 152). Many local authorities have sought to address this through service quality initiatives which incorporate 'customer care' training for front-line staff, and it is particularly important that this is emphasized where service delivery is decentralized to local offices in disadvantaged areas. This is addressed, for example, in Birmingham City Council's strategy.

Conclusion

A number of dimensions of access to services can be addressed in local 'social inclusion' strategies but ultimately it must be acknowledged that deliberate rationing due to resource constraints may be the major factor preventing poor people from gaining access to services to meet their needs. Needs-led resource allocation can improve distributional fairness in the provision of services but concern is often expressed by local authorities about the additional pressure on limited resources which arises from needs-based policy making. Although there is clearly a coherent case on equity grounds for seeking to focus existing resources on groups and areas in greatest need, it can be argued that in order to achieve a major impact on social exclusion a radical increase in the resources, capacities and powers at the disposal of the state will be required.

From this perspective, questions arise about the capacity for collective action to address social exclusion through the emerging model of 'governance' which emphasizes the 'enabling' or 'steering' role of government in building networks and partnerships between all stakeholder groups and interests. Given the imperative in this model to incorporate a wide range of stakeholder interests and to give particular attention to business interests (with a strong emphasis on attracting private finance), what scope is there to build support for social objectives against the perception that economic considerations have 'natural' priority? Moreover, given the now considerable literature on the problems and difficulties of achieving effective partnership working and community involvement, what scope is there to build an effective capacity for collective action which can actually achieve more in terms of welfare impacts than is possible through the diminishing scope of democratic government? Finally, given the increasing emphasis on performance management as the means of ensuring accountability 'upwards' for the use of resources, what scope is there for specifying social inclusion objectives in terms of performance measures, standards and targets?

These are questions upon which research into, and evaluation of, the government's strategy and action plans to address social exclusion will hopefully shed some light. However, it is important that an alternative, more radical policy agenda is retained 'in the frame' for comparative appraisal and assessment and not simply drowned by the dominant discourse. Such an agenda would: adopt a sceptical position on the capacities of the new 'urban governance'; argue for stronger powers of intervention and regulation for government to promote social and equity objectives; argue for enhanced powers and capacities for effective action by local government with strengthened democratic accountability; and argue for a real shift of power 'downwards' to local communities so that those who suffer the hardships of poverty and deprivation gain real influence, involvement and control over the development of action to improve their access to services, facilities and resources which can help to promote social inclusion.

References

Alcock, P., Craig, G., Dalgleish, K. and Pearson, S. (1995) *Combating Local Poverty: The Management of Anti-Poverty Strategies by Local Government*. London: Local Government Management Board.

Bartlett, W., Roberts, J.A. and LeGrand, J. (eds) (1998) *A Revolution in Social Policy: Quasi-Market Reforms in the 1990s*. Bristol: The Policy Press.

Birmingham City Council (undated) *Poverty in Birmingham: City Council Strategy*. Birmingham: Community Affairs Department, Birmingham City Council.

Blair, T. (1998) *Leading the Way: A New Vision for Local Government*. London: Institute for Public Policy Research.

Boardman, B. (1998) *Rural Transport and Equity: Discussion Paper*. London: Council for the Protection of Rural England, Countryside Commission and Rural Development Commission.

Bramley, G. and LeGrand, J. (1992) *Who Uses Local Services? Striving for Equity*, The Belgrave Papers, no. 4. Luton: Local Government Management Board.

Bramley, G. with Lancaster, S., Lomax, D., McIntosh, S. and Russell, J. (1998) *Where Does Public Spending Go? Pilot Study to Analyse the Flows of Public Expenditure into Local Areas*. London: DETR.

Burns, D., Hambleton, R. and Hoggett, P. (1994) *The Politics of Decentralisation: Revitalising Local Democracy*. Basingstoke: Macmillan.

Chapman, P., Phimister, E., Shucksmith, M., Upward, R. and Vera-Toscano, E. (1998) *Poverty and Exclusion in Rural Britain: The Dynamics of Low Income and Employment*. York: Joseph Rowntree Foundation.

Clarence, E. and Painter, C. (1998) Public services under New Labour: collaborative discourses and local networking. *Public Policy and Administration*, 13(3): 8–22.

Cloke, P. (1993) On 'problems and solutions': the reproduction of problems for rural communities in Britain during the 1980s. *Journal of Rural Studies*, 9(2): 113–21.

Cloke, P., Milbourne, P. and Thomas, C. (1995) Poverty in the countryside: out of sight and out of mind, in C. Philo (ed.) *Off the Map: The Social Geography of Poverty in the UK*. London: Child Poverty Action Group.

DETR (Department of the Environment, Transport and the Regions) (1998a) *Modern Local Government: In Touch with the People*, Cm 4014. London: DETR.

DETR (Department of the Environment, Transport and the Regions) (1998b) *A New Deal for Transport: Better for Everyone*, Cm 3950. London: DETR.

DETR (Department of the Environment, Transport and the Regions) (1999) *From Workhorse to Thoroughbred: A Better Role for Bus Travel*. London: DETR.

Donnison, D. (1998) *Policies for a Just Society*. Basingstoke: Macmillan.

Dorling, D. and Woodward, R. (1996) Social polarisation 1971–1991: a micro-geographical analysis of Britain. *Progress in Planning*, 45(2). Oxford: Pergamon Press.

Enoch, M. (1999) Can transport policies help to re-integrate the socially excluded? *Local Transport Today*, 14 January: 6–7.

Fischer, B. and Poland, B. (1998) Exclusion, 'risk', and social control: reflections on community policing and public health. *Geoforum*, 29(2): 187–97.

Ford, J. and Rowlingson, K. (1996) Low-income households and credit: exclusion, preference, and inclusion. *Environment and Planning A*, 28: 1345–60.

Geddes, M. (1997) Poverty, excluded communities and local democracy, in N. Jewson and S. MacGregor (eds) *Transforming Cities: Contested Governance and New Spatial Divisions*. London: Routledge.

Goodwin, M. (1995) Poverty in the city: you can raise your voice, but who is listening? in C. Philo (ed.) *Off the Map: The Social Geography of Poverty in the UK*. London: Child Poverty Action Group.

Gorard, S. (1998) Whither market forces in education? *International Journal of Education Management*, 12(1): 5–13.

Graham, S. and Marvin, S. (1995) More than ducts and wires: post-Fordism, cities and utility networks, in P. Healey, S. Cameron, S. Davoudi, S. Graham and A. Madanipour (eds) *Managing Cities: The New Urban Context*. Chichester: John Wiley & Sons.

Hale, R. (1998) *Local Authority Spending and Services in Rural and Urban England*. London: Rita Hale & Associates.

Hale, R. and Capaldi, A. (1997) *Local Authority Services in Rural England*. Salisbury: Rural Development Commission.

Healey, P. (1995) Infrastructure, technology and power, in P. Healey, S. Cameron, S. Davoudi, S. Graham and A. Madanipour (eds) *Managing Cities: The New Urban Context*. Chichester: John Wiley & Sons.

Healey, P. (1998) Institutionalist theory, social exclusion and governance, in A. Madanipour, G. Cars and J. Allen (eds) *Social Exclusion in European Cities: Processes, Experiences and Responses*. London: Jessica Kingsley.

Healey, P., Cameron, S., Davoudi, S., Graham, S. and Madanipour, A. (1995) Introduction: the city: crisis, change and invention, in P. Healey, S. Cameron, S. Davoudi, S. Graham and A. Madanipour (eds) *Managing Cities: The New Urban Context*. Chichester: John Wiley & Sons.

Kempson, E. (1997) Privatisation of utilities, in A. Walker and C. Walker (eds) *Britain Divided: The Growth of Social Exclusion in the 1980s and 1990s*. London: Child Poverty Action Group.

Kempson, E. and Whyley, C. (1999) *Kept Out or Opted Out? Understanding and Combating Financial Exclusion*. Bristol: The Policy Press.

LeGrand, J. and Bartlett, W. (1993) *Quasi-Markets and Social Policy*. Basingstoke: Macmillan.

Leyshon, A. and Thrift, N. (1996) Financial exclusion and the shifting boundaries of the financial system. *Environment and Planning A*, 28: 1150–6.

LGA (Local Government Association) (1998) *Tackling Rural Poverty and Social Exclusion: The Role of Local Authorities*. London: Local Government Association.

LGA (Local Government Association) (1999) *Local Inclusion: Case Studies of the Local Government Role in Promoting Social Justice and Social Inclusion*. London: Local Government Association.

Lovering, J. (1995) Creating discourses rather than jobs: the crisis in the cities and the transition fantasies of intellectuals and policy makers, in P. Healey, S. Cameron, S. Davoudi, S. Graham and A. Madanipour (eds) *Managing Cities: The New Urban Context*. Chichester: John Wiley & Sons.

McCormick, J. and Philo, C. (1995) Where is poverty? The hidden geography of poverty in the United Kingdom, in C. Philo (ed.) *Off the Map: The Social Geography of Poverty in the UK*. London: Child Poverty Action Group.

Madanipour, A. (1998) Social exclusion and space, in A. Madanipour, G. Cars and J. Allen (eds) *Social Exclusion in European Cities: Processes, Experiences and Responses*. London: Jessica Kingsley.

Marvin, S., Graham, S. and Guy, S. (1999) Cities, regions and privatised utilities. *Progress in Planning*, 51(2). Oxford: Pergamon Press.

NREC (National Rural Enterprise Centre) (1998) *NREC's Vision for the Future of Rural Services: A Discussion Paper*. Warwickshire: National Rural Enterprise Centre.

Philo, C., McCormick, J. and CPAG (1995) 'Poor places' and beyond: summary findings and policy implications, in C. Philo (ed.) *Off the Map: The Social Geography of Poverty in the UK*. London: Child Poverty Action Group.

Pitts, J. and Hope, T. (1997) The local politics of inclusion: the state and community safety. *Social Policy and Administration*, 31(5): 37–58.

Ranson, S. (1995) From reforming to restructuring of education, in J. Stewart and G. Stoker (eds) *Local Government in the 1990s*. Basingstoke: Macmillan.

Ribchester, C. and Edwards, B. (1999) The centre and the local: policy and practice in rural education provision. *Journal of Rural Studies*, 15(1): 49–63.

Roberts, J.A., LeGrand, J. and Bartlett, W. (1998) Lessons from experience of quasi-markets in the 1990s, in W. Bartlett, J.A. Roberts and J. LeGrand (eds) *A Revolution in Social Policy: Quasi-Market Reforms in the 1990s*. Bristol: The Policy Press.

Sanderson, I. (1996) Needs and public services, in J. Percy-Smith (ed.) *Needs Assessments in Public Policy*. Buckingham: Open University Press.

Shucksmith, M. and Chapman, P. (1998) Rural development and social exclusion. *Sociologica Ruralis*, 38(2): 225–42.

Simpson, B.J. (1996) Deregulation and privatization: the British local bus industry following the Transport Act, 1995. *Transport Reviews*, 16(3): 213–23.

Smith, G., Smith, T. and Wright, G. (1997) Poverty and schooling: choice, diversity or division?, in A. Walker and C. Walker (eds) *Britain Divided: The Growth of Social Exclusion in the 1980s and 1990s*. London: Child Poverty Action Group.

Stewart, J. and Stoker, G. (eds) (1995) *Local Government in the 1990s*. Basingstoke: Macmillan.

Van Kempen, E. (1997) Poverty pockets and life chances: on the role of place in shaping social inequality. *American Behavioral Scientist*, 41(3): 430–49.

Wacquant, L.J.D. (1998) Negative social capital: state breakdown and social destitution in America's urban core. *Netherlands Journal of Housing and the Built Environment*, 13(1): 25–40.

White, P. (1997) The experience of bus and coach deregulation in Britain and other countries. *International Journal of Transport Economics*, 24(1): 35–52.

Whitty, G., Power, S. and Halpin, D. (1998) Self-managing schools in the marketplace: the experience of England, the USA and New Zealand, in W. Bartlett, J.A. Roberts and J. LeGrand (eds) *A Revolution in Social Policy: Quasi-Market Reforms in the 1990s*. Bristol: The Policy Press.

8 POLITICAL EXCLUSION

Janie Percy-Smith

Introduction

Most of the chapters in this book are concerned with forms of social and economic exclusion – exclusion from a range of goods, services and activities which are widely considered to be important for individual and collective fulfilment. However, a further facet of social exclusion is the disempowerment of socially excluded groups and individuals which results in their claims to have their social and economic needs met not being voiced, not being heard or not being acted upon. This aspect of exclusion can be termed 'political exclusion' and is the focus of this chapter. Geddes (1995: 8) has defined political exclusion as:

> the isolation of poor people and communities from the mainstream of the political process, and the making of decisions about their lives elsewhere by others. This is particularly the case where geographical concentrations of poverty and deprivation exist – in inner cities, on peripheral housing estates, or in poor rural communities.

It is interesting to reflect that, while there is an increasing literature on social and economic exclusion, there is relatively little on political exclusion. Perhaps it is an aspect of our increasingly non-participative political culture that the fact that a considerable proportion of the population does not choose to, or is effectively prevented from, exercising their political rights does not appear to warrant significant debate or discussion. It is certainly a reflection of the primacy given to economic issues, notably employment, in the social exclusion policy agenda. Indeed, the government's first annual report on poverty and social exclusion (Department of Social Security 1999), despite being extremely wide-ranging, reporting progress on all the myriad initiatives which are being developed to address social exclusion, makes no mention of political exclusion. And yet the increasing literature on social capital makes clear the relationship between forms of civic and community participation, effective governance and prosperity (Putnam 1993). In particular, as Boix and Posner (1998) note, social capital contributes to 'good governance' by helping to develop citizens who are better informed and better able to ensure the accountability of elected representatives. Furthermore 'social capital contributes to effective governance by facilitating the articulation of citizens' demands (Boix and Posner 1998: 690; see also Lake and Huckfeldt 1998).

In liberal democratic states citizenship rights are conferred automatically – typically by virtue of birth – on those residents of a defined territory who meet the nationality criteria of that nation state. Roche and van Berkel (1997: xviii) have defined citizenship in terms of 'the possession of a range of civil, political and social rights and responsibilities – and the ability to exercise these rights and responsibilities – underwritten largely but not exclusively, by nation states'. This definition is useful since it highlights the importance of not only possessing rights but also of having the wherewithal to exercise them.

Universalism is a key aspect of the language of citizenship rights in liberal democratic states. However, despite the appearance of universalism, Taylor (1998: 146) has argued that there is an inbuilt tendency towards exclusion in liberal democratic states 'arising from the fact that democracies work well when people know one another, trust one another, and feel a sense of commitment toward one another'. In particular he identifies the entry of 'new kinds of people into a society' as posing a particular challenge. This has clear implications for minority ethnic groups who may seek citizenship within the host country and accept the responsibilities which that role confers, while at the same time wishing to preserve intact certain aspects of their own culture and way of life. This can be regarded as a challenge to the dominant culture which reacts by seeking to exclude these 'other ways of being' (Taylor 1998: 147).

In a similar vein Halfmann (1998: 513–14) argues that citizenship is simultaneously 'selective' and 'universalist': 'Citizenship is selective because it offers inclusion into the political system, but not necessarily into (all other social systems of) society; it is universalist because, in principle, it provides everyone with membership in a nation-state'. As an example of this duality he highlights the 'oddity' created by migration which might result in an individual being *included* in the labour market or health care system of a country but *excluded* from the political system (Halfmann 1998: 514). So, despite the universalist terms surrounding citizenship, for some groups within the population citizenship is, in fact, partial or circumscribed. This is particularly the case in relation to recent immigrants or temporary workers. However, this group is not the primary focus of this chapter. Rather, it is those people who have full citizenship rights but who, for whatever reason, do not exercise or utilize them fully.

In most liberal democratic states exercise of the rights of citizenship is at the discretion of individuals. While the *responsibilities* associated with citizenship (paying taxes, obeying the law) are enforced, rights are not (there are some exceptions: in a number of countries including Australia, voting in elections is compulsory). Thus it is up to individual citizens to decide whether or not they register to vote, vote in local, general or European elections, join a trade union, stand as a candidate for election, become an activist in a political party, participate in community organizations and so on. If levels of non-participation were not too high and were randomly distributed across social and economic groups it would not, perhaps, be a particular cause for concern. However, this is not the case. As this chapter will seek to demonstrate, non-participation is strongly correlated with social and economic disadvantage. The evidence suggests that a significant proportion of the most vulnerable groups in the population are being systematically denied an effective political voice. In addition, another group has become so disenchanted with democratic political processes that they no longer consider it worthwhile to participate. And, finally, incidents of social disturbance and disorder in some areas suggest a high level of alienation from social and political processes. These factors indicate that political exclusion should be a cause for concern.

This chapter will begin with a consideration of the forms that political exclusion takes and the activities that people are being excluded, or are excluding themselves, from. The chapter will also examine the available evidence on levels of political participation among particular groups and the policy initiatives that are being developed to address political non-participation.

Forms and extent of political exclusion

It is important to recognize at the outset that those who do not participate in the political life of their communities are not a homogeneous group. Within this wider group there are (at least) four categories of people. First, there are those who are *formally excluded* from citizenship rights and who are therefore debarred from having any kind of political voice. This is the situation of asylum seekers in this country and, as Chapter 3 shows, the situation of this group is getting worse as a result of recent changes to rules governing benefit entitlement. Second, there are those people who would participate but who are *effectively excluded* as a result of their personal characteristics or situation. People with disabilities who are unable to attend meetings, read election communications or get to a polling station to vote might fall into this category, as do people such as lone parents or those with other caring responsibilities who may also find it difficult to participate fully in the political life of their community. While these two categories of non-participants may be said to be excluded from participating by external factors (e.g. current legislation, inaccessible political activities) there are two other categories of people who exclude themselves. In the first of these two cases are those people who do not participate as a conscious choice; for whom, in other words, non-participation is a political act. This group includes those people who have assessed political processes, institutions and politicians and decided that there is no benefit in participating. This might be for a number of reasons such as a belief that they do not have an effective voice or that there is no real choice – all political parties are the same. The other group of people who exclude themselves are those who do not participate, not as a result of a conscious decision, but because of one or more of a range of factors such as: lack of information, knowledge and understanding about politics, political processes and the opportunities for participation; participation not being a

Table 8.1 Non-participating groups

Excluded by others	Self-excluded
Formally excluded	Non-participation as political choice
Effectively excluded	Non-participatory culture

part of their everyday experience or expectations; alienation from political institutions and processes; or not feeling that they have a stake in society and, therefore, the way it is governed. These four groups of non-participants are summarized in Table 8.1.

So what is it that people are being excluded, or excluding themselves, from? Political participation takes many forms, both formal and informal. For the purpose of this chapter we will take political participation to involve all or any of the following activities:

- voting in general, regional, local and European elections;
- membership of a political party;
- standing as a candidate for election;
- membership of/activity in a pressure group or campaigning organization;
- participation in a community, residents' or tenants' organization;
- membership of/activity in a trade union;
- participation in local/community decision making (e.g. through an area committee, neighbourhood forum or regeneration partnership).

In the remainder of this section we will consider the available evidence relating to levels of participation and non-participation in both electoral and non-electoral activity.

Electoral activity

For many if not most people, voting in elections is the archetypal form of democratic political participation. It is relatively undemanding of individuals and requires no special skills; elections, especially general elections, receive massive coverage in the national and local press and broadcast media. And yet, election turnout is still relatively low. (However, see Rose 1997 on what constitutes a 'good turnout' and, in particular, the idea of abstention as political choice necessary to a democratic society.)

In general elections in the second part of this century turnout in the UK has averaged at about 75 per cent of registered voters; in the last general election in 1997 turnout was only 71 per cent. In local elections the turnout is generally considerably lower – on average 40 per cent of registered voters, the lowest in the European Union (EU) (Rallings et al. 1996). In the local elections of May 1998 turnout reached an all-time low with only 29 per cent of English electors voting. And in elections for the newly-established and high-profile assemblies in Scotland and Wales, 40 per cent and 54 per cent of electors respectively did not vote.

These rather low turnout figures look even worse when one takes into consideration the fact that not all those who are eligible to vote register to vote. Low voter registration is a particular problem in those areas which are disadvantaged and/or have a highly transient population. Similarly, voter turnout tends to be lower in these areas. Voter turnout is also relatively low among young people (see below).

Traditionally, 'rational choice theory' has been used by political scientists to account for abstentions in elections (Downs 1957; Dunleavy 1991). Rational choice theory suggests that voters will assess the costs (particularly the effort involved in voting) and benefits (notably how likely it is that their vote will affect the outcome of an election) of voting and decide accordingly. 'A rational voter will turn out, therefore, when he or she considers that the benefits outweigh the costs of voting' (Pattie and Johnston 1998: 264). However, in most seats most of the time, a rational assessment along these lines would result in a decision not to vote given the first-past-the-post electoral system which means that the impact of a single vote is limited unless the seat is a marginal. Therefore the fact that around 75 per cent of registered electors do, on average, vote suggests that rational choice is not the only factor at play.

Sociological theories, by contrast, note the differences between social groups as to their propensity to vote. Turnout is generally higher among those in white-collar jobs, among men, middle-aged and older electors, long-standing residents of communities and those who are members of organizations (Pattie and Johnston 1998: 265). Social factors, it is argued, may affect the likelihood of voting because of their relationship to the 'resources' available to electors – for example, the resources necessary to obtain political information, and because such resources relate to the different norms of different groups within the community. A final possible explanation for failure to vote relates to political efficacy. Those social groups which are least likely to vote are most likely to feel most alienated from the political process, to lack confidence in political processes and institutions and to feel that their participation is ineffective.

Recent analysis of data on voter turnout and data from the British Election Survey confirms the link between turnout and marginality, although this is less significant than it used to be (Pattie and Johnston 1998: 268). Local economic conditions were also found to have an impact in the 1992 general election: the higher the unemployment rate in a locality, the lower the turnout. Analysis of the characteristics of voters and non-voters in 1992 showed that voters were disproportionately drawn from particular groups: those who identified as Labour or Liberal Democrat; those who identified strongly with a political party; people in older age groups; owner-occupiers rather than those who rent their home. However, turnout was not found to be linked to other sociological factors such as social class, education or employment status. Finally, electors who care about the outcome of the election are more likely to vote, as are those who feel that politicians care about what they think (Pattie and Johnston 1998: 269).

This data suggests that elements of all three explanations for not voting hold true. However, engagement with and confidence in political processes and institutions is a key determinant and certain groups are more likely to demonstrate these characteristics than others. Furthermore, the data referred to above focuses on the characteristics of those who are registered to vote but do not do so. If we take account of those people who do not even register to vote, it is likely that the relationship between social and economic disadvantage, lack of confidence in political processes and non-participation would be even more marked.

Putting oneself forward as a candidate for election requires considerably more resources than voting. In a majority of cases candidates for election are members of political parties and have been through a process of selection by the party in question to check their suitability as potential candidates. While standing as a candidate for election as a member of parliament (MP) is a particularly demanding commitment and, therefore, by its nature open only to a small minority of individuals, election as a member of a local council should be open to a wider group of people.

In practice, however, councillors are still disproportionately male, white and elderly, and women, younger people and ethnic minorities are all under-represented. Nevertheless there has been some progress in recent years: women doubled their representation between 1964 and 1993 and there has been a steady increase in ethnic minority representation in areas with significant ethnic minority populations (Young and Rao 1994). How important is it that elected representatives mirror the populations which they serve? Stewart and Game (1991: 5) argue that, while elected representatives may not always be 'people like us', they nevertheless should be people who can and will 'act effectively on our behalf'. This is an especially important issue for those communities which are most vulnerable and disadvantaged (see Geddes 1995). Clearly, for some sections of the population, there is little confidence that elected representatives will fulfil this role of community advocates.

Non-electoral political activity

Although, as noted above, participation in (free and fair) elections is commonly seen as a (if not *the*) defining characteristic of a democratic polity, there has been a tradition within democratic theorizing which has recognized the need for more generalized forms of participation to create a democratic society (see, for example, Pateman 1970; Macpherson 1977; Smith and Blanc 1997). This is now being increasingly recognized in policy terms. In particular there is a renewed emphasis on the need for citizen, community and user participation, involvement and consultation. The most recent analysis of political participation in Britain (Parry *et al.* 1992) shows that political activity other than voting is very much a minority activity (however their definition of political activity is limited to 'action by citizens which is intended to influence the decisions of public representatives and officials'). Furthermore it is disproportionately concentrated among particular groups, notably those with access to certain resources, those who identify with a political party, those who feel a sense of political efficacy and those with educational qualifications. In other words, those who are most likely to engage in non-electoral forms of political participation share similar characteristics with those who are most likely to vote.

One of the areas where one would, perhaps, expect there to be relatively high levels of participation at the local level, including in areas of high disadvantage, is in relation to community, residents and tenants organizations. Such organizations are sometimes born out of the situation of disadvantage that people find themselves in. And it is indeed the case that such organizations can often be successful in providing a voice for the communities which they serve, securing much-needed resources for the area or engaging in a range of self-help activities to improve the quality of life of local areas (see Chapter 11 for examples). However, it is also the case that many such organizations also struggle on with a small but committed membership while the majority of members of the community take little or no interest. The Social Exclusion Unit (1998: 68) notes that it has been estimated that only 7 per cent of those living in the most deprived areas are likely to engage in 'voluntary' activities as compared to 20 per cent of those living in the most affluent areas. Furthermore, community groups representing marginalized areas may be seen by the local state not as allies in the fight against social exclusion, but as threats to the established order. Moreover, Campbell (1993: 247) has argued that community activity in areas of high disadvantage is essentially gendered: 'The redoubts of active citizenship on these estates were run by women whose improvised self-help systems denied their reputation as lairs inhabited by an inert underclass'.

Throughout the 1980s and 1990s a number of pressures have combined to make local authorities seek ways of making their services more accessible and responsive to local people and their decision-making structures more inclusive. As a result many, if not most, local authorities now employ a range of different methods for engaging more effectively with local people (see Lowndes et al. 1998). These include: administrative decentralization; political decentralization; one-stop shops; user forums; surveys of citizens; community needs assessments; citizens panels; interactive web sites and youth councils. All of these initiatives, if implemented appropriately, are useful additions to the system of political representation and offer some opportunities for direct participation of local people either as citizens, residents or service users. However, a recurring theme in assessments of consultation, involvement and participation initiatives is that they involve only a minority of local people and that those groups who are most disadvantaged are the least likely to participate. Furthermore, they may not be sufficient to overcome the profound sense of disempowerment felt by many disadvantaged users of local public services – especially those which are means-tested or felt to be stigmatizing – in their encounters with officials who control access to provision (Van Kempen 1997). One of the themes of regeneration initiatives in recent years (see Chapter 9) has been the need to work in partnership with local people in the regeneration of local communities. As a result most regeneration initiatives now require the establishment of a local partnership body responsible for overseeing the activities of the initiative. These boards almost always have seats for community representatives. This is the case for both UK regeneration initiatives such as Single Regeneration Budget and European initiatives.

For many working-class people working in traditional industries membership of a trade union went with the job and provided not only a collective voice in negotiations with employers but also membership of a political party, opportunities to discuss issues, information on important issues and a range of social and welfare benefits. However, the changing structure of employment, particularly the demise of traditional manufacturing industry, the attack on trade unions during the Thatcher years and high levels of unemployment have all resulted in a severing of the link between work and trade union membership. Those people who are either totally excluded from participation in the labour market as a result of unemployment or whose link with the labour market is tenuous as a result of part-time working or temporary contracts are unlikely to be members of a trade union and, as a consequence, they lack a voice through which to express their employment-related grievances.

Social disorder and violent disturbance

As was noted above, for some people alienation from political organizations, institutions and processes has been accompanied by social disorder and incidents of violent disturbance. In an analysis of 13 recorded incidents that occurred in Britain in 1991 and 1992, Power and Tunstall (1997a) identified the characteristics of such disturbances, the people involved and the nature of the local communities. All of the places affected were areas of significant disadvantage with high levels of unemployment and poverty, considerable evidence of social problems and a poor image in the wider locality. In addition, all involved estates with a higher than average concentration of young people. It was generally boys and young men (aged 10 to 30) who were actively involved in the disturbances. Only one of the 13 areas had significant numbers of ethnic minority residents – the vast majority of those involved were white. Power and Tunstall summarize these characteristics as follows: 'the areas contained a dangerous combination of large numbers of out of work young males with no status or stake in society, living in low-income work-poor households, in areas suffering from a high social stigma' (1997b: 12). Furthermore the researchers note that all of the areas had a history of disorder, violence and law breaking among young men:

> Causing trouble was a commonly known way of asserting an alternative, defiant, anti-authority and destructive image to compensate for the inability to succeed or participate in a more organised way in mainstream society . . . They accepted and some claimed to admire violent, aggressive, illegal actions which set them apart from the mainstream from which they felt excluded.
>
> (Power and Tunstall 1997b: 12)

Although some commentators have attempted to recast violent disturbances and riots as overtly or consciously political acts, this seems to ignore the underlying conditions which have given rise to these events and the characteristics of the perpetrators. Rather, they should perhaps be viewed as essentially *apolitical* acts reflective of deep-seated alienation from mainstream political processes and the breakdown of social controls. Power and Tunstall again:

> The underlying causes of riots in the 1990s appear to stem from demographic, economic and social factors. The demographic factors are an unusually youthful population with high levels of transience and very

high numbers of lone-parent families separated into large, isolated areas. The economic factors are lack of work opportunities for young males, lack of marketable skills and lack of any useable work experience. The social factors are poverty, family breakdown, weak social controls, an acceptance of law-breaking, and poor relations with the police. These factors can act together to undermine normal community controls.

(1997b: 13)

Pitts and Hope (1997: 53) link social disorder, including criminal victimization, interpersonal violence and drug misuse, not only to lack of economic resources but also to the marketization of welfare services:

the marketisation of the welfare infrastructure in impoverished areas in Britain has substituted 'exit' for democratic 'voice' as the medium of communication and the criterion for resource allocation. As such, public services are ceasing to deliver the cultural capital to the community which might enable residents to resist social dislocation and, importantly, have ceased to become the medium whereby private troubles could be translated into public issues.

Similarly, Campbell (1993) argues that places which have experienced outbreaks of social disorder have been effectively abandoned by political parties, local government and other agencies.

Excluded groups

What can we conclude from this brief review of political participation? First, it is undoubtedly the case that those people who are most disadvantaged socially and economically have relatively low levels of participation. While disadvantage may not be the only reason for non-participation it is clearly an important variable. In this section we consider participation in relation to three specific groups for whom participation appears to be problematic: young people, minority ethnic groups, and disabled people. However, before doing so it is worth mentioning the situation of a more disparate group who, it could be argued, are effectively being denied the rights of citizenship as a result of an unwillingness to conform to dominant views of what constitutes an acceptable lifestyle. This group includes rough sleepers, travellers and certain people with mental health problems. Worrall (1998) has argued that the current focus in social and criminal justice policy on 'public protection' is resulting or will result in the effective denial of citizenship rights to such groups. This view echoes the concerns about the underlying moral agenda in relation to policies addressing social exclusion referred to in Chapters 1 and 10.

Young people

A survey of the political activity of young people carried out for the British Youth Council (cited in Clipson 1998) found that:

- 50 per cent of those entitled to vote didn't vote in the last general election;
- 60 per cent of those entitled to vote didn't vote in local elections;
- the main reasons given for not voting were: not being interested in politics, not knowing enough about politics and not being registered to vote;
- 54 per cent said that their MP rarely or never listened to them;
- 58 per cent said that their local council didn't listen to their views;
- 64 per cent felt that government rarely or never listens to young people;
- 75 per cent felt that they were rarely or never consulted by their community.

Politicians are, in the eyes of young people, the least respected of all public figures; only 4 per cent named politicians as the public figures they respected most; 78 per cent of young people could not name their local MP; 10 per cent did not know who the prime minister was.

These findings suggest that, in many cases, young people are choosing not to participate in political activity for a variety of reasons including: a feeling that their participation is, or is likely to be, ineffective; that politics is of no interest (or possibly relevance?) to them; and that they lack information and knowledge about politics. Although this evidence does not take account of pressure group activity which may be a more attractive option to at least some young people, there is cause for concern that so many young people appear to lack confidence in formal political processes. Given all that we know about political participation it is reasonable to assume that this tendency towards non-participation among young people will be significantly more pronounced among those young people who lack educational qualifications, are unemployed and live in disadvantaged areas.

The need to engage with young people in relation to the policy process has been recognized by at least some local authorities and regeneration partnerships who are trying to find ways of engaging with young people, finding out their views and developing more effective policy responses to their needs. In addition to surveys and focus groups, some councils are co-opting young people onto policy advisory groups or setting up youth councils. Again these are important initiatives but, in most cases, they are not designed to engage with the most disadvantaged or disaffected young people.

Minority ethnic groups

The evidence relating to the political participation of minority ethnic groups is contradictory, highlighting the importance of not treating minority ethnic groups as one, undifferentiated category. A survey of electoral registration in 1991 found that 24 per cent of blacks, 15 per cent of south Asians and 24 per cent of other ethnic groups were not registered to vote as compared to 6 per cent of white people (Anwar 1994: 24). Various explanations have been offered for the relatively high rate of non-registration among ethnic minority groups including:

- lack of familiarity with political processes;
- language difficulties experienced by some groups;
- general alienation of some groups;
- fear of racial harassment and racial attacks on the part of Asians, Chinese and others through identification by their entry on the electoral register;

- policies of registration offices which do not meet the needs of a multicultural electorate (Anwar 1994: 24).

It is very difficult to calculate the relative turnout rates of different ethnic minority groups. However, various pieces of local research demonstrate a fairly consistent trend of relatively high turnout rates for Asians as compared to other ethnic groups, while turnout rates among African Caribbeans is relatively low (Anwar 1994: 24–32). Indeed the turnout of Asian voters in areas like Bradford and Rochdale is sometimes twice that of white voters. This may be reflective of a greater sense of political efficacy in such areas where there is a significant concentration of minority ethnic voters arising out of historical patterns of settlement relating to labour market needs at the time of immigration. Put bluntly, where there are large concentrations of ethnic minority residents in an area, their needs and concerns are likely to figure more prominently in the agendas of local politicians. However, this does not explain the differential rates of participation across different ethnic groups. A more detailed analysis of social and economic circumstances is likely to be necessary to account for this phenomenon.

Although the selection of ethnic minority candidates by the main political parties to stand in, particularly, winnable seats has increased, the number of ethnic minority MPs is still relatively low. Similarly, at local level, ethnic minority groups are underrepresented on local councils. However, there is also evidence of significant ethnic minority community mobilization through voluntary and community groups including both those which are specific to a minority ethnic group and those which are multi-ethnic (Anwar 1994: 116).

Disabled people

Oliver (1995) has identified a number of barriers which effectively prevent people with disabilities from participating fully in political life. These include: difficulties of physical access to premises (e.g. the House of Commons, offices of local constituency parties), 'lip-service' paid to the concerns of disabled people in party manifestos and lack of political information for visually impaired people. He concludes: 'So in the twentieth century we have been excluded from the political system, from the political institutions and parties which are supposed to represent our views and our wishes and our needs, from the political process in which our views are articulated' (p. 21).

Clearly there is a lot that still should, and could, be done to dismantle the barriers preventing disabled people from playing a full and active part in the political life of communities. Some of these things are relatively simple issues concerning access – making buildings fully accessible to people with disabilities, ensuring that political publications are available in an appropriate form for those with sensory impairments. The fact that such issues have not been addressed fully can only reflect a lack of political will. Other changes would require more complicated modification of political processes. For example, greater use of electronic media for political debate, consultations and voting, together with provision of computers and modems for people with impaired mobility has the potential for considerably enhancing their participation.

In practice, the barriers confronting people with disabilities are reflective of a more fundamental cultural and political problem – namely the fact that, while equality of citizenship rights is widely trumpeted as a 'badge' of a democratic society, the fact that they are imperfectly realized in practice suggests that, in reality, many people have a rather weak attachment to them.

Policy responses to political exclusion

Despite the high profile given to social and economic exclusion and the range of policy responses that are currently being developed and implemented, political exclusion is receiving little attention. Indeed, it can be argued that the essentially non-participatory political culture that has developed in this country is such that non-participation is not widely viewed as a problem. There is a tradition within political science that views low levels of participation as an indicator of overall satisfaction. However, this complacency has been challenged by exceptionally low turnouts in local, regional and European elections, evidence to show that young people are especially disinterested in and/or distrustful of politics and politicians, and social disorder and violent incidents in some areas. To the extent that there are policy responses to these manifestations of low levels of participation they are ad hoc, uncoordinated and given a relatively low profile. As such there is little data available to evaluate their effectiveness. It is hoped that the recently established Economic and Social Research Council (ESRC) research programme, *Democracy and Participation* (ESRC 1998) will give a higher profile to some of these issues and produce data and research findings on the nature and extent of participation and non-participation, their relationship to social exclusion and effective responses to political exclusion.

Voter registration and turnout

The government's current drive to 'modernize' local government includes voter turnout as one indicator of success. As a result many local authorities are introducing measures to improve voter registration and turnout. These include:

- advertisements stressing the importance of electoral registration;
- explaining the electoral process to young people in colleges and schools;
- using more canvassers to call on residents who have not returned their registration form;
- better designed registration forms and explanatory leaflets including the use of minority ethnic languages.

Certain other changes are being considered, but will require legislation before they can be introduced. These include:

- The introduction of a 'rolling register' allowing constant updating of the electoral register.

- Relocation of polling stations to make them more accessible and to allow voting wherever it is most convenient. Such a change would necessitate an electronic system for recording who has voted to ensure that votes were only cast once. Indeed it is likely that in the future voters will be able to cast their votes electronically (see Percy-Smith 1996). Electronic voting will be piloted in the first election for the mayor of London.
- Increasing the availability of postal voting.

However, while these sorts of changes might have a limited impact on voter registration and turnout on those groups who identify the costs of voting as being too high or those whose characteristics, circumstances or personal situation currently make voting difficult, they will have little or no impact on those groups who do not vote or register to vote because they lack confidence in, or feel disconnected from, political processes. One initiative that might have more potential in terms of creating a more participatory political culture is the current plan to include teaching on 'citizenship' within the National Curriculum. However, while this might address some of the issues relating to young people's lack of knowledge about politics and political processes, it is unlikely to address the deep-seated sense of alienation clearly felt by the most disaffected young people. Indeed, since many of these young people fail to attend school on a regular basis (or are excluded from school), they may not in practice participate in these classes.

Community involvement

People are more likely to participate around local issues than national issues (Parry *et al.* 1992). This suggests that there is, in principle, a willingness to get involved among at least certain sections of the population. It is this willingness that many local authorities are trying to tap into by creating new non-electoral opportunities for participation. Such initiatives are positively encouraged by the current government as a means of enhancing democratic legitimacy, creating a more active and involved citizen body and contributing to more effective local services. At the local level, at least, there is now widespread acceptance of the view that while elected local government is an important channel for political expression it is not, and should not be, the *only* channel. In particular there is a growing emphasis on the importance of, and need for, various forms of community involvement. A consultative paper, *Modernising Local Government*, published in 1998 states: 'The Government has a clear vision of successfully modernised local government. It will be characterised by councils which once again engage directly with their local communities. Such councils will actively promote public participation' (DETR 1998: 6).

The involvement and participation of citizens at the local level is a central plank of a number of the government's policy initiatives including Best Value, the requirements of the Crime and Disorder Act, 1998 and Health Action Zones. The Social Exclusion Unit (1998: 69) has set up a Policy Action Team on 'community self-help' with an objective to draw up an action plan with targets to:

- raise the numbers involved in volunteering and community activity in poor neighbourhoods;
- increase the viability of community groups and the services they deliver;
- encourage the growth of informal mutual support.

Furthermore, as we have seen, partnership working (including partnership with local communities) is now a firmly-established requirement of regeneration initiatives and is accepted by most local players. As Geddes (1995: 10) writes: '"Partnership with the community" in local area-based regeneration and anti-poverty initiatives is becoming an important element of local governance, as a preferred method of enabling local communities to voice their needs, become involved in decision-making and hold agencies accountable for their actions'. However, it is not clear whether such community involvement is as effective or empowering as it is claimed to be. For example, it is questionable whether partnerships between public agencies, the private sector and community organizations can ever be equal (Geddes 1995: 12). Community activists may be suspicious of the motives of agencies which have previously been seen to be at best unresponsive and at worst even hostile to their concerns. Furthermore it is questionable to what extent these initiatives engage the attention of those groups who are socially excluded. Failure to do so will exacerbate the extent and depth of their exclusion.

Concerns about the effectiveness of community involvement in these types of initiative have led to 'capacity building' initiatives to develop the ability of community activists and representatives to participate effectively and deliver programme outputs. Indeed, the Social Exclusion Unit (1998: 40) has itself recognized that community involvement has often promised more than it has actually delivered:

> It is now well-recognised that for local regneration to be effective, communities need to be involved. But too often community involvement is paid no more than lip-service. Not enough has been done to build up skills and institutions at neighbourhood level, and often pressures to implement policies quickly have meant that bureaucrats fall back on their own assumptions rather than consulting the community.

Conclusion

The government is currently increasing the opportunities for political participation at a number of levels and in a variety of forums. These include: enhanced opportunities as a result of constitutional reform (e.g. elected assemblies for Scotland and Wales); local government reform (e.g. annual elections, a new assembly for London); the modernization agenda (e.g. a renewed emphasis on consulting and involving citizens in relation to key policy and service delivery areas); and encouragement of experimentation and innovation through citizens' juries and panels, policy forums and so on. For many people in society these changes offer real opportunities for enhanced participation in the government of their localities, regions and country. However, as we have seen, there is a significant number of individuals for whom further opportunities for participation will have little impact. For these individuals and groups, who do not participate in existing political processes, new participative mechansisms may well prove as exclusionary as existing ones. And, to be excluded from further categories of decision making and governance could have the effect of deepening and intensifying existing feelings of alienation and dissatisfaction and creating, in effect, two classes of citizens – those who have the rights, resources and motivation to participate and those who do not.

In those areas which lack social capital (see Chapter 1) political insitutions are less likely to be effective. Thus, in order to address political exclusion it may be necessary not only to enhance opportunities for participation and ensure that those opportunities can be effectively exercised by all groups in society, but also to invest in the processes necessary to build up social capital. Failure to do so will result in those people who are most likely to be the targets of a range of policy interventions having the least involvement in their formulation or implementation, thus exacerbating their exclusion and feelings of alienation and increasing the risk of further outbreaks of social disorder and violent disturbance.

While all the mainstream political parties have views on and policy agendas for social exclusion, none could seriously claim to *represent* those people who are socially excluded. Indeed, as all the main political parties increasingly compete for the centre ground in politics, it could be argued that while the socially excluded are increasingly the focus for policy interventions, they are at the same time denied an effective political voice in the development of those policy interventions. And, as a number of the chapters in this volume have shown, many of these policy interventions include an element of compulsion or coercion and are reflective of a particular view of what constitutes an acceptable lifestyle. In other words, social policy and the welfare state are no longer (if they ever were) an expression of social citizenship rights but are rather an instrument of social control wielded by the included towards the excluded. As such they imply a 'conditional' form of citizenship for certain people (Dwyer 1998), with clear implications for diversity.

References

Anwar, M. (1994) *Race and Elections: The Participation of Ethnic Minorities in Politics*, Monographs in Ethnic Relations no. 9. Coventry: Centre for Research in Ethnic Relations, University of Warwick.

Boix, C. and Posner, D.N. (1998) Social capital: explaining its origins and effects on government performance. *British Journal of Political Science*, 28(4): 686–93.

Campbell, B. (1993) *Goliath: Britains' Dangerous Places*. London: Methuen.

Clipson, C. (1998) State of the young nation: encouraging responsibility in young people. *Childright*, 149: 1–2.

Department of Social Security (1999) *Opportunity for All: Tackling Poverty and Social Exclusion*, Cm 4445. London: The Stationery Office.

DETR (Department of the Environment, Transport and the Regions) (1998) *Modernising Local Government: Local Democracy and Community Leadership*. London: DETR.

Downs, A. (1957) *An Economic Theory of Democracy*. New York: Harper & Row.

Dunleavy, P. (1991) *Democracy, Bureaucracy and Public Choice*. London: Harvester Wheatsheaf.

Dwyer, P. (1998) Conditional citizens: welfare rights and responsibilities in the late 1990s. *Critical Social Policy*, 18(4): 493–517.

ESRC (Economic and Social Research Council) (1998) *Democracy and Participation: Research Programme, Programme Specification*. ESRC: http://www.esrc.ac.uk/demoparspec.htm.

Geddes, M. (1995) *Poverty, Excluded Communities and Local Democracy*, CLD Research Report, no. 9. London: Commission for Local Democracy.

Halfmann, J. (1998) Citizenship, universalism, migration and the risks of exclusion. *British Journal of Sociology*, 49(4): 513–33.

Lake, R.L.D. and Huckfeldt, R. (1998) Social capital, social networks and political participation. *Political Psychology*, 19(3): 567–84.

Lowndes, V., Stoker, G., Pratchett, L. *et al.* (1998) *Enhancing Public Participation in Local Government*. London: DETR.

Macpherson, C.B. (1977) *The Life and Times of Liberal Democracy*. Oxford: Clarendon Press.

Oliver, M. (1995) *Disability, empowerment and the inclusive society*. London: Policy Studies Institute.

Parry, G., Moyser, G. and Day, N. (1992) *Political Participation and Democracy in Britain*. Cambridge: Cambridge University Press.

Pateman, C. (1970) *Participation and Democratic Theory*. Cambridge: Cambridge University Press.

Pattie, C. and Johnston, R. (1998) Voter turnout at the British general election of 1992: rational choice, social standing or political efficacy? *European Journal of Political Research*, 33: 263–83.

Percy-Smith, J. (1996) Downloading democracy? Information and communication technologies in local politics. *Policy and Politics*, 24(1): 43–56.

Pitts, J. and Hope, T. (1997) The local politics of inclusion: the state and community safety. *Social Policy and Administration*, 31(5): 37–58.

Power, A. and Tunstall, R. (1997a) *Dangerous Disorder: Riots and Violent Disturbances in Thirteen Areas of Britain 1991–92*. York: York Publishing Services.

Power, A. and Tunstall, R. (1997b) Riots and violent disturbances in Britain: police clashes with young men. *Childright*, 138: 12–13.

Putnam, R. (1993) The prosperous community: social capital and public life. *American Prospect*, 13: 35–42.

Rallings, C., Thrasher, M. and Downe, J. (1996) *Enhancing Local Electoral Turnout: A Guide to Current Practice and Future Reform*. York: York Publishing Services.

Roche, M. and van Berkel, R. (1997) European citizenship and social exclusion: an introduction, in M. Roche and R. van Berkel (eds) *European Citizenship and Social Exclusion*. Aldershot: Ashgate.

Rose, R. (1997) *Evaluating Election Turnout*, Studies in Public Policy no. 290. Glasgow: Centre for the Study of Public Policy, University of Strathclyde.

Smith, D.M. and Blanc, M. (1997) Grass-roots democracy and participation: a new analytical and practical approach. *Environment and Planning D: Society and Space*, 15: 281–303.

Social Exclusion Unit (1998) *Bringing Britain Together: A National Strategy for Neighbourhood Renewal*, Cm 4045. London: *The Stationery Office*.

Stewart, J. and Game, C. (1991) *Local Democracy: Representation and Elections*. The Belgrave Papers no. 1. Luton: LGMB.

Taylor, C. (1998) The dynamics of democratic exclusion. *Journal of Democracy*, 9(4): 143–56.

Van Kempen, E. (1997) Poverty pockets and life chances: on the role of place in shaping social inequality. *American Behavioural Scientist*, 41(3): 430–49.

Worrall, A. (1998) Laws and orders: public protection and social exclusion in England and Wales. *Current Issues in Criminal Justice*, 10(2): 183–96.

Young, K. and Rao, N. (1994) *The Local Government Councillor in 1993*. York: Joseph Rowntree Foundation/LGC Publications.

9 URBAN POLICY AND SOCIAL EXCLUSION

Jo Hutchinson

Introduction

The introductory chapter in this book identified a number of dimensions of social exclusion and noted the importance of the spatial dimension. Economic restructuring and social progress are experienced differently by people in different places. Typically the processes of social exclusion can result in large numbers of disadvantaged people living together in a poor area. This observation alone provides justification for searching for policy responses to exclusion which can be applied to particular areas – generally inner cities or peripheral estates. However, the type of intervention and the process through which it is applied has been the subject of a series of experiments and incremental policy initiatives over the past three decades. This chapter first traces some of the arguments regarding the degree to which being in a particular place at a point in time contributes to the processes of social exclusion. The perspective which policy makers take on this issue is reflected in their response. The key dilemma is whether an intervention should focus on people or on places. The chapter then examines some of the specifically spatial policy initiatives which have been implemented over the past two decades, before turning to the new agenda and how new policies are being shaped to respond to the experiences of the past.

Does geography matter?

Social exclusion has a spatial dimension. It is common practice to map areas to indicate levels of poverty and of social exclusion, and then to use these as a basis for targeting assistance on particular areas. An exercise by the London Research Centre (Edwards and Flatley 1996) used factors such as low income, unemployment, health, housing and homelessness, and levels of crime and drug-taking to identify at a borough and ward level, areas where people experienced social exclusion. Unsurprisingly the research identified a general pattern that the closer to the centre of London, the more concentrated were the factors of exclusion. However, the use of maps, and more specifically the factors that are mapped either individually, or as part of an index, can be controversial. The application of different indices to the same area using the same data sets can show different patterns of disadvantage. The application of the Z-Score Index and Jarman's Underprivileged Area Index across the Greater London wards demonstrated a slightly different spatial pattern of deprivation between the two indices. The choice of variables and the method through which they are combined explain the different outcomes (Edwards and Flatley 1996). The choice of index therefore has significant implications for policy and resource allocation.

Perhaps more importantly though, the use of these maps to allocate resources betrays the limits of understanding of the nature of processes of exclusion. First, indices are only as good as the data on which they are based, and with the use of the decennial census, the data provides a snapshot which, given the dynamic nature of social processes, can quickly date. Second, the indices map proxies of exclusion, rather than necessarily reflecting the actual experience of people who are excluded. For example, while indices may use information on income levels and housing, not all people on low incomes and living in high-density accommodation are socially excluded (students are a clear example).

The final problem with using maps as spatial analyses of exclusion is that they can show concentration but, as Townsend's (1979) studies of poverty showed, not everyone in a poor area is in poverty (or excluded), and not everyone who is in poverty (or excluded) is in a poor area. So, policies which concentrate on areas may not necessarily reach disadvantaged people in those areas. Furthermore, to focus policy exclusively on defined areas would then exclude disadvantaged people living outside those boundaries.

The extent to which geography is a factor which contributes to poverty, disadvantage and, now, social exclusion has been explored in various academic circles for a number of years. Three key areas of discussion are examined briefly in turn. The first perspective looks towards a structural explanation of social exclusion. Within this set of ideas the processes of social exclusion/inclusion happen anywhere and places are simply a neutral arena for these events to take place. A study for the Joseph Rowntree Foundation thus concluded that 'the inner city/periphery, religious/ethnic, high rise/low rise, public/non-profit/private sector, old/new distinctions . . . are not in themselves determinants of deprivation and their existence in a particular neighbourhood should not be mistaken for the central problem, which remains poverty caused by economic restructuring' (Thake and Staubach 1993: 54).

Globalization of trade has led to economic restructuring. The latter does have a spatial dimension but the behaviour of capital in the global environment is largely independent of geography. So, the international restructuring of coal mining, ship building and, more recently, textiles will have an impact on places such as Wales, Tyneside and the East Midlands (respectively), but the explanation for the subsequent manifestation of social exclusion lies with the imperative of capital and not something that is specifically local.

The forces driving this trend are too large for national and sometimes even international coalitions to influence or redirect. The appropriate response for area-based policy in this global environment is for cities to compete for capital and investment to pursue goals of local economic development. The reason for this is that 'more global events, largely economic in character but sometimes political too, loom large' (Cox 1995: 214) and any local intervention to overturn them would inevitably fail. Solesbury (1993) has also argued that urban policy should focus on competitive place-marketing which would, in his view, increase diversity between places, and improve international competitiveness.

The second area of discussion regarding the effect of geography on social exclusion can be found in the ideas of environmental determinism. The idea that a clean, healthy, attractive environment will create a good community is the acceptable face of environmental determinism. The great urban social reformers such as Ebenezer Howard and Titus Salt believed that creating healthy environments would encourage healthy communities and they set out to prove their ideas. Garden cities such as Letchworth and Welwyn and the capitalist philanthropist towns (such as Saltaire, Bourneville and Port Sunlight) are still seen as models of design which have proved sensitive to the needs of people since they were built. The appeal of these places is, however, as much to do with the facilitation of the processes through which people live as it is to do with building well-proportioned houses. The urban social reformers recognized that people needed both opportunities and access to employment, to socializing, to buying food and clothing, and to religious, cultural and artistic expression. The degree to which these experiments in living were purely philanthropic is questionable (Gauldie 1974). They generally demanded conformity and would have excluded those who could not adapt to the ways of living demanded by the landlord-employer. Nonetheless the idea that the quality of your living environment affects the quality of your life is hardly controversial. The *extent* to which a quality living environment defines the quality of life is much less clear.

In the mid-1980s there was a brief interlude of interest in the ideas of Coleman (1985) who proposed the converse of the garden city ideal. She argued that the physical conditions on estates shaped the behaviour of people who lived there, and in particular that some aspects of design positively encouraged crime. The living conditions found on 'problem estates' in effect created the problem. However, after debate academics concluded that 'it was clear that while inhuman design played a part, far more complex social and economic pressures were at work, making "design-determinism" an oversimplified escape from the long-term landlord task of management' (Power 1996: 1547).

The two previous analyses of the importance of space as a factor of exclusion have presented the polarities of the argument. First, that exclusion is an inevitable consequence of global industrial restructuring, that capital does not recognize geography, and therefore that while its effects are felt differently in different places the policy response needs to be at a macroeconomic level, and anything less than that is a 'zero-sum game'. The second argument is that place is a factor in causing exclusion and that if nice places create sound communities then the corollary is also true. The policy response in this case must be to develop a range of good quality urban and rural environments for everyone.

Unsurprisingly, a third perspective lies somewhere between these two. This is that the interaction of social and economic processes together create places, and that the nature of those places in turn affects the interaction of social and economic processes (both inclusionary or exclusionary) through time. According to this perspective place can be a factor of considerable import- ance because it represents identifiable patterns of polarization or alienation. These patterns can then become part of the processes of social exclusion which create a spatial concentration of excluded people in a particular place at a particular time. Living in a particular location can both intensify and reinforce the experience of social exclusion.

The look of a place is important. Urban policy in the 1980s focused on improving the environment of run-down areas, as a means of attracting inward investment. More recent research shows that this is important because of the way it affects the spirit of the people who live there. Robinson and Shaw (1998: 7) comment that a negative image leaves the people of an area 'burdened with a poor image founded on stereotypes'. A report by the Joseph Rowntree Foundation (1999: 4) talks of the factors affecting social cohesion within neighbourhoods based on research projects in four areas in Teesside, London, Liverpool and Nottingham. The report finds that:

> one of the most significant factors undermining local confidence was a strong sense of physical deterioration, loss and abandonment by the statutory services. Older, historic buildings, are fundamental to residents' sense of place and the loss or decline of such 'landmark' buildings led to an acute feeling of lost heritage, pride, status and identity.

The daily sight of physical decay reinforces residents' own experiences of decline and abandonment.

Being in a particular place may also reinforce the experience of exclusion from mainstream activities. A simple example of this is post-code discrimina- tion. Lawless and Smith (1998) highlight cases of this on two estates in Sheffield and York where there was a perception that 'employers may possess discriminatory attitudes towards individuals living on stigmatised estates which affect labour market participation' (p. 211). This perception is then reinforced by negative media accounts of the area. In other cases the barriers to employment, education and training may be reinforced by being in an area with inadequate public transport links to places which offer these opportunities, inadequate services (so that people may not know about them anyway) and social relationships which reinforce the feelings of alienation. Gaffikin and Morrisey (1994) call this a process of 'social containment'.

Healey (1998: 69) also emphasizes the importance of the social experience of people in the place in which they live:

> The social experience that develops in places where those in particularly difficult situations find themselves concentrated adds to the difficulties people already experience. Some people in some neighbourhoods in such conditions do find ways to maximise their chances of flourishing. A key variable in whether this happens or not is the social world which builds up through social interaction in the living place.

In other words, limited opportunities for social interaction on a daily basis, or a limited range of opportunities to meet with a range of people, can further alienate particular groups from the mainstream of society.

Van Kempen (1994) also emphasizes the importance of the social in relation to the spatial. She notes that the changing sociospatial structure of cities cannot be adequately explained by analyses of social polarization. Rather, one's position in the social strata of the city or the community is a function of one's occupation, industry, income or wealth. The key to effecting change in one's social position lies in the nature and extent of one's personal relationships. The degree to which individuals can gain access to these 'relational resources' which affect their 'life chances' has a strong influence on the degree to which they experience inclusion or exclusion.

Policies designed to change the nature of social interaction can be problematic. Attempts to intervene in areas to build new social networks can be prone to difficulty, as the experience of Scottish Homes, who integrated owner-occupiers with social renters on the same estate with no great effect, demonstrates (Atkinson and Kintrea 1998).

These cases show that place is a factor in developing social exclusion, either through physical alienation, the exclusion of people on the basis of the perceptions of outsiders, or the nature of social interaction that develops in a particular place. Just as the processes of social exclusion are dynamic, so are their interactions with place. Geography alone does not necessarily cause exclusion – but neither can changing a place overcome it. This perspective generates an understanding of social exclusion that recognizes the importance of place. The challenge for policy is to develop a response that tackles the social and economic processes of exclusion in the place *and* at the time when they occur.

Policy responses to the geography of social exclusion: an overview

So far, it is argued that place is a factor in the process of social exclusion. The fact that groups of people live in a particular place can both sustain and intensify their experience of social exclusion. This is recognized in the development of policies that are spatially targeted. A raft of policies and programmes with an explicitly spatial dimension have been developed over the past few decades and are generally combined under the heading of 'urban policy', or more latterly 'regeneration policy'.

Cameron and Davoudi (1996) have traced the development of urban policy through a series of phases. The late 1960s focused on social problems; in the 1970s employment problems came to the fore; then the 1980s targeted economic objectives; and the 1990s moved towards people-centred urban policy. In all these periods of policy trial and experimentation the dominant political paradigm or prevailing understanding of the causes and consequences or urban problems has, to some degree, shaped policy.

However, before moving on to discuss some of the issues regarding the development and progress of spatial policy responses to exclusion it is worth clarifying some aspects of what is meant by 'urban policy'. The use of the term urban policy disguises the fact that it covers a wide range of policies, emanating from a number of government departments, operating at different spatial scales and addressing a series of issues. Indeed, there is debate about whether at any particular time 'urban policy' is any more than the 'patchwork quilt' of initiatives noted by the Audit Commission (1989) – at best a series of discrete initiatives with some common underlying themes.

A second important qualifying point to make before discussing the development and implementation of urban policy is that not all policies that affect urban life (including exclusion) are necessarily urban policies. Experience from the USA has demonstrated that the shape and character of cities is much less influenced by city-level policy than by federal programmes. For example, the unintended consequences of policies designed to promote home ownership and protect the environment have resulted in urban sprawl and the separation of people from jobs. In other words, there are national policy initiatives which may have an impact on social exclusion in an area which goes far beyond anything intended or unintended by more local policy efforts. The thrust of more localized policy initiatives may then be either to build on national policy developments to bring their benefits to the excluded, or even to ameliorate negative local impacts.

Third, it is misleading to characterize social exclusion as a purely urban phenomenon and therefore one to be addressed by urban policy. Exclusion is also a fact of rural life. Rural communities can be characterized by low levels of income, economic activity and opportunity; poor health provision; drugs problems; lack of physical mobility and other aspects of exclusion. Policies developed through the former Rural Development Commission (for example, Rural Challenge) were designed to address issues of social exclusion which were exacerbated by the realities of the geography in which they occurred. These policies received comparatively limited financial support (Rural Challenge was worth £6 million between six winners in 1994) but could nevertheless be locally significant.

It is important therefore to note that urban policy is not a coherent set of initiatives based on a thorough understanding of the nature of evolution and change within areas. Also, it is not as influential in affecting those changes as some national policy and wider economic trends. And finally, the characteristics of urban policy are also reflected in the more limited range of policies to address exclusion in rural areas. Given this context however, there are a number of key issues which policy makers need to address when developing ways to tackle the spatial dimension of social exclusion. These are outlined in the following section.

◯ Key issues for urban policy development

At what spatial level should policy be addressed?

There are policy initiatives that aim to tackle the processes of social exclusion in the places where they are experienced. Some of these policies aim to address issues at a regional level, some at a sub-regional or urban level and some at a neighbourhood level. The appropriate level of spatial intervention is a matter of debate. Thus Imrie and Thomas (1992) stress the locality,

Solesbury (1993) the city, and Stewart (1994) the regional or even European scale. In practice there are policies which address each of these various spatial levels.

The European Regional Development Fund (ERDF) is the prime example of regional policy and it aims to ameliorate some of the consequences of industrial restructuring. More specifically, two of its objectives are:

- to promote the development and structural adjustment of regions whose development is lagging behind (Objective 1); and
- to convert the regions, frontier regions or parts of regions (including employment areas and urban communities) seriously affected by industrial decline (Objective 2).

Only Objective 1 status is allocated to areas as large as regions (for 2000–6, Merseyside, Cornwall, South Yorkshire and West Wales and the Valleys qualify for Objective 1 status in Britain).

Most urban policy initiatives focus attention on parts of cities, typically inner cities or peripheral estates. City Challenge aimed to transform specific run-down inner-city areas. Its successor, the Single Regeneration Budget Challenge Fund, was available to any partnership anywhere – the designation of areas for support was left to the locality, though in practice the interim evaluation found that 68 per cent of partnerships focused on areas no larger than the local authority district (DETR 1998a). Both of these policies sought to address the multi-faceted nature of the problems experienced within the designated areas. As such they represented the beginning of the move towards 'holistic', partnership-based approaches to tackling urban problems. The underlying premise of both was a need to regenerate areas both socially and economically.

These aims are also complemented by some of the European Union's (EU) community initiatives, in particular the URBAN Initiative which is designed to help find solutions to the serious socioeconomic problems experienced by many urban areas by supporting schemes for economic and social revitalization and environmental improvement.

What resources should be allocated?

Government spending on regeneration amounts to £1.3 billion in 1999/2000 and is due to rise to £1.7 billion by 2001/2 (Robinson and Shaw 1998). This incorporates funding for a number of different initiatives including New Deal for communities, the Single Regeneration Budget Challenge Fund and New Single Regeneration Budget, English Partnerships, Housing Action Trusts, Estate Action and ERDF.

These resources are significant although they should be seen within the context of overall public spending. Exploratory research work (DETR 1998c) into the flows of money into particular areas has found that the volume of public spending resources in three study areas was very significant at £10,750 per household, or between £30–£60 million per ward. Expenditure per head on services for poor areas is above the national average by 17 per cent (c. 30 per cent in Liverpool, c. 4–7 per cent in Brent and Nottingham). The additional

Table 9.1   Single Regeneration Budget Challenge Fund expenditure allocation by region, 1995/6–1998/9 (£ million)

| | Lifetime totals | | | | |
	Rounds 1 + 2	Round 3	Round 4	All rounds	% of total
North East	240.8	141.5	20.5	402.8	11.0
North West	276.4	98.4	28.5	403.3	11.1
Merseyside	165.5	42.8	24.7	233	6.4
Yorkshire and the Humber	354.5	130.6	57.8	542.9	14.9
East Midlands	112.8	29.7	22.3	164.8	4.5
West Midlands	303.9	55.3	50.0	409.2	11.2
Eastern	56.0	18.6	8.7	83.3	2.3
South West	72.0	23.1	10.4	105.5	2.9
London	547.5	280.5	73.0	901	24.7
South East	303.9	76.0	23.0	402.9	11.0
England	**2433.3**	**896.5**	**318.9**	**3648.7**	

Sources: Regional Policy Commission (1996: 51); DETR (1998c).

resources provided by specifically spatial policies are therefore important, however they are by no means sufficient to address the needs of those living in poor areas – they 'will still only scratch the surface of the complex and deep-seated problems' (Robinson and Shaw 1998: 11).

The allocation of these resources varies by region and by programme. For example, the total ERDF allocation to the English regions between 1994 and 1999 was £2346 million. The West Midlands received the largest share of £439 million while the eastern region got £20.4 million (DETR 1999a). This type of funding is underpinned by the premise that inequalities across the EU can be (partly) addressed by developing the infrastructure and changing the underlying industrial structure of a region. The ERDF has been complemented by using other Social Fund monies for softer 'people-oriented projects', such as retraining under Objective 4 or tackling long-term unemployment under Objective 3. However, these latter two funds were not spatially targeted.

In total, the Structural Funds allocation for the UK from 2000–6 will be £10 billion, of which Objective 1 accounts for £3 billion. Merseyside will receive £844 million, South Yorkshire £742 million and Cornwall £315 million.

National funding for additional support is also spatially targeted, but the level and focus of support has changed over the years. The national budget for regeneration and other spatially targeted funding is allocated to each region. The criteria for this allocation is somewhat enigmatic, but regions whose economies are relatively healthy receive a lower allocation than those with economic problems. Table 9.1 shows the allocation of the Single Regeneration Budget Challenge Fund by region over the first four years of operation (1995/6 to 1998/9). The table shows that there has been less new money available to projects under the Single Regeneration Budget Challenge Fund in recent years, and that some regions have much greater allocations than others.

How should resources be allocated?

The allocation to projects within regions has changed over the past decade. Initially, City Challenge was open to 56 urban authorities. The Single Regeneration Budget Challenge Fund was then available to any authority. The New Single Regeneration Budget (the fifth round) has set aside 80 per cent of resources to be targeted on the most deprived wards.

A characteristic of all these funds has been that while the different areas are eligible to apply for them, their allocation is not automatic. The 'challenge' aspect of urban policy has become increasingly widespread. It has established the principle that regeneration funds (and increasingly other types of fund) will be allocated on the basis of a strategic bid, developed by a partnership, with clearly outlined targets, costs and outputs. These bids enter a competition, decided by ministers through the filter of the regional government office, and some authorities win, while others lose (Hutchinson 1995).

The competitive nature of urban policy resource allocation has been the subject of debate. First, observers have questioned the equity of creating winners and losers (De Groot 1992; Oatley 1995). Second, the competition has been characterized as a 'beauty contest' where bidders are 'driven to emphasise presentation at the expense of openness, and to pander to central government preferences rather than local priorities' (Dickson 1997: 3). The third element of the debate has been the extent to which it is appropriate or desirable to allocate resources on the basis of 'need' versus 'opportunity'. Part of the decision-making criteria for bid selection is the rank of the area on the Index of Local Deprivation, which has recently replaced the Index of Local Conditions, and which is a measure of 'need'. However, in addition, bids also have to demonstrate that there are social or economic opportunities in those areas that could provide the stimulus for change. Partnerships therefore have to decide whether to put forward a bid which addresses the needs of their poorest areas (where they might not feel able to promise high levels of output), or areas where they might be fewer problems, or less intensely-felt needs, but where there are more opportunities for 'success'.

Integrating policy

Urban policy is not a coherent whole and in fact has been used to achieve many goals, not all of them mutually reinforcing. Goals for urban policy have included:

- increasing economic growth;
- increasing employment;
- increasing the levels of skills and qualifications of the workforce of the city;
- improving the physical infrastructure the city;
- enhancing the living conditions, health and well-being of the poorer communities within the city;
- empowering underrepresented groups to participate more fully in decision-making structures;
- reducing levels of crime and fear of crime within the city.

More implicitly the goals of policy can be political or designed to effect institutional change. Different policy initiatives have been informed by a range of perspectives on what is happening in the urban arena and have used different instruments of intervention. Therefore it is important to note that not all urban policies have been tackling or are designed to tackle social exclusion.

Many urban policy initiatives have been developed by various departmental sponsors – for example, Section 11 funding from the Home Office, pursuit of inward investment through the Department of Trade and Industry (DTI), and physical renewal of derelict or run-down sites through English Partnerships, initially sponsored by the Department of the Environment (DoE). The lack of coordination of such activities, combined with variable responsiveness to the needs of local communities, has been a criticism of urban policy as a whole. Indeed the Single Regeneration Budget, established in 1994, brought together 20 different regeneration programmes which were being administered by five different government departments.

Spatially targeted, relatively unconstrained, 'pump-priming' funding offers great potential to address the range of processes occurring in an area which generate problems of social exclusion. It is this holistic nature of Single Regeneration Budget funding, combined with a requirement to bring the key agencies together in partnership working which is a key strength. It represents an opportunity for the key players in an area, including community representatives, to generate an understanding of the problems in their area, to think of ways of overcoming those problems and then to pull together existing and new resources to action projects and manage change.

However, while the budgets may have been brought together for disbursement at the regional level, it can be the case that at a local level the single budget becomes 're-departmentalized' through local authority, Training and Enterprise Council (TEC) and other agencies' structures. If this is the case the local TEC will offer various training courses, housing associations will build new homes, local authorities will improve their existing stock and community capacity building initiatives will encourage local people to get involved with the process of delivery and management of projects. In other words, the 'holistic' programme can simply become a series of projects. The Single Regeneration Budget is then used opportunistically as a new form of funding to compensate for losses elsewhere rather than as a vehicle for looking at the problems of an area and tackling them holistically (Fordham et al. 1999).

Integrating people

Resources to implement urban policy are allocated on the basis of deprivation scores that are used to target areas. One of the key issues for policy makers is the extent to which the funding reaches excluded people in those places. Studies have shown that the creation of private wealth in an area can completely bypass local people (Brownill 1990). Spatially-based initiatives therefore need to develop approaches to exclusion which not only develop opportunities within the locality but also build mechanisms to link them with local people. An example is the creation of Joblink schemes that aim to match the needs of the unemployed with those of local employers (Foley and Hutchinson 1994). Thus, at a local level the challenge is to connect emerging opportunities with the socially excluded. A concern of urban policy intervention is that mobile individuals and businesses are better able to exploit the advantages created by intervention than those who are socially excluded.

The boundaries of targeted areas are permeable to the economically successful. Mobility of people is a key issue for spatially targeted interventions as population turnover will thwart initiatives where there is no geographical community that binds people to a place (Duffy and Hutchinson 1997). For example, Tao and Feiock (1999) found that the Community Redevelopment Act in the USA, which was designed to improve poor neighbourhoods and reduce the income disparities evident within cities, was in fact increasing income disparities as areas became gentrified and higher income groups took advantage of the area improvements. Such examples demonstrate the need for integrating place and people within urban policy.

Impact

The efficacy of spatially targeted policies is also an important issue. The interim evaluation of the Single Regeneration Budget Challenge Fund found the following:

> Early indications are that each £20,000 of Exchequer costs generates 0.5 additional jobs, 11 pupils with enhanced educational attainment, 0.7 people trained with qualifications, 3 young people receiving personal development training, 17 residents benefiting from community safety measures, 3 residents using additional health, sports or cultural facilities along with other smaller benefits to the target area and its residents.
>
> (DETR 1998: 12)

It is interesting to note the 'people-oriented' emphasis of these findings. This stands in contrast to earlier area regeneration initiatives such as urban development corporations where regeneration was to be achieved by changing the physical structure of an area without affecting the prevailing social structures.

The sustainability of these outputs, however, is a particular problem. There is concern that successful projects (even in terms of value for money) have not survived the withdrawal of central government support, either because of lack of revenue funding or over-reliance on voluntary or community groups that do not have the capacity to continue with projects without support (Fordham 1995).

Overall, evaluations of the impact of urban policy are at best ambiguous. Evaluating the impact of policy has to have regard for issues of additionality (what extra the policy has induced), deadweight (what might have happened anyway), and attribution (what can be attributed to the policy and what might have occurred as the result of other factors). In their evaluation of urban policy for the (then) DoE, Robson et al. (1994) concluded that the impact of policy instruments used in the 1980s was more positive than negative but its overall impact was almost negligible.

Summary

This section has reviewed past urban policy and identified a number of important issues. These can be summarized as a series of questions:

- At which level is intervention most appropriate: local, city-wide, regional or national?
- What level of funding is necessary?
- Should resources be targeted at areas of need or of opportunity?
- Should resources be allocated in a competition?
- Can policies targeted at poor areas reach socially excluded people?
- Can policy that is place-bound address social and economic processes that are not?
- Can successful projects be sustained without additional support?
- Can area-based policies generate an increase in economic well-being as well as reducing social exclusion?

These questions derive from a review of EU and UK area-based regeneration policies. These policies have not necessarily, either implicitly or explicitly, been designed to address 'social exclusion'. However, many regeneration partnerships will have focused on the needs of the disadvantaged and their experience will be valuable in the next phase of policy development which is discussed in the following section.

Current policy trends

Social exclusion is neither caused by the fact of where people live, nor can changing that place overcome the processes associated with social exclusion. However, this chapter has argued that being in a particular place at a particular time can deepen and intensify the processes of exclusion. The policy response to this is generally known as urban policy or regeneration policy. This policy is changing and evolving, and the election of the Labour government in May 1997 has increased the pace of change, the institutional context, the nature of policy making and the nature of urban policy. These issues form the basis of the discussion in this penultimate section.

New institutional structures

The geography of the boundaries of public sector agencies has been changing over the past decade with local government reorganization. However, the Labour government has changed the geography of institutions whose remit includes aspects of both regeneration and urban policy quite significantly. First, the creation of the Scottish Parliament and the Welsh Assembly bring some legislative power closer to those regions. However, prior to this, both Wales and Scotland had their own structures of engagement in the Welsh Development Agency and the Scottish Office, so their experience of area-based policy has always been different to that of England in certain respects.

In addition, the amalgamated DoE and Department of Transport (DoT) was given an additional role of overseeing the regions. The activities of the

Department of the Environment, Transport and the Regions (DETR), under the aegis of the deputy prime minister, John Prescott, has been strongly shaped by the findings of the Millan Report – the Regional Policy Commission which reported in 1996 when the Labour Party was in opposition. This report set out the regional agenda and outlined the needs and potential role of regional development agencies. Subsequently the creation of regional development agencies (from April 1999) in England, and the development of regional chambers marked a significant shift towards building a regional voice and regional strategies for development.

The regional development agencies have assumed responsibility for the Single Regeneration Budget, for English Partnerships and inward investment agencies. All RDAs spent the spring and summer of 1999 pulling together regional strategies which are expected to set the strategic framework for regional development. Their influence at a regional level is anticipated to grow over the next few years as they become embedded and assume wider responsibilities.

Regional development agencies are not the only new regional agencies. The Countryside Agency, formed in April 1999, represents a merger of the Rural Development Commission and the Countryside Commission. It has eight regional offices and works to promote, among other things, 'social equity and economic opportunity'. The recent White Paper, *Learning to Succeed* (DfEE 1999), outlines new proposals for post-16 training provision. The implication of the move from 82 TEC areas to about 50 local Learning and Skills Council areas is to again redraw the geographical boundaries of local and regional institutions.

The creation of these new institutions could be increasingly significant if the strategies which are generated by the new bodies are genuinely set within the regional context and are both coherent and comprehensive. Given these circumstances the locus of decision taking for area priorities could move towards the regions, while macro-level decisions remain at the centre. Whether the effect of this is 'joined-up government' at the local level or an increase in competition and 'turf wars' between neighbours remains to be seen.

New area-based policy initiatives

Regeneration policy is being reshaped under the new Labour government. The DETR's 1997 White Paper, *The Way Forward for Urban Regeneration*, had two key themes: to emphasize government priorities of tackling social exclusion and to develop a collaborative, targeted, partnership approach at the regional level.

The DETR also published its *Index of Local Deprivation* (1998b) to replace the Index of Local Conditions. This has informed the priority for regeneration funding, which is to concentrate resources on the 'worst' areas. Consequently, 80 per cent of the funding of the fifth round of the Single Regeneration Budget is to be targeted on schemes in the most deprived wards.

More recently the DETR's Urban Task Force, under the leadership of Lord Rogers, published its findings under the title *Towards an Urban Renaissance* in July 1999 (DETR 1999b). The report proposes 104 recommendations across a broad range of issues. These include the creation of new urban priority areas where special regeneration measures would apply, plus more flexible local responses to local problems. The findings of the Task Force will influence the proposed urban White Paper which is due to be published in late summer 2000. The first such paper in 20 years, it will:

- describe the policies to improve the quality of life in our towns and cities;
- look at the combined effect of a wide range of issues, such as social exclusion, with the aim of enabling communities in urban areas to prosper;
- consider policies on, for example, housing, competitiveness, delivery of public services, regional development, planning, transport, community involvement and sustainable development;
- link in with work being taken forward by other departments on issues such as education, training and crime reduction – all of which are essential to enabling communities to achieve their full potential.

The proposed urban White Paper will also build on work currently underway on the UK Sustainable Development Strategy.

There is however, some speculation about the ability of the DETR (and the deputy prime minister) to deliver the legislation which the White Paper may propose, given the lack of progress of the transport White Paper. This will be particularly true if the large financial costs associated with the Task Force report recommendations are also reflected in the White Paper.

New Deal for communities

The New Deal for communities represents a way forward for the government in bringing together the themes of tackling social exclusion into small focused areas through a locally-based, partnership approach. New Deal for communities is initially being developed in 17 'pathfinder' areas. The government identified 17 local authority districts but has left it to local partnerships to identify which neighbourhoods (typically representing between 1000 and 4000 households) within those cities should become the New Deal for communities areas.

The programme addresses one of the criticisms of previous regeneration initiatives in that it has provided a longer lead time to build strategies, and has provided funding (£12 million in total) to facilitate this process. Thus between September and December 1998, local partnerships were charged with selecting a suitable neighbourhood and working up outline proposals. The second phase, between January and June 1999 was to produce a detailed plan setting out a strategy for longer-term regeneration of the area. This process was supported financially by the government. From July 1999, successful partnerships would receive an offer of funding for up to ten years. In the event, 10 of the 17 partnerships were given the go-ahead to produce their strategies in the new year, while the remaining 7 who took a little longer began that process in June 1999.

The programme is worth £800 million for these 17 neighbourhoods over three years. The DETR has set aside £100 million to support the programme in 1999/2000, a further £250 million in 2000/1 and £450 million in 2001/2. In the initial phase the programme seeks to address the four themes of:

- tackling worklessness;
- improving health;
- tackling crime;
- raising educational achievement.

This reflects a bias towards people-based themes rather than the more traditional physical renewal emphasis of previous regeneration policies. Consequently the emphasis of this area-based policy is more strongly focused on engaging the local community and building bottom-up approaches to promoting change than the policies preceding it. However, should local people want to add a fifth theme – improving their housing – then government guidance allows for this.

A further feature of the New Deal for communities is that it positively encourages links to 'work with the grain' of other policy initiatives. There is a need to join up policy at the local level to enable local areas to learn from the experience of existing initiatives, to reinforce the activities of other initiatives and to develop linkages through partnerships that facilitate this most effectively.

New Deal for communities is different from previous area-based regeneration policies: it is focused on smaller areas; it is more people-oriented; it places greater emphasis on community participation and engagement; it actively seeks innovative management systems; it will last over a longer time period; and it positively encourages links with the wider policy agenda.

While the policy addresses some of the key issues outlined in the review of past urban policy, the degree to which it will overcome others will need to be evaluated. In particular, the need to build bridges between smaller areas and the wider social and economic systems of the city, and the need to maintain community stability to build momentum within the community to capture the longer-term benefits must both be addressed by local partnerships. Furthermore, whether New Deal for communities will reach those people within areas who are socially excluded and the degree to which the effects are sustainable in the longer term will become crucial factors in any retrospective evaluation of the initiative.

The zones

The New Deal for communities is one of a raft of smaller, experimental, area-based initiatives emanating from various government departments (and discussed in more detail in other chapters). These include Employment Zones, Education Action Zones, New Start, Sure Start, crime reduction strategies and Health Action Zones. These zones are, in contrast to New Deal for communities, set up to explore different approaches to specific single problems or issues such as those facing young children and their parents, or poor educational performance.

Many of the zones are relatively small and localized. Education Action Zones include about 20 schools (two or three secondary schools and a cluster of feeder primaries). The five Employment Zones cover some 5000 people in all. Health Action Zones cover wider areas, but focus on particular health issues such as community-based diabetes in Bradford and under-age pregnancies in Lambeth, Southwark and Lewisham. In the initial 'pathfinder' phase of New Deal for communities the chosen neighbourhoods are also small, typically covering between 1000 and 4000 households. Smaller more localized targeting can be more successful at ensuring that the resources do reach socially excluded people, as the boundaries are more tightly drawn.

However, determination of the size and location of zones is still problematic. The Social Exclusion Unit (1998) note the difficulty of putting a figure on the number of very poor neighbourhoods. They cite reports which estimate that there might be anything between 1370 and 4000 neighbourhoods which are very poor, varying in size from between 50 households to as many as 5000.

The choice of areas is also akin to the processes of challenge bidding. Criteria are put forward by government for areas which might be eligible for special zone status, partnerships are invited to bid, and then these bids are assessed by ministers. As with Challenge funding there are more bidders than 'winners'. Sixty applications for Education Action Zone status were received with 5 initially being successful in September 1998 and a further 20 running by January 1999.

The sums of money available are also relatively small compared with the scale of the issues with which they are dealing. The first ten Health Action Zones have shared £30 million between them. Meanwhile other sources of funding are declining. Nevin *et al.* (1997: 12) point out that 'the Single Regeneration Budget has been reduced by 40 per cent in five years and housing capital investment will be substantially lower at the end of the decade when compared with the start – even allowing for capital receipts'. However, ministers and civil servants are keen to argue that the financial support available within zones is really to facilitate better use of resources which are already committed to an area, and to encourage 'joined-up action' in local areas. The areas are also given greater freedom from policy constraints to align resources with local priorities.

These zones could be considered to be area-based policies. However, they are not intended to be integrated responses to social exclusion. Exclusion is a multi-faceted process and while tackling health or education or employment issues in small areas is necessary it is not sufficient to combat exclusion. The Social Exclusion Unit report (1998: 56) states that 'many zones will cover the same areas'. This is as yet true in only a couple of areas (including Plymouth) and may therefore represent a step backwards in terms of building a holistic approach to area-based exclusion. As the zones are only a few in number, and cover small areas, they are perhaps better considered as policy experiments or 'pilots' rather than area-based policy.

Evidence-based policy making

Recent government initiatives have changed the institutional structure of the regions, and have begun to reshape urban policy. The way that these changes are being developed in particular places is an interesting theme. The work of the Social Exclusion Unit has been instrumental in the re-examination of the processes of social exclusion and their interaction with policy. The work of the Social Exclusion Unit has developed a spatial element. Its strategy for neighbourhood renewal was published in 1998, and set out the need to coordinate national programmes to tackle the causes of social exclusion with area programmes. It promises that 'the combination of new national policies alongside new area programmes will ensure more energy, more resources and more commitment to dealing with social exclusion' (p. 57). It then goes on to out-line an ambitious programme of activity involving ten Whitehall departments in 18 cross-cutting teams to provide policy recommendations on how to fill in the policy gaps which many poor neighbourhoods inhabit. The work of these 18 Policy Action Teams was completed in 1999 (Policy Action Team on Skills 1999).

The Social Exclusion Unit is coordinating a re-examination of the processes of social exclusion. It is building on research undertaken by academics and by consultants and is engaging government civil servants and ministers very closely in the research process and its analysis. The zones discussed in the previous section are essentially experiments and are part of the major programme of policy development which is being coordinated by the Social Exclusion Unit.

It is hoped that this will result in evidence-based strategy development, with actions developed from proven practice. The extent to which the result-ant strategies are radical shifts in policy or incremental developments of past experience remain to be seen. The Employment Action Zones may be par-ticularly interesting in the way that lessons from these areas inform national policy. Employment Action Zones are not pilots, they are 'prototypes'. The way in which these zones 'challenge the rules which stifle current programmes or constrain the effectiveness of much public spending' (DfEE 1998: 1) may well inform the primary legislation which is required to deliver manifesto promises through the notion of a 'personal job account'.

This experimental approach could provide valuable input into designing the processes through which policy is delivered at a local level. It will however be guilty of one of the key criticisms of 'Initiative-itis' in that there will be insufficient time to evaluate the impacts of the experiments on the people in the area, or the sustainability of the approach, or the impact on the wider area. In terms of experimental design, the approach may also be criticized because of the tendency to induce the 'Hawthorne Effect'. Individuals and groups who are the focus of attention from media, senior policy makers and their peers may well act differently from those who are charged with a task and left to get on with it. Lessons from experiments can then be difficult to mainstream, as expectations may be raised.

In the past, the strong political and social imperatives which encourage policy makers and practitioners to 'do something' to respond to an urgently felt need have tended to discourage extensive exploration of the causes of problems and the consequences of actions. The exploration of issues, evaluations and experiments is a characteristic of the approach of the cur-rent government to developing policy. While the fact that policy is being developed at the same time as this activity is ongoing (rather than waiting for conclusive findings) is a result of political imperatives; nevertheless the move towards more evidence-based decision making is a positive one.

Conclusions

Most of the other chapters in this volume have examined particular aspects of social exclusion, all of which have a spatial element. In this chapter the aspect of place has been discussed as a factor which will not by itself lead to social exclusion but which will both reinforce and intensify the processes of exclusion as they develop through time.

National policy responses to social exclusion will have different effects in different areas. Initiatives to raise school performance for example find that the greatest challenges exist in particular communities. The logic towards targeting particular areas is thus strong, particularly with scarce resources. However, area-based policies alone will not overcome social exclusion. Rather, they can be used to bend mainstream policies in to an area or to link that area with the mainstream economy and society.

Area-based policy has been associated with 'urban policy'. This policy has developed in incremental phases and while in the past has focused on physical renewal, it is now moving towards increased community participation and is more explicitly acknowledging its role in addressing social exclusion. For example, Ginsburg (1999) points out that the bidding guidance for New Single Regeneration Budget (Round 5) talks of tackling social exclusion and promoting equality, neither of which were part of the Conservative's Single Regeneration Budget guidance.

Area-based policy must work with mainstream policy; it must also be clear that its objectives are social as well as physical. However, lessons from prior experience show that the capacity of policy to intervene in an area to overcome exclusion is constrained. These constraints come not just from inadequate financial resources but also from a lack of social capital. The lack of capacity within an area is one of the reasons for its decline (for example, a lack of skills, poor health, low educational achievement and low mobility) and the need to build these elements up within an area is one of the prerequisites for area renewal.

New area-based policy initiatives are beginning to identify the need to link physical with social renewal. The regional development agencies, for example, are bringing an overview of key issues to develop regional priorities for regeneration. The revised Single Regeneration Budget is now more attuned to areas of need and to building community capacity. The New Deal for communities is strongly associated with building 'bottom-up' approaches to area-based problems. The development of local structures which are rooted in their area and which can capture mainstream policy to the advantage of their area could be a very important legacy of some of these programmes.

The success or failure of any integrated and locally-based approach to area-based social and economic regeneration is strongly associated with the nature of partnership working in those areas. Social exclusion is multi-faceted and so agencies associated with all those facets need to work together. The effectiveness of such arrangements are seen at a local level and can be affected by the geographical remit of the organizations, their own priorities and resources, their culture and modes of communication and their commitment to the area (Hutchinson 1994). Where these factors come together, partnerships can be very powerful agencies for change but this is neither automatic nor inevitable.

Finally, some of the features of recent policy developments resonate with those of the 1970s:

The emphasis on deprived neighbourhoods, acknowledgement of the complex nature of deprivation and efforts to promote increased co-ordination, multi-agency working and bending of main programmes . . . hark back to the 1970s experiences of the Urban Programme, Community Development Projects and Comprehensive Community Programmes.

(Robinson and Shaw 1998: 11)

If this is part of a 30-year cycle of urban policy there are two main conclusions: first to ensure that lessons of success are learned and that the reasons for failure first time around are not repeated; second that while urban problems may change their morphology, they are persistent. Zones and experiments have a role but they are no substitute for long-term, strategic intervention at the local level.

References

Atkinson, R. and Kintrea, K. (1998) *Reconnecting Excluded Communities: The Neighbourhood Impacts of Owner Occupation*, Research Report no. 61. Edinburgh: Scottish Homes.

Audit Commission (1989) *Urban Regeneration and Economic Development: The Local Government Dimension*. London: HMSO.

Brownill, S. (1990) *Developing London's Docklands: Another Great Planning Disaster?* London: Paul Chapman.

Cameron, S. and Davoudi, S. (1996) Social exclusion and British urban policy. Paper presented to seminar on Evaluating Policies to Combat Social Exclusion, Bristol, 12–13 September.

Coleman, A. (1985) *Utopia on Trial*. London: Hilary Shipman.

Cox, K. (1995) Globalisation, competition and the politics of local economic development. *Urban Studies*, 32(2): 213–24.

De Groot, L. (1992) City Challenge: competing in the urban regeneration game. *Local Economy*, 7(3): 196–209.

DETR (1997) *The Way Forward for Urban Regeneration*. London: DETR.

DETR (1998a) *Regeneration Research – Summary Evaluation of the Single Regeneration Budget Challenge Fund: A Partnership for Evaluation*. London: DETR.

DETR (1998b) *Index of Local Deprivation: A Summary of Results*. London: DETR.

DETR (1998c) *Where Does Public Spending Go? Pilot Study to Analyse the Flows of Public Expenditure into Local Areas*, Regeneration Research Report no. 20. London: DETR.

DETR (1999a) *The Government's Expenditure Plans 1999–2000 to 2001–02*. <http://www.detr.gov.uk/annual99>. London: DETR.

DETR (1999b) *Towards an Urban Renaissance*. London: DETR.

DETR (1999c) Single Regeneration Budget Challenge fund: Round 4 – Successful Bids. London: DETR.

DfEE (Department for Education and Employment) (1999) *Learning to Succeed. A New Framework for Post-16 Learning*, Cm 4392. London: DfEE.

DfEE (Department for Education and Employment) (1998) *Employment Zones*, briefing paper. London: DfEE.

Dickson, J. (1997) *Making Regeneration Work*, London Housing Unit briefing report. London: London Housing Unit.

Duffy, K. and Hutchinson, J. (1997) Urban policy and the turn to community. *Town Planning Review*, 68(3): 347–62.

Edwards, P. and Flatley, J. (1996) *The Capital Divided: Mapping Poverty and Social Exclusion in London*. London: London Research Centre.

Foley, P. and Hutchinson, J. (1994) Joblink schemes: matching the needs of the employers and the unemployed. *Regional Studies*, 27(7): 686–91.

Fordham, G. (1995) *Creating Sustainable Neighbourhood and Estate Regeneration*. York: Joseph Rowntree Foundation.

Fordham, G., Hutchinson, J. and Foley, P. (1999) Strategic approaches to local regeneration: the Single Regeneration Budget Challenge Fund. *Regional Studies*, 33(2): 131–41.

Gaffikin, F. and Morrisey, M. (1994) In pursuit of the holy grail: combating local poverty in an unequal society. *Local Economy*, 9: 192–206.

Gauldie, E. (1974) *Cruel Habitations: A History of Working-Class Housing 1780–1918*. London: Allen & Unwin.

Ginsburg, N. (1999) Putting the social into urban regeneration policy. *Local Economy*, May: 55–71.

Healey, P. (1998) Institutionalist theory, social exclusion and governance, in A. Madanipour, G. Cars and J. Allen (eds) *Social Exclusion in European Cities. Processes, Experiences and Responses. Regional Policy and Development*, series 23. London: Jessica Kingsley.

Hutchinson, J. (1994) Operational issues for partnerships in local economic development. *Local Government Studies*, 20(3): 335–44

Hutchinson, J. (1995) Can partnerships which fail succeed? The case of City Challenge. *Local Government Policy Making*, 22(3): 41–51.

Imrie, R. and Thomas, H. (1992) The wrong side of the tracks: a case study of local economic regeneration in Britain. *Policy and Politics*, 20(3): 213–26.

Joseph Rowntree Foundation (1999) *Social Cohesion and Urban Inclusion for Disadvantaged Neighbourhoods*, Foundation Report 4109. York: YPS.

Lawless, P. and Smith, Y. (1998) Poverty, inequality and exclusion in the contemporary city, in P. Lawless, R. Martin and S. Hardy (eds) *Unemployment and Social Exclusion: Landscapes of Labour Inequality*. London: Jessica Kingsley.

Nevin, B., Patel, B. and Hillier, M. (1997) Setting the targets for change. *Housing Today*, 53 (2 October): 12–13.

Oatley, N. (1995) Competitive urban policy and the regeneration game. *Town Planning Review*, 66(1): 1–14.

Policy Action Team on Skills (1999) *Final Report*. London: The Stationery Office.

Power, A. (1996) Area-based poverty and resident empowerment. *Urban Studies*, 33(9): 1535–64.

Regional Policy Commission (1996) *Renewing the Regions*. Sheffield: Regional Policy Commission.

Robinson, F. and Shaw, K. (1998) Joined up urban policy: a new deal for disadvantaged communities. *Northern Economic Review*, 28: 4–14.

Robson, B., Bradford, M., Deas, I. et al. (1994) *Assessing the Impact of Urban Policy*. London: HMSO.

Social Exclusion Unit (1998) *Bringing Britain Together: A National Strategy for Neighbourhood Renewal*, Cm 4045. London: The Stationery Office.

Solesbury, W. (1993) Reframing urban policy. *Policy and Politics*, 22: 133–45.

Stewart, M. (1994) Towards a European urban policy. *Local Economy*, 9(3): 226–77.

Tao, J. and Feiock, R. (1999) Directing benefits to need: evaluating the distributive consequences of urban economic development. *Economic Development Quarterly*, 13(1): 55–65.

Thake, S. and Staubach, R. (1993) *Investing in People: Rescuing Communities from the Margin*. York: Joseph Rowntree Foundation.

Townsend, P. (1979) The difficulties of policies based on the concept of area. Barnett Shine Foundation Lecture, Department of Economics, Queen Mary College, University of London.

Van Kempen, E. (1994) The dual city and the poor: social polarisation, social segregation and life chances. *Urban Studies*, 31(7): 995–1015.

10 RESPONDING TO SOCIALLY EXCLUDED GROUPS

Tom Burden and Tricia Hamm

Introduction

This chapter will examine the exclusion of groups and the policy responses of New Labour. Socially excluded groups are those whose members have a high chance of not being accorded full membership of society. Their exclusion can involve economic, social, political, neighbourhood, individual and spatial aspects (see Chapter 1). Social exclusion can usefully be thought of as existing when groups of people are unable to achieve what are viewed as 'normal' levels of social acceptance and participation. This usually involves the lack of one or more of the following:

- accepted levels of material well-being and of social benefits;
- commonly held legal and civil rights;
- a positive estimation of social status and identity.

This chapter will start by considering theoretical perspectives on the processes by which these various forms of exclusion of groups occur. It will then examine aspects of the character of exclusion for two groups, ethnic minority communities and the disabled. These examples have been identified as they are significant in contemporary public and policy debate, and raise issues which have implications for the adequacy of current policy. Finally, the chapter will consider the underlying ideological assumptions behind the New Labour approach to social exclusion and to broader social policies, and the impact of policy responses towards particular groups.

Processes of exclusion

Exclusion, in the form of the attribution of a degraded status given to particular groups, the failure to grant full rights of citizenship and the existence of institutionalized discrimination and prejudice, is a common feature of our history. While the term 'social exclusion' is relatively new, the idea which it expresses is found in various traditions of social thought. The generation of the conditions which lead to exclusion has been related to interlinked processes which are economic, political, cultural and social. Key aspects of these processes are outlined below.

Economic processes

In advanced industrial societies, wealth and income are highly valued and a dominant ideology normally emphasizes the importance of independence and of paid work, which is viewed as productive labour, unlike other forms of work such as domestic labour, caring and voluntary work.

For many radicals social exclusion is seen as a 'normal' part of an industrial society. It is a feature of the economic, political and social subordination of the working class, and of fluctuations in the operation of the capitalist economy. According to this view, during times of economic crisis, increases in inequality, intolerance and social authoritarianism occur. During these periods, divisions within the working class mean that marginalized groups – typically including women, migrant workers, youth and older people – will often experience the worst conditions within the labour market and may be excluded from it altogether (Burden and Campbell 1985; Byrne 1997). This notion of the 'reserve army of labour' is, however, overlaid by the realities of late twentieth-century capitalism. Here, globalization, the decline of manufacturing industries and increased casualization of work has brought about large-scale male exclusion from the workforce and a situation which has been termed the 'feminization of the labour market'.

Industrialization brought about the separation of home and work and led to particular group exclusions. Disabled people became perceived as unproductive because they were unable to undertake the full-time work which the factory system required. For both economic and ideological reasons women were largely excluded from the labour force. Despite major increases in womens' economic participation in the second half of the twentieth century, they still occupy an unequal position in the world of work and in the household. Feminists have described the 'feminization of poverty' in which women's proportionately greater experience of poverty is related to a continued marginalization in the private sphere and to the unequal distribution of income within the household.

Consumption is another process involved in social exclusion. The consumption of goods and services, in particular the consumption of commodities produced by the industries involved in cultural production, has become an essential part of modern life, and indeed of identity. Those who do not visibly participate in this culture may be marginalized. This process can be related to the definition of poverty developed by Townsend (1979) which sees the poor as lacking the resources necessary to lead what is seen as a 'normal' lifestyle.

Political processes

The state itself plays an important role in establishing processes of inclusion and exclusion. An important theme in the literature of critical social policy in the last two decades is the way in which policies in many capitalist societies are based on restrictions on the social rights of those who are defined as not being members of the national community. Laws on social security entitlements, nationality, immigration and the treatment of 'aliens' and asylum seekers are all involved in this (Williams 1987). In the Victorian era, those in receipt of poor relief lost the right to vote.

Another aspect of the state's role in exclusion involves the process of criminalization. Where behaviour is defined as criminal, those involved may be viewed as outside society and as having earned a degree of deliberate exclusion by the state. A criminal record may be used to discriminate between applicants for employment. For a long time male homosexuality was a crime and gay men were therefore subject to legal sanction, as well as social discrimination and stigmatization.

Cultural and social processes

The negative depiction of groups who are seen to be different from the norm is a feature of many societies. Categories such as disability, gender and race, while constructed as 'normal', inevitable and essential, are inventions of cultural practice and 'rather than being taught to accept difference, we are taught to categorise into sameness and protect the sanctity of sameness' (Kitchin 1998: 344).

In Young's (1990) 'classification of oppression', power relations between dominant and oppressed groups are maintained through means which are political, social and violent, and through a system of cultural imperialism which involves:

> the universalization of a dominant group's experience and culture, and its establishment as the norm . . . Since only the dominant group's cultural expression receives wide dissemination, their cultural experiences become the normal, or the universal and thereby the unremarkable. Given the normality of its own cultural expressions and identity, the dominant group constructs the differences which some groups exhibit as lack and negation. These groups become marked as Other.
> (Young 1990: 59)

Some writers have also examined how 'discourses' or 'narratives' have been constructed around a number of aspects of identity, including ethnicity, bodily appearance, sexuality and household arrangements (Leonard 1997). One important area of social definition is the possession or absence of attributes associated with what is seen as a 'normal' human being. Here 'normality' is represented by the body and its 'appropriate' forms which relate to appearance, 'race', bodily demeanour and health. Those who deviate from 'norms' defining physiological or psychological normality, or those with learning difficulties, may also fail to achieve full social acceptance (Ryan and Thomas: 1980). Eugenics, a notion based upon assumptions about biological inferiority, still plays a role in the exclusion of disabled people. 'Hereditarian' theories have also been developed in several areas finding expression, for example, in debate about 'racial differences'. The discourse of sexuality defines 'normal' and 'deviant' forms of sexuality. Related to this are powerful norms in societies which define the normality of the nuclear family household and may degrade the status of those who differ from this.

Contexts of exclusion

Above we identified some theoretical understandings of how economic, political, cultural and social processes operate to exclude particular groups. Many interrelated factors shape these processes of social exclusion: economic shifts on global, national and local levels; ideologies of governments and their social policies; the nature of institutions, in particular the welfare state; and the strength and influence of social movements in identifying and challenging their experiences of marginalization.

The approach taken here combines elements of cultural theory with ideas from Marxism, feminism and other social movements. These ideas are drawn on in current debates about citizenship which are also central to our understanding of group exclusion. These debates challenge the assumption of universal equality behind the depiction of the twentieth-century citizen, and demonstrate how the construction of citizenship as rooted in the public sphere has operated to exclude those marginalized groups who have limited access to it (Marshall 1963; Mishra 1990; Lister 1997).

Understanding social exclusion: ethnicity and disability

The first section of this chapter has looked at ideas about exclusionary processes in societies and at the contexts in which they operate. This section examines how some of these processes operate in a contemporary context, using ethnic minority and disabled groups as examples. It considers evidence of the exclusion of these groups using the dimensions of social exclusion outlined in Chapter 1. It also considers structural and institutional processes which may affect people in these groups, and suggests that a focus on how inequalities are produced is central to understanding and addressing group exclusion.

Ethnic minorities

In Chapter 1 it was suggested that there were a number of dimensions of social exclusion including economic, social, political, neighbourhood, individual and spatial aspects. It was also suggested that a concentration of characteristics within particular groups would create a greater risk of exclusion.

Using this typology we can see considerable evidence of the economic exclusion of those from ethnic minority groups. There are major socioeconomic differences between ethnic groups but it is still the case that black people are overall more likely than white people to be living in poverty (Modood *et al.* 1997). Unemployment and concentration in low-pay occupations are more likely to be higher, particularly for the Pakistani and Bangladeshi communities (Berthoud 1998), and women from certain ethnic groups are more likely than others to be homeworkers or in casual employment networks (Bhavnani 1994).

There is evidence about ethnic minority groups which relates to other aspects of social exclusion. For example, under social dimensions, there is evidence of increasing homelessness among those from ethnic minority groups, particularly single people aged 16–24 affected by benefit changes and high levels of unemployment (Ratcliffe 1999). Under individual dimensions there is striking evidence of educational underachievement among certain ethnic groups, of overrepresentation of Caribbean boys in school exclusion figures and of Caribbean men in the mental health and criminal justice systems (Law 1996; Modood *et al.* 1997). Under neighbourhood dimensions there is evidence of relatively poor living conditions, including overcrowding, again particularly within the Pakistani and Bangladeshi communities (English House Conditions Surveys 1986 and 1991 cited in Ratcliffe 1999). And under spatial dimensions there is evidence of a concentration of Muslim South Asians in wards with a high level of relative deprivation and with a high ethnic minority concentration (Dorsett 1998).

At the start of this section, we argued that an examination of structural processes is important in understanding and addressing the particular character of exclusion for different groups. In the area of race and ethnicity, a focus on 'institutional racism' has been useful in shedding light on aspects of the 'lived experience' of exclusion. The Stephen Lawrence Inquiry recently defined institutional racism as:

> the collective failure of an organisation to provide an appropriate and professional service to people because of their colour, culture or ethnic origin. It can be seen or detected in processes, attitudes and behaviour which amount to discrimination through unwitting prejudice, ignorance, thoughtlessness and racist stereotyping which disadvantage minority ethnic people.
>
> (Macpherson 1999: 28)

Many commentators have contested the view that institutional racism is the primary or sole cause of ethnic group disadvantage, arguing that class or economic factors also play a large role (Castles and Kosack 1973; Phizacklea and Miles 1980; Law 1996). In addition, exclusionary institutional processes are not universal 'in the sense of applying to all places, at all times and to all individuals of minority origin' (Ratcliffe 1999: 16). Ethnic minority disadvantage is too complex to be attributed solely to racialized policies and processes. However, strong arguments can nonetheless be made for looking at these processes in greater depth, particularly in view of the strong associations which have been made between them and social exclusion in the form of vulnerability to poverty, unemployment and related risks. For example, Richardson (1999: 10) talks of an 'iceberg structure of institutional racism in education' which shows how the disproportionate levels of school exclusions of African Caribbean pupils and students at the 'tip of the iceberg' lead to social exclusion and institutional racism in wider society.

Institutional exclusion may contribute to understandings about the over- or underrepresentation of those from ethnic minority communities in some arenas. Monitoring of institutional processes has suggested, for example, that the overrepresentation of Caribbean young men in the criminal justice system may be partly explained by evidence of differential rates of 'stop and search' actions and patterns of sentencing (Campbell 1999). The over-representation of the same group in the mental health system may also in part be explained by differential diagnoses and hospital admissions (see Westwood 1994; Law 1996). Ethnic monitoring of this kind has been given a renewed impetus by the Stephen Lawrence Inquiry and there has been recent acceptance that institutional racism is operating within various institutional domains (e.g. Brindle 1999).

Other kinds of analyses of institutional processes have also shed light on the lived experience of 'exclusion'. The overrepresentation of Caribbean pupils in school exclusion figures has been attributed to racialized processes of low teacher expectation, negative stereotyping and disproportionate levels of criticism and control (Grant and Brooks 1996; Gillborn 1998) as well as to broader associations with class or economic factors. Another example of an approach which contributes to this kind of understanding is Westwood's (1994) study exploring 'identity', 'mental illness' and the 'institutional', which puts the experience of black people at its centre, and which demonstrates the way that racism can have a direct impact in the development of mental ill health.

Disabled people

'Social exclusion is the general collusion (whether conscious or unconscious) on the part of society to deny to disabled people the respect it automatically gives to able-bodied people' (Knight and Brent 1998: 5).

Social policy towards disabled people has generally been based on an 'individual' model in which needs are met through providing benefits. This approach has tended to associate disabled people with notions of 'dependency' and 'care'. It is linked to the idea of disability as a category of 'need' within the welfare state. It has involved the promotion of a benefits culture rather than a work culture. It has also encouraged the segregation of many disabled children in 'special' education establishments and adults in residential and other institutions.

An alternative 'social' model emphasizes 'rights' and views disability as resulting from the failure of society to adjust to different impairments experienced by people. In this view, disabled people do not need a mobility allowance; instead, society requires a transport system free of the barriers which restrict those with mobility impairments. The rights approach emphasizes citizenship, civil rights, anti-discrimination, self-determination and support for independent living.

The economic disadvantage of disabled people as a group is well established. There is a consensus that disabled people – including those with physical impairments, learning disabilities and those with a severe mental illness – are overrepresented among the poor and that strikingly high proportions of this group are not in employment (Beresford 1996; Sayce 1998). The evidence suggests that people who are disabled experience many of the dimensions of social exclusion outlined in Chapter 1. However, this alone does not adequately reflect the experience of exclusion for those from this group. Again, a focus on structural inequalities associated with 'disabling' processes in society is key to understanding exclusion in this context.

Priestley (1998: 9) states that the disabled people's movement has 'struggled hard to gain acceptance for the idea that disability can be considered as a form of institutional discrimination or collective social oppression'. For many activists and academics within the disability movement who advocate a social model (see, for example, Oliver and Barnes 1998), structural processes arising from an individual and medical model of disability have been funda-mental in shaping the experiences of exclusion of disabled people from many aspects of public and even from private life. Linked to this, Young's (1990) notion of cultural imperialism (see p. 186) has been used to examine the effects of 'disabling' representations in excluding disabled people from culture itself and from fundamental citizenship rights of sexuality, relation-ships and parenting. Kitchin (1998) and Imrie and Kumar (1998) have used the social model and Young's notion of dominant cultural values to describe how the built environment has been designed to exclude people with phys-ical or mobility impairments.

Discrimination and negative social attitudes are central to the experience of 'social exclusion'. Knight and Brent (1998: 6) emphasize the economic dis-advantage and exclusion of disabled people but describe social attitudes as a vital element in the lived experience of exclusion: '[being] patronised, avoided, ignored, abandoned, mocked by strangers, assumed to be stupid, treated as an inconvenience and regarded as unfit for public view'. Sayce (1998) refers to the discrimination faced by users of mental health services in various areas of life which include employment, parental rights, housing, immigration, insurance, health care and access to justice.

The examples of both ethnic minority communities and disabled people show how fundamental inequalities are produced and reproduced in society which denies to certain groups full citizenship and legal rights, which operates discriminatory institutional processes and which associates group members with negative stereotypes. In both cases, exclusion is exemplified by low levels of participation and visibility in many aspects of social and public life includ-ing in politics and the professions. We argue here for a broad conceptualization of exclusion which has inequality at its centre, but which also includes the lived experience of excluded groups as a focal point. If this is done, a focus on excluding structures and institutions, and on discrimination and attitudes, as well as on the effects of exclusion, becomes central. This kind of approach will have implications for a broad range of policy interventions.

New Labour, social exclusion and 'groups'

'I want to renew faith in politics through a government that will govern in the interest of the many, the broad majority of people who work hard, play by the rules, [and] pay their dues' (Labour Party 1997: 1).

The ideas of New Labour work with the ideological and policy legacy of the past. New Labour is also constrained by the need to keep the support of its diverse constituency which, very importantly, includes its new 'Middle England' voters. How New Labour defines social exclusion and socially excluded groups is a key determinant of policy. In this section, we examine how this is being done.

Levitas (1996) traces the development of social exclusion policy, noting that it is based on assumptions about the importance of social integration and cohesion and their relationship to economic efficiency. More recently she has discussed how the New Labour social exclusion agenda has keyed into elements of three competing discourses around social exclusion which she names: 'RED, the redistributionist discourse', historically a key component of Labour policy but largely set aside by this government; 'SID, the social integrationist discourse' which emphasizes the primacy of work; and 'MUD, the moral underclass discourse' which includes a focus on the behaviour of the poor and their presentation as culturally and morally distinct from the 'mainstream', assumptions about state benefits dependency and about 'idle, criminal young men and single mothers' (Levitas 1998: 9–21).

For New Labour, social inclusion is viewed as an aspect of social cohesion rather than of economic and social equality. Approaches to facilitate this form of 'inclusion' bring together labour market re-entry and a rejection of dependency on state benefits, along with policies to control the behaviour of those seen to threaten social cohesion.

In the rest of this section we explore policy developments in relation to a range of groups, both those which are targeted within an 'inclusion' agenda and others which, using the concepts employed in this chapter, may also be seen as vulnerable to exclusion. New Labour's response to groups is inevitably complex. A number of themes which characterize emerging policy, stemming both from the social exclusion programme and from other agendas, are examined below.

Redefining citizenship: inclusion as work, responsibility and independence

'The language of welfare to work being about ending dependency is quite offensive to people for whom benefits are a way to make them independent' (Lorna Reith, cited in Daniel 1998: 23).

An evolving notion of what it is to be a citizen is an important element of the New Labour programme. A key aspect of the duty of a citizen is to take the responsibility to provide for themselves where they can, to avoid state dependency and to be in paid employment if at all possible (Dwyer 1998; Heron and Dwyer 1999). New Labour's interest in citizenship reflects the direction taken by the last Conservative government and by the New Right in policy initiatives such as the *Citizens' Charter* of 1991 and the notion of the 'active citizen'. Elements drawn from communitarianism and its idea of the 'moral community' also form part of New Labour's stance (Heron and Dwyer 1999).

Communitarianism has become an important idea in those versions of reformism which downplay economic egalitarianism and emphasize moral improvement. Its goal is to promote community rather than equality. A central assumption is the need to balance individual rights and community responsibilities, as unrestrained individualism is seen to have undermined family and community relationships. Communitarian ideas include the 'peer marriage' which endows parents with equal rights and responsibilities towards their children, and an approach to dealing with crime which emphasizes the creation of strong social bonds and partnerships between communities and the enforcement agencies. The influence of these ideas can be seen clearly in particular New Labour initiatives.

For Dwyer (1998), New Right and communitarian ideas contribute to a notion of citizenship for welfare recipients which has an increasingly 'conditional' element, in which coercion and a willingness to withdraw various welfare state benefits are seen as acceptable strategies to facilitate compliance. Examples of 'conditional citizenship' translated into policy can be seen in the probationary tenancies and the Job-Seekers' Allowance introduced by the Conservatives and in Labour's New Deal, in which those eligible must participate or risk loss of benefit rights. It is certainly true that the Conservatives and subsequently New Labour have imposed a number of conditions which relate to personal morality or lifestyle on those who are to receive various social benefits. However, this is not a new approach. The refusal of benefits to those seen as 'work shy' or otherwise undeserving has been a key principle of the state benefit system throughout the twentieth century. The punitive treatment of single mothers was a strong component of the Victorian poor law and the stigmatization of the long-term unemployed also has a long history (Golding and Middleton 1982).

The treatment by the Labour government of disabled people provides an example of its somewhat mixed approach to addressing the exclusion of particular groups. Undoubtedly some policy initiatives, such as the establishment of the Disability Rights Commission, support for anti-discrimination measures and support for principles of independence, are designed to address 'disabling' exclusionary barriers in society. However, other aspects of policy may reinforce the exclusion of disabled people. Proposals in the Welfare Reform and Pensions Bill published in November 1998 include a comprehensive plan for the reform of benefits for the disabled. Benefits for those judged to be severely disabled are to be increased and additional assistance to be provided for disabled children. Incapacity benefit is to be means-tested and eligibility for it narrowed to those who have worked within the last two years. This major change is based on the notion that many current claimants are not actually incapable of work, but use the benefit as a means of subsidizing what is, in effect, an early retirement. The 'all work test' (whose emphasis was on proving an inability to work) is to be replaced by a 'capacity test' which will assess what work the person *is* capable of doing. A disability income guarantee and disabled working tax credit will also be introduced.

Concern has been expressed about the tone of these policy initiatives and the underlying assumptions of 'work for those who can and security for those who cannot'. Knight and Brent (1998: 3), for example, cite Lord Plant who suggests that the emphasis on work as 'the passport to social and economic citizenship' is leading to a danger that the government will 'undermine the legitimacy of unconditional benefits even for those unable to work'. Critics have also identified a contradiction between government claims to be addressing social exclusion while at the same time reducing benefits for an extremely deprived group. There are fears that thousands will lose out as a result of increased means-testing, changes in eligibility for incapacity benefit and the abolition of severe disablement allowance for new claimants over 20. The disabled person's tax credit and income guarantee may make only a marginal rather than substantial difference to the income of disabled people (Scott and Bray 1998; Vaux 1999).

Inclusion as conformity and conformism

Cooper (1998) contrasts the approach of the New Urban Left (NUL) of the 1980s towards a diverse range of social groups with that of New Labour. In her view, the former emphasized minority rights and the latter the rights of the majority. She suggests that the notion of community under New Labour has been 'inverted from NUL understanding', no longer identifying 'a constellation of minorities' but rather a 'cultural majority whose security is jeopardised by the continued existence of a dispossessed other' (p. 470).

The message from Tony Blair in the 1997 election manifesto is that we are, or are aspiring to be, part of the many who are decent, work hard and 'pay their dues'. This is part of the understanding that 'we are all middle class now', and it is about an assumption of shared values and acceptable norms. The assumption of a general consensus in society which prescribes a particular style of life involving paid employment and the nuclear family can be viewed as an attempt to promote a high degree of moral conformity. This runs counter to the notion of a wide-ranging acceptance of 'difference'.

Current interest in social exclusion and social inclusion does not pay attention to the means by which the 'mainstream' of society generates social exclusion. The focus is upon those groups which are deemed to be 'excluded'. For Cooper (1998), whose interest is in the use of urban space, this is manifested in the prioritizing of 'respectable majority' interests over those who are seen not to 'belong'. This is exemplified by aspects of current policy and by comments such as those made by Jack Straw prior to the election about 'winos, addicts and squeegee merchants'. Employing these ideas in the wider context, it is possible to see a number of policy developments and proposals as reinforcing social exclusion rather than reducing it.

For New Labour, an emphasis on the safety of the wider community is a critical element of an inclusive society. Aspects of the 'tough on crime' approach include harsh sentencing policies and the range of exclusion orders brought in by the Crime and Disorder Act 1998. Levitas (1998: 166) argues that: 'some of the mechanisms for delivering these outcomes rely not only on repression but forms of repression which are themselves directly exclusionary . . . it is important to recognise that the inclusion of some is predicated on the further exclusion of others'. Various policy initiatives make clear assaults on social citizenship rights and further marginalize groups whose citizen status is already at risk. Proposals have been made to detain people with 'personality disorders' even where there is no evidence of criminal acts (Travis 1999). Plans were also proposed to deny benefits to people who break their bail orders (White 1999). The Asylum and Immigration Bill 1999 proposed to prevent asylum seekers from being able to choose where they stay and to replace benefits with vouchers. These represent concrete, material exclusions which rest substantially on appealing to public safety fears and which stigmatize groups which through behaviour, mental health or citizen status do not 'belong'.

The hint of 'social cleansing' in this range of policy developments can also be seen in some of the proposals emerging from the Social Exclusion Unit. Reports on rough sleeping and teenage pregnancy contain some imaginative and 'joined-up' proposals to address severe exclusion effects for particular groups, but they also include less progressive measures. As one commentator has said, proposals in the report on *Rough Sleeping* (Social Exclusion Unit 1998a) that hostel places be linked to participation in the New Deal and that resistance to a zero tolerance of rough sleeping be met by police intervention risk putting 'the clock back a long way [and] increasing the exclusion and alienation' experienced by this group (Ghosh 1998: 7). This authoritarian tone can also be seen in the recent report on teenage pregnancy, which has generally been well received for its pragmatic acceptance of teenage sexuality. The ideas contained within the report are generally radical by comparison to past attempts to deal with such issues. However, progressive measures of improving the provision of sex education and the availability of contraception are combined with harsher proposals, including the suggestion that the option of local authority housing should no longer be given to pregnant teenagers who instead are to be offered supervised hostel places and 'on-site' access to job search and parenting skills support.

The continued promotion of norms defining, among other things, 'acceptable' household arrangements is also a feature of policy and can be seen in New Labour's ambivalence towards lone parents. New Labour's apparent wish to avoid stigmatizing this group is contradicted by a number of its actions. The abolition of the lone parent premium in December 1997 is the most obvious example. In the Foreword to the *Supporting Families* consultation paper (Home Office 1998) the home secretary himself acknowledged that families 'do not want to be lectured or hectored, least of all by politicians' (p. 2), but within that document and in various other contexts ministers have continued to make references to marriage as the optimal situation in which to raise children. Comments from Jack Straw in January 1999 about the need for pregnant teenagers to consider adoption for their babies may have been overtly about the lack of emotional and financial stability of many young mothers, but they also strongly keyed in to notions of adequate and inadequate parenting models. The tone of proposals like these also strengthens traditional ideas of 'deserving' and 'undeserving' groups, while the willingness to use coercion reinforces New Right notions of those who 'will not be helped' as a self-excluding underclass.

The limits of New Labour policy

There are clear limits to New Labour's willingness to deal with the exclusion of groups. If New Labour is guided by the need to promote economic efficiency and social cohesion, it is perhaps not surprising that there is little apparent concern about groups which are outside the labour market and which are not seen as a threat to social order or to the moral consensus. One of these groups is the elderly. At the current time the government has still not made a decision about how to pay for the long-term care of older people. It has not accepted the recommendations of the Royal Commission on Long-term Care that public money should be used for this purpose. The level of the basic state pension is not to be increased in terms of its spending power although the government has introduced what is, in effect, a more generous means-tested addition to the pensions of those with little or no additional sources of income. Older people are also not to receive legal protection through a law which makes discrimination on the basis of age and crime. Instead there will be a voluntary code of practice.

New Labour has made some progress in recognizing diversity and support-ing claims to equal rights. Examples of this can be found in the attempts to reduce the age of consent for gay men, to address certain further aspects of the discrimination towards lesbians and gay men embodied in the law and in various initiatives aimed at addressing the exclusion of disabled people. Labour has pledged to review the limited Disability Discrimination Act 1995 brought in by the Conservative government; it has lobbied successfully for the inclusion of disabled people in forthcoming European directives on dis-crimination and it has proposed to establish a Disability Rights Commission which supporters hope will give 'teeth' to the 1995 Act (Benn 1998; Daly 1998). Other initiatives support the independence of disabled people. For example, the extension of direct payments promised in the White Paper, *Modernising Social Services* (Department of Health 1998a), will enable a wider age range of disabled people to select and pay for the help they require. The White Paper also supports the principle that users should have a say in the way that services are provided.

Support for some limited formal rights is acceptable to a slowly liberalizing public opinion, reflects Labour's historical commitments to social justice and marks a change to or even a reversal of Tory agendas on certain 'marginalized' groups. However, in general, these initiatives fall short of signifying a move towards truly including those groups or opening up citizenship rights in any fundamental way.

The initiatives which New Labour have taken remain at a great distance from the 'identity politics' of the NUL which celebrated 'difference' (Cooper: 1994). The government has appeared happy to support its quota of 'out' gay MPs. It has also adopted a strong moral stance against prejudice – for example in relation to the Stephen Lawrence Murder Inquiry and in its response to the nail bombings of black and gay communities in Brixton, Brick Lane and Soho in April 1999. However, New Labour has been quieter or more ambival-ent about thornier issues concerned with further aspects of citizenship and the implications of 'group' identity. For example, Paul Burston (1999) high-lighted the initial failure of the government to repeal Section 28 of the 1988 Local Government Act, which prevents those in education from 'promoting homosexuality' as an equal lifestyle choice and denotes lesbians and gay men who choose to bring up children as 'pretend families'. More recently, how-ever, New Labour has made an explicit commitment to repeal Section 28.

This somewhat uneasy and ambivalent approach to issues of group identity can be seen in policy responses to black and ethnic minority communities. There is undoubtedly a greater recognition of the implications of racism under this government than under the Conservatives. The Stephen Lawrence Inquiry has brought an impetus to addressing some aspects of institutional racism. There has, for example, been an immediate commitment to extending the Race Relations Act of 1976. In other broad policy areas there may also be scope for the needs of ethnic minorities to be addressed more effectively. Guidance on race equality has, for example, been produced to be used with the New Deal for communities programmes. The greater emphasis on community participation under 'Best Value' (DETR 1998), among other initiatives, may provide more opportunity for ethnic minority communities to have a say in local matters. In addition, greater resources directed towards the inner cities – for example, through Education Action Zones and through the *Excellence in Cities* programme (DfEE 1999) – might also offer some benefits for such communities.

However, in other areas there is concern about inadequate targeting of ethnic minority groups in policy. There has been criticism of the limited attention given to ethnic minority communities in family policy in view of the evidence that families within many communities are more likely to have children and to live in poverty (Butt 1998). There has also been criticism of the failure of *The Quality Protects Programme* (the programme to improve children's services) (Department of Health 1998b) and of other policy proposals to highlight the problems arising from the overrepresentation of young black people in care (Community Care 1998).

In the field of education New Labour has continued with an essentially 'colour-blind' and 'deracialized' policy agenda (Hatcher 1997; Gillborn 1998). For Richardson (1998: 23):

> Race equality, in the parlance and priorities of New Labour, is said to be a second term issue . . . Social exclusion and the so-called underclass are on the political agenda but to suggest that they cannot be tackled without also looking at issues of racism, nationalism and Islamophobia is to be seriously . . . off-message.

A recognition of the importance of disadvantage and diversity does distinguish Labour from Conservative policy in this area. In the 1997 White Paper *Excellence in Schools* (DfEE 1997) there is some discussion of ethnic minority underachievement and of the need to address racial harassment. The Department for Education and Employment (DfEE) has established a task force to report on community mentoring for ethnic minority groups. There is also now a greater emphasis by the DfEE on the need for ethnic monitoring as a result of the Stephen Lawrence Inquiry. Another key initiative is the replacement of Home Office Section 11 funding, largely used for English as an Additional Language support, by the Ethnic Minorities Achievement Grant. The effects of this are yet to be seen, but the focus on achievement may overall be beneficial.

Many of the concerns about policy in this area are related to New Labour's continued commitment to the 'marketization' of education implemented by the Conservatives. New Labour's embrace of a managerialist policy, focused on 'raising standards', downgrades notions of social and racial justice and may actually reinforce inequalities to the detriment of working-class and ethnic minority pupils (Hatcher 1997). The government has committed itself to 'setting' as part of 'raising standards' in *Excellence in Schools* (DfEE 1997) and again in *Excellence in Cities* (DfEE 1999). However, this policy may instead 'replicate and further entrench existing social divisions based on class and ethnic differences' (Gillborn 1998: 723). The expansion of 'specialist' and 'beacon' schools proposed in *Excellence in Cities* is likely to further widen the differences in status and resourcing between schools (Blair *et al.* 1999: 13). Another concern linking again to a deracialized agenda and to a lack of explicitness in policy relates to school exclusions. In the Social Exclusion Unit (1998b) report, *Truancy and School Exclusion*, there are no specific targets set for the reduction of ethnic minority exclusions. At the end of 1998, Herman Ouseley of the Commission for Racial Equality stressed the danger that without such target-setting it would be: 'possible to meet the SEU [Social Exclusion Unit] target of reducing exclusions by one-third by 2002, while still allowing massive over-representation of ethnic minorities to lurk beneath apparently favourable and decreasing overall levels of exclusion' (Ouseley 1998: 13). This has in fact already happened. Current evidence suggests that high levels of exclusions among certain ethnic groups persist, despite a small overall decrease at the present time (Thornton 1999).

Conclusions

For Northway (1997: 164), who examines debates about integration and inclusion within the field of disability: 'An inclusive society is . . . one which embraces a wide range of diversity rather than requiring conformity or assimilation within a narrow interpretation of "normality". Inclusion conveys a right to belong'. As this chapter has argued, for New Labour social inclusion is a rather narrower concept. Social inclusion is viewed as facilitating social cohesion rather than addressing inequality. The approach to date is to provide opportunity for labour market participation and to deal with or prevent certain behaviours resulting from exclusion – homelessness, teenage pregnancy, crime and school misdemeanours. The New Labour social exclusion agenda thus sets limits to the scope of policy, to which groups are to receive policy intervention and to which approaches can be used.

The overall focus is not on the causes but on the effects of exclusion. New Labour orthodoxy views the ability to compete in the global economy as of supreme importance and its programme of 'reform' and 'modernization' is set within this context. The fundamental inequalities which are part of a market society are not being addressed despite growing evidence that they are a factor in health, crime, alienation and stress. This is an issue for consideration of exclusion generally. For those groups whose members may be disadvantaged by specific structural processes it has particular implications.

Policies on social exclusion which do not address specific institutional processes will certainly be limited in impact. For example, the New Deal is unlikely to help young people from ethnic minorities when employer resistance to the recruitment of black people is still a major barrier, and when referral organizations collude in 'anticipatory discrimination' by failing to refer these clients on (Youthaid *et al.* 1997). Similarly, a range of barriers (including employer resistance, inflexibility of work patterns and lack of access to work environments) currently prevent many disabled people from working. Unless these are dismantled, employment opportunities for disabled people will not increase.

The emphasis on work as the main route to inclusion is problematic for many reasons (Walker 1998). There is a risk that it will be very difficult to draw a line between those whom the government requires to be available for work and those who are viewed as having a legitimate reason for not undertaking it. The characterization of work as the most important form of social participation through which citizenship status and social inclusion can be earned is itself potentially exclusionary. This may be a problem for groups such as disabled people and lone parents, for whom existing work opportunities will not necessarily lead to improvements in their circumstances. The depiction of work as a moral obligation and as a necessary part of self-esteem is also problematic when opportunities are scarce in particular occupations and geographical locations. As Levitas (1998) has pointed out, in a climate of high unemployment the strengthening of connections between self-esteem, work and social status may be particularly damaging for young men, who are less likely than young women to gain a positive sense of identity through other means, such as caring responsibilities. As Levitas says, this creates an argument for separating paid work from self-esteem, rather than reinforcing this association.

New Labour differs from its Conservative predecessors in supporting limited claims for improved rights for some groups. However, it has an ambivalent attitude towards group identity and to the wider implications of group 'difference'. Indeed, the assumption of a homogeneous cultural majority has mitigated against an interest in genuine diversity, and the assumption of support for a conventional moral framework reinforces this. This assumption has in fact served further to reinforce the boundaries between those who are, and those who are not, 'included'.

The main focus of government policy is on work and on support for conventional lifestyles and morality. There is also a determination to maintain a strong appeal to the values of Middle England. This, combined with a rejection of policies designed to produce a major redistribution of income, suggests that under New Labour a range of groups are likely to continue to experience social exclusion.

References

Benn, M. (1998) Changing perceptions. *Community Care*, 17–23 September: 12.

Beresford, P. (1996) Poverty and disabled people: challenging dominant debates and policies. *Disability and Society*, 11(4): 553–67.

Berthoud, R. (1998) Incomes of ethnic minorities. *Findings*, November: N48.

Bhavnani, R. (1994) *Black Women in the Labour Market: A Research Review*. Manchester: Equal Opportunities Commission.

Blair, M., Gillborn, D., Kemp, S. and MacDonald, J. (1999) Institutional racism, education and the Stephen Lawrence Inquiry. *Education and Social Justice*, summer: 1–3.

Brindle, D. (1999) NHS priority is an end to 'culture of racism', *Guardian*, 12 March: 9.

Burden, T. and Campbell, M. (1985) *Capitalism and Public Policy in the UK*. London: Croom Helm.

Burston, P. (1999) *Tony's Fairy Tales*, Channel 4, 13 March.

Butt, J. (1998) Family policy – remember minorities. *Community Care*, 19–25 November: 13.

Byrne, D. (1997) Social exclusion and capitalism: the reserve army across time and space. *Critical Social Policy*, 17(1): 27–51.

Campbell, D. (1999) Stop and search leaps by 20pc, *Guardian*, 8 March.

Castles, S. and Kosack, G. (1973) *Immigrant Workers and the Class Structure in Western Europe*. Oxford: Oxford University Press.

Community Care (1998) Government failing black homeless. 3–9 December: 4.

Cooper, D. (1994) *Lesbian and Gay Politics Within the Activist State*. London: Rivers Oram Press.

Cooper, D. (1998) Regard between strangers: diversity, equality and the reconstruction of public space. *Critical Social Policy*, 18(4): 465–92.

Daly, N. (1998) A commission with teeth. *Community Care*, 30 July–5 August: 9.

Daniel, C. (1998) Radical, angry and willing to work. *New Statesman*, 6 March: 22–3.

Department of Health (DoH) (1998a) *Modernising Social Services: Promoting Independence, Improving Protection, Raising Standards*, Cm 4169. London: The Stationery Office.

Department of Health (DoH) (1998b) *The Quality Protects Programme: Transforming Children's Services*. London: DoH.

DETR (1998) *Modern Local Government : In Touch with the People*, Cm 4014. London: DETR.

DfEE (Department for Education and Employment) (1997) *Excellence in Schools*, Cm 3681. London: HMSO.

DfEE (Department for Education and Employment) (1999) *Excellence in Cities*. London: DfEE.

Dorsett, R. (1998) *Ethnic Minorities in the Inner City*. Bristol: The Policy Press.

Dwyer, P. (1998) Conditional citizens? Welfare rights and responsibilties in the late 1990s. *Critical Social Policy*, 18(4): 493–517.

Ghosh, S. (1998) From rough to smooth? (rough sleeping). *London Housing News*, 73: 6–7.

Gillborn, D. (1998) Racism, selection, poverty and parents: New Labour, old problems? *Journal of Education Policy*, 13(6): 717–35.

Golding, P. and Middleton, S. (1982) *Images of Welfare*. London: Martin Robertson.

Grant, D. and Brooks, K. (1996) Exclusions from school: responses from the black community. *Pastoral Care in Education*, 14(3): 20–7.

Hatcher, R. (1997) New Labour, school improvement and racial equality. *Multicultural Teaching*, 15(3): 8–13.

Heron, E. and Dwyer, P. (1999) Doing the right thing: Labour's attempt to forge a new welfare deal between the individual and the state. *Social Policy and Administration*, 33(1): 91–104.

Home Office (1998) *Supporting Families: A Consultation Paper*. London: Home Office.

Imrie, R. and Kumar, M. (1998) Focusing on disability and access in the built environment. *Disability and Society*, 13(3): 357–74.

Kitchin, R. (1998) Out of place, knowing one's place, space, power and the exclusion of disabled people. *Disability and Society*, 13(3): 343–56.

Knight, J. and Brent, M. (1998) *Access Denied: Disabled People's Experience of Social Exclusion*. London: Leonard Cheshire.

Labour Party (1997) *New Labour: Because Britain Deserves Better – The Labour Party Manifesto*. London: Labour Party.

Law, I. (1996) *Racism, Ethnicity and Social Policy*. London: Prentice Hall.

Leonard, P. (1997) *Postmodern Welfare*. London: Sage.

Levitas, R. (1996) The concept of social exclusion and the new Durkheimian hegemony. *Critical Social Policy*, 16(46): 5–20.

Levitas, R. (1998) *The Inclusive Society? Social Exclusion and New Labour*. London: Macmillan.

Lister, R. (1997) *Citizenship: Feminist Perspectives*. London: Macmillan.

Macpherson, W. (1999) *The Stephen Lawrence Inquiry*, Cm 4262–1. London: The Stationery Office.

Marshall, T.H. (1963) *Sociology at the Crossroads*. London: Heinemann.

Mishra, R. (1990) *The Welfare State in Capitalist Society*. Hemel Hempstead: Harvester Wheatsheaf.

Modood, T., Berthoud, R., Lakey, J. *et al.* (1997) *Ethnic Minorities in Britain: Diversity and Disadvantage*. London: Policy Studies Institute.

Northway, R. (1997) Integration and inclusion: illusion or progress in services for disabled people. *Social Policy and Administration*, 31(2): 157–72.

Oliver, M. and Barnes, C. (1998) *Disabled People and Social Policy: From Exclusion to Inclusion*. London: Longman.

Ouseley, H. (1998) Black exclusions scandal, *Times Educational Supplement*, 18 December: 13.

Phizacklea, A. and Miles, R. (1980) *Labour and Racism*. London: Routledge & Kegan Paul.

Priestley, M. (1998) *Disability Politics and Community Care*. London: Jessica Kingsley.

Ratcliffe, P. (1999) Housing inequality and 'race': some critical reflections on the concept of 'social exclusion'. *Ethnic and Racial Studies*, 22(1): 1–22.

Richardson, R. (1998) Inclusive societies, inclusive schools – the terms of debate and action. *Multicultural Teaching*, 16(2): 23–9.

Richardson, R. (1999) Unequivocal acceptance – lessons from the Stephen Lawrence Inquiry for education. *Multicultural Teaching*, 17(2): 7–11.

Ryan, J. and Thomas, F. (1980) *The Politics of Mental Handicap*. Harmondsworth: Penguin.

Sayce, L. (1998) Stigma, discrimination and social exclusion: what's in a word? *Journal of Mental Health*, 7(4): 331–43.

Scott, J. and Bray, E. (1998) Funny money, *Guardian*, 15 December.

Social Exclusion Unit (1998a) *Rough Sleeping*, Cm 4008. London: The Stationery Office.

Social Exclusion Unit (1998b) *Truancy and School Exclusion*, Cm 3957. London: The Stationery Office.

Thornton, K. (1999) Exclusion still highest in minority groups, *Times Educational Supplement*, 9 July: 2.

Townsend, P. (1979) *Poverty*. Harmondsworth: Penguin.

Travis, A. (1999) Psychopaths to be denied liberty, *Guardian*, 16 February: 9.

Vaux, G. (1999) The devil is in the detail. *Community Care*, 11–17 March: 29.

Walker, R. (1998) Does work work? *Journal of Social Policy*, 27(4): 533–42.

Westwood, S. (1994) Racism, mental illness and the politics of identity, in A. Rattansi and S. Westwood (eds) *Racism, Modernity and Identity*. Cambridge: Polity Press.

White, M. (1999) Benefits may be cut for criminals, *Guardian*, 8 February: 5.

Williams, F. (1987) Racism and the discipline of social policy. *Critical Social Policy*, 20: 4–29.

Young, I.M. (1990) *Justice and the Politics of Difference*. Princeton, NJ: Princeton University Press.

Youthaid, Barnado's and The Children's Society (1997) *New Deal – Fair Deal? Experiences of Black Young People in the Labour Market*. Ilford: Barnado's.

11 COMMUNITY RESPONSES TO SOCIAL EXCLUSION

Gabriel Chanan

> I like a lady to be exclusive; I'm dying to be exclusive myself. Well we *are* exclusive, Mother and I. We don't speak to everyone – or they don't speak to us. I suppose it's about the same.
>
> (Henry James, *Daisy Miller*)

Introduction

Like most political slogans, 'social exclusion' is a slippery phrase. It implies that there is a mainstream form of society and that the only thing wrong with it is that some people aren't in it. What is it that people are being excluded from? Although the phrase was invented to overcome limitations in the concept of poverty it is still assumed that what everyone wants to be included in is prosperity. And the dominant concept of prosperity is still ever-rising gross domestic product (GDP), stimulated by ever more globalized world trade. Critics of the mainstream model (e.g. Waring 1988, Jones 1990; Korten 1995) suggest that it is the very way that we pursue prosperity that generates an increasing amount of exclusion. The experience of the European Structural Funds over the last decade of the twentieth century is that prosperity, as measured by GDP, can increase while the number of people unemployed remains the same or increases (EU 1999). Over the 1980s and 1990s Britain developed one of the highest employment rates in the European Union (EU), at 73 per cent – and at the same time child poverty increased to the highest in the EU (Macpherson 1999). So increasing GDP alone does not put an end to unemployment, and in any case employment alone (much of it part-time and low paid) does not abolish poverty.

We must recognize exclusion at several different levels of collectivity: an individual may be excluded from local society; a whole locality or neighbourhood may be largely excluded from wealth and influence in a city or region; a whole city or region may be somewhat excluded from national prosperity; and the pattern is evident again on a global scale, with whole countries at a severe disadvantage compared with others.

The exclusion of individuals, therefore (which is usually the primary meaning attributed to social exclusion) may be massively compounded by their concentration within other levels of disadvantage. It is because of a concentration of excluded people that certain neighbourhoods are designated as disadvantaged, but this is not a merely statistical phenomenon. There is an interaction between people and place: people with less money go to (or stay in) cheaper areas where they can afford to live; areas with a critical mass of poorer people have less money circulating, fewer opportunities, more stigma. The individual trying to overcome exclusion is therefore faced with a 'cascade' of obstacles which need to be addressed by a corresponding multi-layered approach to solutions.

This chapter looks at the perspective 'from the bottom': it examines how people spontaneously try to tackle exclusion in their local context, and what implications this has for official anti-exclusion policies. But the implications are ultimately global as well as local. In the age of globalization it is inadequate to focus on community participation without also looking at the macro forces that impinge on this. Of these, the most extensive is the dominant pattern of world trade. 'Free trade' is not simply a natural system, it is a highly managed and regulated system, replacing the rules of protection with even more complex rules against protection (Lean 1999). These rules need to be reframed to give a central place to ensuring the best conditions for local communities. Meanwhile, where does community activity fit into official anti-exclusion practice?

A requirement to ensure the active involvement of the community is a prominent feature of several major regeneration and social inclusion schemes launched in the UK in 1998 and 1999. Examples are the New Deal for communities, the fifth and sixth rounds of the Single Regeneration Budget, the healthy living centres, the Sure Start programme for helping under 5s in disadvantaged families and the Social Exclusion Unit itself. A similar trend in European social and regional funding (the Structural Fund 'objectives' and 'community initiatives') takes the form of encouragement rather than requirement (Chanan 1998).

While most policy initiatives addressing social exclusion are top-down, people in disadvantaged local communities are struggling with the same issues in a fragmented, low-profile way. Experienced community organizations sometimes develop formal initiatives, but most people who spontaneously strive to improve their situation are not aware that their efforts could form part of an official programme. It is easy for official schemes to ignore these seemingly small, scattered efforts. Indeed, they are unlikely to even know about them unless they specifically look for them. But these are precisely the signs and seeds of the involvement which official schemes need, and often find hard to generate themselves.

The prominence of the theme of community activity in new regeneration policies, responding largely to 'grass roots' feedback from previous social programmes, suggests that the government believes it is an important component in overcoming exclusion. There are two implicit concepts here.

In the first concept, community activity is about the involvement of local inhabitants in innovative development schemes, regeneration partnerships and job creation initiatives. It is a means of obtaining active consent and cooperation for official schemes and of mobilizing voluntary effort to help make them 'stick'. In the second concept community activity is a good in itself, knitting communities together, furnishing friendships and acquaintanceships, invigorating local democracy and creating social cohesion.

This chapter argues that while the two concepts are complementary it is only the first one that has really been assimilated in new policy, whereas the second is more fundamental: the intrinsic value of community activity is not only the basis for any major involvement in official policies, but has more far-reaching implications for the future. The more important changes are in the people themselves – better skills, employability, more capacity for mutual aid. New ideas about the importance of 'social capital' (EU 1999) draw attention to these less tangible but no less real factors in the viability of localities.

This chapter therefore looks in turn at these questions:

• What is inclusion?
• What does community activity contribute to inclusion?
• Can community activity be quantified?
• What strategies should be adopted for maximizing community activity and what timescale is required to implement them?

What is inclusion?

What does inclusion look like? The first factor would be having a job – or having had one, and, largely in consequence, possibly having some property or assets; or living in a household which has at least one person in employment. This factor immediately indicates a different relationship to the locality from that which applies to excluded people. Included people have maximum opportunity for local community involvement but are not dependent on it. In contemporary conditions a fully active citizen is someone who participates at a wide variety of levels and frameworks in civic society: as a voter both locally and nationally; as an informed member of the public reading national and international news and having views on all such issues; as an employee possibly of a multinational company, perhaps through a national, regional or local subsidiary; as a leisure consumer (possibly being as much a commuter to city centres, cultural or entertainment centres as locally); as a friend or member of networks (as much through the telephone and the computer as face to face in the neighbourhood).

The privileged person can engage with his/her locality to a variable, freely chosen degree. Well-off localities are generally safer, people are more mobile, there are more and easier places to meet. The ultimate sanction is that people have the option of not being there at all – they have a saleable property, they have the means to move elsewhere, their whole psychological orientation in relation to the place is one of positive choice. And if they are indeed committed to staying there, they have the skills and the means to combine to defend the territory from unwelcome 'development', thus protecting both their privileges and the value of their property. This is not to say that the voluntary activities of well-off people are purely selfish. Many also combine to exert influence for the benefit of society as a whole. Some, no less than people in poor communities and often more, support environmental, human rights and political organizations with national or global agendas.

In poor localities the relationship of the individual with the locality is more obligatory and more fraught. This is not only a matter of joblessness. Much of the housing is more likely to be publicly owned (or owned by a housing association), and even the housing that is privately owned will not have the same marketability as housing in well-off areas, so there is already a limitation on the ease of moving into or out of the locality. More people in the locality, being poor, are likely to have a 'structural' relationship with the public services – whether as claimants, tenants or social service clients, or all three. People are likely to be more pinned down to the locality by lack of the means to be mobile, to commute, to have wide leisure choices. But while these factors might tend in some ways to help bind people together in a locality, in other ways they militate against this – fear of crime and harassment, lack of easy meeting places and poor transport keep them apart.

What does community activity contribute to inclusion?

Most community activity is so intrinsic to daily life that its achievements are taken for granted: household cooperation, family life, friendships, acquaintanceships, good neighbourliness. Beyond the household and informal networks come the semi-formal organizations of the community sector: low profile but sometimes quite large groups carrying out some form of mutual aid or joint interest activity – sports clubs, social clubs, religious groups, babysitting circles, health circles, drama clubs, rambling clubs, choirs. Beyond these again are the formal charities, whether wholly local or branches of national organizations, and there is also the volunteering that takes place around statutory agencies – schools, hospitals, youth clubs, welfare services.

The government has declared a positive concern to strengthen communities. However, it is still inclined to confuse increasing the strength of communities with promoting opportunities for volunteering (NCVO 1999). In the sense of freely devoting time to an activity for the common good, 'volunteering' and 'community activity' are similar. But 'volunteering' generally carries the connotation of 'doing good for others without regard to self', while 'community activity' focuses on pursuit of joint interests, mutual aid or problem solving. These two ways of being active have important differences. People who are secure and well resourced are in a better position to 'volunteer', and surveys always show more volunteering among these groups. Surveys of volunteering invariably claim to include community activity but tend to underestimate it because the language and assumptions are different. People who see themselves as volunteers will respond to questions about giving time or money to good causes. People who spend as much or more time on community activity often do not see themselves as volunteers. They are more likely to see themselves as spending time on *meeting shared needs* or *solving joint problems*. The element of public-spiritedness is still there (and conversely there is often an element of self-interest in volunteering). But strategies to assess and increase 'opportunities for volunteering' will be less effective in overcoming social exclusion than strategies to *improve conditions* for community activity.

There are numerous ways in which the benefits of community activity could be assessed. Traditionally it has hardly been felt necessary to assess a factor so fundamental to social life, but when it breaks down we soon become aware that the social 'glue' has come unstuck. One way to assess it is to call it volunteering and assess how much of it there is. The National Commission on the Future of the Voluntary Sector (NCVO 1996) quoted estimates of the total cash equivalent value of volunteering as being £25 billion a year. This was twice as much as their estimate of the cash turnover of the sector.

However, this estimate depends on a definition of volunteering (developed by the National Centre for Volunteering) which excludes activities carried out for close friends or family – the very heart of community activity. This restriction is strongly influenced by the legal definition of charities as organizations which carry out good works for others: the 'doer' is not allowed to benefit personally. This in turn derives from the nineteenth-century concept of morality as being the good we do to others, whereas the good we do to ourselves is self-interest and therefore legitimate in business and personal advancement but not in charitable activities or public works.

It would be timely to re-examine how this morality jibes with the more common contemporary view that true morality is based in pursuing the common good, self-sacrifice often being an illusion. However that may be, the attempt to subsume community activity under the category of charitable good works undoubtedly leads to a huge underestimate of its extent. In reality the great majority of voluntary organizations are small local community groups, whose ethos is frequently both public spirited *and* self-interested.

Many of these groups, however, do not seek to register as charities, which saves the Charity Commission the embarrassment of refusing their applications. The irony is that whereas these organizations are overwhelmingly voluntary, have very few assets and are largely dedicated to some form of public improvement, some parts of the formal voluntary sector (which consists almost universally of registered charities) are highly professionalized and act increasingly as businesses, albeit on a non-profit basis. This is manifestly necessary if they are to carry out the specialist public service functions for which they are now relied upon, but it is important to see that they thereby become in effect a variant of the public sector, and may be remote from community activity. They cannot be at the same time both the deliverers of public services, paid from public funds, and the customers of those services.

Most community activity is clearly not amenable to direct policy intervention, nor should it be. However, there is every reason to think that it flourishes where conditions are propitious – and conditions *are* amenable to policy. A Community Development Foundation (CDF) study in Wrexham in 1992 (Bell 1992) showed that 1 hour of community development mobilized 15 hours of volunteering. A study in Sandwell in 1996 (Dale and Humm 1996, 1997) showed that after five years' community development a disadvantaged area of 27,000 people had 96 community organizations producing over 2064 volunteer hours per week – the equivalent of 56 full-time jobs, compared with far fewer in adjacent areas.

But what does community activity deliver in terms of benefit to society? For this we have to look at specific examples of community organizations. A recent study in 12 European countries (EU 1997) showed that many of the types of social benefit from community activity that we are familiar with in Britain are quite universal:

- In 'Punt 50' in the Feijenoord district of Rotterdam, the Netherlands, a group of 20 women on low incomes ran a centre for training, advice, mutual aid and social activities used by over 200 women and children.
- In Osterholz-Tenever, Bremen, Germany, residents created and ran a mothers' centre, tenants' meeting place, youth café and young people's cultural centre.
- In 'Wotepa', in the Antwerpen district of north-east Antwerp, Belgium, residents converted a disused school into a furniture renovation and distribution service.
- In Barcelona, in the Ciutat Vella (old city) district, residents' groups campaigned successfully to improve conservation and obtain subsidies to ensure that poorer residents could stay in the locality as property values rose due to renovation.
- In the 'BIK' project, in Aalborg East, Aalborg, Denmark, a dormant neighbourhood council reinvigorated by resident participation obtained a new local bus service, making life cheaper and easier for less well-off residents.
- In Glasgow, tenants on the Greater Easterhouse estate carried out a long campaign which eventually persuaded the local council to install a more efficient heating system throughout the damp, unhealthy flats. Their success saved tenants thousands of pounds a year in heating bills, more than paid for its cost to the council in savings on repairs, and saved the health authorities a lot of expense as well.

Each of these relatively high-profile and well documented examples is paralleled by hundreds of smaller and generally undocumented initiatives. The Easterhouse heating campaign was unusual in documenting its economic effects, but it is quite obvious that all such activities must have a considerable economic value. However, it is not the kind of value that is registered in GDP. On the contrary, community activity *reduces* GDP because it consists largely of unpaid activity, prevention of waste and the production of direct value that is not traded through the market. Like most environmental improvements, this merely shows the inadequacy of GDP as a measure of real value, and the danger of basing major policies on it (Waring 1988).

While all countries have their own characteristic types of community organization, the functions that they perform are recurrent everywhere. These could broadly be characterized as:

- Self-help/mutual aid (e.g. Alcoholics Anonymous, women's health groups, child care groups, self-build housing).
- Campaigning (e.g. to save common land, obtain a swimming pool, get improvements in public housing).
- Representative (e.g. residents' association, parents' association, patients' association).
- Recreational (e.g. sports, arts, youth clubs).

- Faith (e.g. religious groups).
- Social economy initiatives (e.g. local exchange trading systems (LETS) credit unions, community businesses).
- Infrastructure (e.g. support bodies, development projects, forums).

Other than, or in addition to, getting a job, the foundation-stone of social inclusion is involvement in some form of community activity. However, it cannot be assumed that the population of any given locality is automatically a 'community'. In the era of globalization, and perhaps for some time past, local social networks (many of which, in urban areas, had only been forged over three or four generations or less) have been dissolving at an exponential rate, for a variety of reasons. Television globalizes, standardizes and isolates; the disappearance of local anchor industries dissolves major occupational networks and the social networks that attach to them; the expansion of opportunities, communications and mobility for well-off people has made their networks more diffuse as well as more optional.

The 'community', therefore, is not necessarily a pre-existing entity in the sense of a cohesive, organic whole. There is a physical locality and there are people living in it. If it has had a fairly stable history much of the population may have been there for several generations and be interwoven by ties of family, friendship and common experience. If there are dominant occupations or a dominant industry, there may be extensive work-based networks and a sense of commonality. Women may have extensive additional networks concerned with child care or extended family. All these factors help to create a community in a profound sense, but communities in this sense are no longer the norm, especially in urban areas. Large numbers of local inhabitants may have been there for a generation or much less. Families may have been split up, with invisible but far-reaching further consequences in extended family networks. Industries may have collapsed, suddenly dissolving wide occupational networks.

In situations where a deep sense of community has disappeared or never yet materialized, many individuals and families may be in effect barely living in 'the community'. People experience their problems primarily as personal misfortune. The idea that their problems are partly problems of the locality as well as themselves may hardly have occurred to them, and the further idea that it is possible to do something constructive about them on a joint basis with their neighbours and the public authorities might well strike them as being in the realms of science fiction.

Most disadvantaged localities are probably somewhere between the extremes of time-honoured cohesiveness and complete artificiality or dislocation. The first lesson that should guide a strategy of community involvement is to know the history of the area and look at existing signs of 'embedded' or reactive community activity: what joint activities, networks and organizations already exist on the inhabitants' own initiative? What practical help can they call on? What obstacles do they face?

We can safely assume that in these conditions community activity is not easy to sustain, and therefore even small organizations are an important sign of people's strong motivation to create a sense of community in their lives. It is vital to give this motivation every encouragement and assistance. A certain sheer density of community activity – of people knowing each other, acting together, extending their awareness of what's going on around them – is essential before one can speak meaningfully of 'involving the community' in a higher forum.

Involvement in 'the regeneration of the locality' makes huge assumptions: that people identify with their locality; that they understand how public policies work; that they know how to plan and follow through a project; that they are well motivated towards other inhabitants and understand the reciprocity that comes from this; and – perhaps most neglected of all – that they are willing to devote a great deal of their own time to pursuing these ends. Wonderfully, all these conditions are in fact met, time and time again, by small groups of people in every locality – a phenomenon which community workers call 'ordinary people doing extraordinary things'. But it cannot be taken for granted and it cannot be created instantaneously. The watchword for involvement policies therefore is: individuals have to be involved in the community in order for the community to be involved in public policies.

Can community activity be quantified?

Increasing community activity, and increasing its effectiveness in overcoming social exclusion, is one of the primary objectives of community development. Variant versions of this process (with shifting boundaries currently) are capacity-building, community involvement and participation (CDF 1999). But if we are to be able to set targets for improved community activity we need some baselines and norms. What incidence of 'natural' involvement can be expected in a disadvantaged locality? A pioneering study in the early 1990s (Chanan 1992) examined data from an average of 230 households in each of seven matched areas in different European countries to examine the proportion and characteristics of local people who got actively involved in community groups and voluntary organizations. All the samples were in disadvantaged areas known to have a fair number of voluntary and community organizations operating – an average of three organizations per thousand people.

The total sample of 1590 respondents were clustered according to their awareness of, and level of involvement in, local groups or organizations. Just under half (46 per cent) were involved in at least one local organization as users. People helping at least one group or organization consistently over the preceding year and who were aware of a variety of local groups were regarded as highly active. People who helped groups intermittently and had a limited awareness of local groups were rated moderately active. 'Not active' people helped only occasionally if at all, and knew few or no local groups. Five per cent of the sample were found to be highly active, 9 per cent moderately active and 86 per cent not active. All the categories were spread across the seven case studies.

Most active and moderately active people were also users, so the general picture which emerged was of about one in seven people (14 per cent) being the ones who ran the sector, who 'made it happen'; a further two or three out of seven (32 per cent) using the groups without being actively involved in running them; and three or four out of seven (54 per cent) neither using nor helping them (Chanan 1992: 46–7).

The active minority was made up of roughly equal numbers of men and women, and marital status made little difference. There was an increasing level of activity, however, among people over 40, suggesting that a long-term association with the locality, or the expectation of staying there, could be a factor. People with care responsibilities were more likely to be active. Retired people and those not looking for work were less likely to be active than those who were unemployed, employed full-time or employed part-time, and activity was higher among white-collar workers and professionals than among skilled or unskilled manual workers.

A supplementary study (Bell 1993) looked at how far activism was related to whether the respondent was personally affected by the issue addressed in the activity – in other words, how far community activity was driven by personal need and how far by altruism or interest. Four types of position emerged. Forty-two per cent of respondents had little interest in local issues, even when they affected the household, and did nothing about them. Another large group, 45 per cent, had a high level of concern with local issues, and about a quarter of the issues affected their household directly, but they did little about them. A third group of 7 per cent were both concerned with local issues, were frequently affected by them and were active about them. The final group of 5 per cent were little personally affected by the issues but were characterized by concern for local issues and a high level of activity with respect to them.

This pattern suggests that the minority of local populations who make the local community and voluntary sector what it is are a number of fairly exceptional people, some motivated by need and others by altruism and interest. The great majority of people are not 'connected' in a practical way, though about half are consciously concerned with local issues whereas the other half are not interested even when affected by the issues.

Any regeneration scheme which seeks to 'involve the community' against a background such as this will no doubt be able to engage the interest of the exceptional minority quite quickly but will have difficulty engaging the majority. The main obstacle is not just inertia or lack of interest but the simple but overwhelming fact that there has never been, in most such areas, a concerted strategy to recognize and foster widespread community activity, to facilitate it by practical means (not just by exhortation) and to create a climate which conveys to people the feeling that the way the locality develops is amenable to their own joint wishes and efforts.

Two later UK studies drawing on these techniques extended their inquiries to assessing the potential for greater activity by local people. Studies in seven neighbourhoods in Sandwell, West Midlands, in 1996 (Dale and Humm 1996) elicited a massive 70 per cent of residents wanting more local groups and around 30 per cent saying they themselves were willing to be more active, where current activity levels were around 10 per cent. Similarly a survey in Southwark in 1997 elicited 45 per cent of people saying they would be willing to be more involved in improving local conditions if there was better information about activities and facilities to meet and a dialogue about development between local people and public services (Southwark/ OPM 1997).

It seems therefore that there is almost certainly a huge potential for increased community activity if the right conditions and support can be created, and that ways can be found to measure it.

Strategies and timescale

Given the multifarious benefits of community activity, and its new prominence in policy, one would expect that it should be seen as a self-evidently fundamental mechanism for overcoming social exclusion. In most programmes, however, community activity is still seen only as an auxiliary to other outcomes – participation in partnerships, delivering parts of public services and, in particular, creating jobs.

The European programmes, in particular, are devoted to the goal of job creation. It is difficult to get access to Structural Fund support unless there is some connection with job creation. Getting a job is undoubtedly one of the greatest steps to overcoming exclusion. Nevertheless, in far too much of the literature, overcoming unemployment is used almost synonymously with regeneration. This would condemn most people in such areas to continuing exclusion, because in most cases only a minority of those not employed are foreseeably going to get jobs, even with the help of regeneration programmes. The impeding factors are many: new jobs in disadvantaged areas frequently do not go to local unemployed people; the poverty of the locality affects also those who are not in the labour market, who are often far greater in number than the unemployed; it also affects the low paid; deliberate job creation is expensive and the number of jobs created in such areas even with substantial regeneration funding is rarely enough to provide work for more than a fraction of local unemployed and non-employed people; and even when job creation programmes are successful this does not automatically result in improvement to the life of the locality as a whole – the increased income may flow rapidly out of the locality, or the employed individuals may leave (CDF 1999).

New employment remains a vital component in regeneration and social inclusion but a much wider strategy is needed to accompany action on unemployment. While a local employment scheme would be doing well to provide new work for 20 per cent of unemployed or non-employed people in the disadvantaged locality for a few years, this will be of little lasting benefit to the life of the locality as a whole unless other major measures are taken at the same time to amplify other ways of being included which can be directly accessed by the majority of the population. These activities, and the climate they create, are equally necessary for those who already have, or newly obtain, a job.

The economic value of community activity needs to be assessed in terms of costs saved, services improved, life-skills developed as well as jobs created. All these things can contribute to getting or making paid employment as well, but their full implications are lost if they are regarded only as sub-activities of job creation. Most community organizations do not have the aim of job creation. Their aims are to do with the direct improvement of local life, pursuit of common interests, facilitating friendships, enjoyment and – though they wouldn't use such a term – social cohesion. If they were given enough money – and money-handling skills – to fulfil these functions on a bigger scale they could certainly create jobs – at least as many jobs as are created with the same money in the business sector – and with much more likelihood that those jobs would go to local people. But if you asked community organizations whether they could contribute to a job creation programme most would say no.

Without necessarily knowing it, community groups are often being more realistic than the job creation programmes. Even with the fairly impressive sums allocated by the Structural Funds and the domestic programmes, there isn't enough money in the system to create the number of jobs that would be required to turn around the most disadvantaged areas where unemployment is concentrated. Fluctuations in the job market at macro level dwarf the local remedial programmes. With fully a third of the world population of working age unemployed or seriously underemployed, according to the United Nations (UN 1998), the lasting solution has to be redistribution of work as well as creation of work. The loss of income to some must be tempered by a huge boost in the direct social and economic benefits of local community activity. We need a 'community wage' in terms of healthier, safer, pleasanter localities with maximum local production for local use. This is also the way the environmental imperative points, though many environmentalist organizations seem curiously unclear that their constituency is therefore all local community organizations, not just the ones that call themselves 'environmental'.

Politicians don't like to admit that they cannot decisively overcome unemployment, but also avoid committing themselves to full employment. The macroeconomists among them would in any case regard such an aim as dangerously inflationary. Meanwhile society is becoming increasingly part-time. While much of the USA and UK success in creating employment comes in the form of part-time jobs, France, Italy and Germany are shortening the working week, overcoming initial opposition by demonstrating that a household can often increase its income by getting another member to take advantage of the increased employment opportunities, while some individuals lose a few hours' work a week as a result. This is also a nudge towards more equal gender roles in the household. Yet all this, whether Continental or Anglo-Saxon, is taking place without any specific policy link to the positive corollary of a day a week for the community. A policy link could help both sides of the equation – but the community part must stay voluntary, under people's own control and to their own and others' mutual benefit.

We need a vision of post-industrialism as the advent of a well-paid, well-protected, part-time society. In such a society it will be seen that the full range of ordinary community activity is the sector's distinctive contribution to sustainable economic development. This 'community wage' will not be mainly transacted in jobs, cash and GDP but in mutual aid, free activities, social cohesion and democratic invigoration. All this will also, as a spin-off, equip people better for their part-time jobs – but its primary contribution will be impaired if job creation has been made into its raison d'être.

Regeneration policies follow a political timetable. They look for results in unrealistically short times, compared with how long it takes to develop a community. But this is no mere foible of policy planners. The problems are urgent, and no one feels this more keenly than the local inhabitants themselves. So urgency is not an arbitrarily imposed imperative, though particular top-down objectives often are. The answer is that involvement, and regeneration as a whole, has to undertake several different tasks in parallel. That part of the local population which is 'up to speed' on local issues and which has experience of involvement (probably the one in seven people whom the 1992 European study identified as active in the community sector) is likely to be ready to be engaged in dialogue immediately. It must be remembered, however, that these people are also likely to be fully stretched in carrying out the activities they are already involved in. They will not have 'budgeted' for spare capacity to get involved again at a 'meta' level. If a partnership wants their input it should be prepared to compensate the local micro-organizations to which they are already giving their energies, by some form of resources or technical assistance – which in any case may be needed to help strengthen those organizations for a larger role.

The second task to be carried out at the same time is to optimize the conditions and stimuli to get a larger proportion of local people involved in community activity of virtually any kind. This means looking at the profile of current activity and finding all means possible to boost it: strengthening existing organizations, assisting people who are trying to start new ones, fostering a climate of awareness and demand for community activity. It may mean instituting – or strengthening if it already exists – a local community sector umbrella body whose job is to foster the growth of the sector as a whole.

A third task is to take further special measures to involve the most excluded individuals. These are people who for one reason or another are not likely to be reached by the general stimulus of the second measure or who are not in a position to respond to it. This may be because they are particularly poor, homeless, lacking in skills, immobile or facing discrimination. For people in this situation it is not necessarily realistic to expect that they can simply get involved in community activity at will. They may need help in establishing even the most basic bonds of human connection, and there have to be special measures to assist them to do so. Initially this assistance is therefore likely to take the form of social work rather than community work; but as soon as the basic bonds are being created the option of community involvement can also come onto the horizon. Sometimes community involvement can itself be a means of reintegration into local society, but the initial vehicles usually have to be small, close at hand and unthreatening. The move from 'How can I possibly cope with my problems?' to 'How can I contribute to solving the problems of the locality?' is nothing short of a psychological revolution – yet can also be the most therapeutic treatment conceivable.

Conclusion

The task of building up community involvement at these simultaneous levels is therefore no sideshow: it is a tremendous challenge and requires substantial and highly skilled resources. All this might be thought hardly worthwhile if community involvement were merely a minor accompaniment to a programme of renewal that is primarily an extension or galvanization of public services. Sometimes this is all that 'regeneration' becomes. But if so, the opportunity for a much more profound and lasting change has been missed. What makes a locality thrive from within is the state of mind, capability and activity of the inhabitants themselves. To facilitate a change from, say, one in seven to one in three being active on local public issues is not merely a preparation for consensus on certain physical plans. It is the very stuff of regeneration. No large commercial company would invest substantial resources in renewing plant, premises and equipment without a corresponding investment in staff skills and attitudes, yet regeneration schemes still frequently invest millions of pounds in physical amenities and job creation with barely one or two per cent for the development of local community activity.

The 'objective' or 'instrumental' way of looking at the local community and voluntary sector is admittedly unfamiliar, even in community development tradition. It is imperative not only to reveal the hugely impressive achievements from small resources but also to get some sense of overall scale, coverage and gaps: neither the individual organizations nor the sector as a whole (which frequently does not conceive itself as a whole) claim systematic coverage either of the population or of issues. On the contrary, the sector grows from within and any attempt to coerce or systematize this process would undoubtedly destroy it. This would also nullify the democratic value of the sector as constituting a distinct public space free of all obligation to the state or the market. But this does not prevent a strategy to stimulate and support it.

The issue of timescale is more significant than simply the question of how long it takes to achieve certain objectives. It has a fundamental bearing on the question of the relationship between community involvement and overall regeneration. The overall aims of regeneration projects are normally stated in terms of improvements in social, economic and material conditions and as preconceived objectives. Thus the creation of jobs, improvement of x houses, reduction of x per cent in crime levels is equated with the regeneration of the locality. Community involvement is seen as one of the means to achieve this, not as an objective in itself. The community has to be 'involved' in official actions to assist those actions to improve the material conditions which result in a better community. But what is a better community? It is a community that is involved precisely in processes such as these. Community activity is the very stuff of social cohesion. Community involvement is therefore an objective as well as a means. But how long does it take to move from the active involvement of one in seven to the critical mass of involvement which would make regeneration irreversible, and what would that critical mass be? What improvements in material conditions are essential to facilitate this level of involvement?

Can an injection of £200 a year per head of population in a disadvantaged area for a five-year period (the kind of sum that is often available for regeneration purposes) overcome the deep-rooted problems of the locality in terms of low educational attainment, high crime, joblessness and poor amenities? There are already vastly greater sums than this being spent in the locality in the form of public services and benefits. How should it be possible to 'regenerate' a locality of 10,000 people with £2 million of public money a year when it is not achieved by the regular input of £20 million or £30 million a year in other public money?

What is feasible is that the extra £2 million, shrewdly and creatively used, would be able either to begin or to continue to achieve a stage in a longer process. To formulate regeneration-scheme aims in more modest and realistic terms has important implications for the element of community involvement and for changes of culture among authorities and agencies. If the achievements of five years are demonstrative, not decisive, it is clear that one of the main objectives must be not just that the community 'has been involved' in making decisions and assisting processes but that at the end of the period the community is in a better condition to drive the next stage of regeneration itself.

It is natural for communities to seek to control the development of their own economic and social conditions, much as a household does – by determining what balance to exercise as between buying and selling, making and doing, earning and spending. But it is difficult to see how communities can increase their control if nations are losing theirs – or, to be more precise, negotiating it away in the name of globalization. The rules of the proposed Multilateral Agreement on Investment, which the Organization for Economic Cooperation and Development attempted to lay down in 1998, would have given multinational companies the right to sue governments if the governments placed virtually any conditions whatever on their trading and investment in that country, or fostered any form of 'unfair competition' (Petley 1999). This agenda – still very much alive in global financial planning – would be about as natural as if there were laws against growing your own potatoes because this would impinge on the trading rights of your local supermarket. We will not have found really effective policies against exclusion until these are joined up 'vertically' as well as 'horizontally' – until, that is, active citizenship comes to be a multi-layer concept, addressing the interactions of localities, regions, government, blocs and international bodies, and ensuring, in Colin Hines' phrase, that we 'protect the local globally' (Hines forthcoming).

References

Bell, J. (1992) *Community Development Teamwork: Measuring the Impact.* London: Community Development Foundation.

Bell, J. (1993) The Activist and the Alienated. London: Community Development Foundation (unpublished). (The main findings were also reflected in Chanan 1992.)

CDF (Community Development Foundation) (1999) *Regeneration and Sustainable Communities.* London: Community Development Foundation.

Chanan, G. (1992) *Out of the Shadows: Local Community Action and the European Community.* Dublin: European Foundation for the Improvement of Living and Working Conditions.

Chanan, G. (1998) *The New Structural Funds: What Development Model for Europe?* London: Community Development Foundation.

Chanan, G. (1999) *Community Involvement: A Handbook for Good Practice.* Dublin: European Foundation for the Improvement of Living and Working Conditions.

Dale, P. and Humm, J. (1996) Community Involvement in Two Areas of Sandwell. Sandwell: Sandwell Regeneration Partnership and Community Development Foundation (unpublished).

Dale, P. and Humm, J. (1997) Community Activity in Sandwell's Estates Renewal Challenge Areas: Overview. Sandwell: Sandwell Regeneration Partnership and Community Development Foundation (unpublished).

EU (European Union) (1997) *Community Involvement in Urban Regeneration: Added Value and Changing Values*, Regional Studies no. 27 (DGXVI). Luxembourg: European Union.

EU (European Union) (1999) *Sixth Periodic Report on the Regions: Summary of Main Findings*, European Commission fact sheet DGXVI (Cx-20-99-688-EN-C). Luxembourg: Office for Official Publications of the European Communities.

Hines, C. (forthcoming) *Protect the Local Globally*. London: Earthscan.

Jones, B. (1990) *Sleepers, Wake! Technology and the Future of Work*. Melbourne: Oxford University Press.

Korten, D. (1995) *When Corporations Rule the World*. London: Earthscan.

Lean, G. (1999) The hidden tentacles of the world's most secret body, *Independent on Sunday*, 18 July.

Macpherson, N. (1999) *Child Poverty*, presentation to HM Treasury, 14 July. London: HM Treasury.

NCVO (National Council of Voluntary Organizations) (1996) *Meeting the Challenge of Change: Voluntary Action into the 21st Century*, report of the National Commission on the Future of the Voluntary Sector. London: National Council of Voluntary Organizations.

NCVO (National Council of Voluntary Organizations) (1999) *Speech by the Prime Minister to NCVO Conference, 21 January*. London: National Council of Voluntary Organizations.

Petley, J. (1999) MAI-day! *Vertigo*, summer: 9. See also *Trade and Industry Report* (HC112), London: The Stationery Office, and website <http://www.mai.flora.org>.

Southwark/OPM (1997) *Community Survey*. London: London Borough of Southwark and Office for Public Management.

United Nations (UN) (1998) *Overcoming Human Poverty*. New York: UNDP.

Waring, M. (1988) *If Women Counted*. London: Macmillan (subsequently republished as *Counting for Nothing*).

12 EVALUATING INITIATIVES TO ADDRESS SOCIAL EXCLUSION

Ian Sanderson

Introduction

As social exclusion achieves growing salience in national and local policy arenas, increasing attention is being given to issues of measurement and evaluation. Of course, this is to be expected; standard models of policy making tell us that monitoring and evaluation must be undertaken to 'close the loop' and ensure that lessons are learned from experience and fed back into ongoing policy formulation and adjustment. There is, indeed, an increasing emphasis in government on securing evidence of 'what works' and on accountability for performance on the basis of measurable indicators which is pushing evaluation from its traditional 'backstage' role into the spotlight (Martin and Sanderson 1999).

However, the picture is varied. Although there is an emphasis in the government's *Bringing Britain Together: A National Strategy for Neighbourhood Renewal* (Social Exclusion Unit 1998: 75) on 'learning lessons . . . of how policy impacts at ground level and affects those in poverty', and reference to the need to measure success in outcome terms, the development of an evaluation strategy is not given a high profile. The situation is better in Scotland where the development of the Social Inclusion Strategy (Scottish Office, undated) includes action by the Scottish Social Inclusion Network (1999) to formulate an evaluation framework which addresses both the use of indicators to 'measure success' and the need for evaluation research to understand 'how and why success is achieved' (or not).

Generally, this latter concern with understanding, explanation and learning is subordinated in discussions of evaluation in official circles to issues of measurement and accountability. Thus, in the government's 'modernizing government' agenda, at both central and local levels, the emphasis is on the establishment of performance measurement frameworks to allow monitoring of progress against targets. It can be argued that this displays more of a concern for achieving central accountability and control than for promoting learning and improvement (Sanderson 1998). Indeed, Henkel (1991a) has referred to the 'new evaluative state' in which performance is scrutinized at different levels through a variety of means: in terms of outputs through systems of performance measures and indicators; in terms of managerial systems and processes through inspections and quality audits; and in terms of contract performance through monitoring of standards. This emphasis on control implies the development of a particular form of evaluation:

> Government policies now promoted evaluation as a contribution to the control of the periphery by the centre, particularly in the management of resources. It stressed values of economy, efficiency, 'value for money' and effectiveness or performance. As a corollary, it assumed that evaluation would be summative, delivering authoritative judgements, based as far as possible on performance indicators or quantitative measures of input-output relationships and outcomes and set against predefined targets and standards.
>
> (Henkel 1991b: 20)

The fact that evaluation has become closely associated with 'top-down' control and accountability may help to explain why it is not strongly developed in the decision-making and management processes and cultures of public sector organizations. It is seen largely as 'something we have to do for government' rather than 'something we should do to help us perform better'. Indeed, in local government, where many initiatives to address social exclusion are being developed, evaluation capacity is very uneven (Sanderson *et al.* 1998). Moreover, such initiatives are commonly developed on a cross-service and multi-agency basis, producing an institutional context in which evaluation can be problematical. Accountability for performance is required in Single Regeneration Budget (SRB) and European Union (EU) programmes but this tends to reinforce an orientation to 'performance measurement' rather than broader evaluation. Finally, evaluation in the field of social exclusion is undoubtedly a complex and difficult enterprise which is conceptually and methodologically challenging and which therefore places considerable demands on public agencies in terms of knowledge, skills and resources.

This chapter considers approaches to evaluating initiatives to address social exclusion. The next section briefly discusses perspectives on the purpose of evaluation, arguing for a view of evaluation as a form of 'practical reason'. This has implications for both the 'cognitive' and 'normative' bases of evaluation which are then considered, with a focus on the case for a realist approach which adopts a critical stance in relation to the ends of human action. The following section develops the argument for theory-based evaluation which seeks to test and develop the theoretical underpinnings of policies and programmes and presents a framework for evaluation in the context of social exclusion. Key evaluation challenges are then discussed: 'capturing' and measuring outcomes and effects; attributing effects to programme measures; explaining how outcomes and effects are caused by programme 'mechanisms'; and valuing the 'net worth' to society of public action. The concluding section briefly addresses the broader 'political' context of evaluation, arguing for a 'participatory' approach to evaluation in the context of social exclusion on 'ideological' grounds and because it is an important condition for effective utilization.

The purpose of evaluation

Dominant conceptions of evaluation are tied to the notion of effectiveness, the dominant concern being 'how well do policies and programmes achieve the objectives which have been set for them?' This concern with the effectiveness of means to given ends can be seen as embodying 'instrumental rationality', underpinned by positivist notions of objective knowledge derived through accepted canons of scientific enquiry (Sanderson 1998). When Patton (1982: 15), for example, talks about 'confusion' over what evaluation is, and about evaluation involving 'systematic collection of information' to 'reduce uncertainties, improve effectiveness and make decisions', he presents evaluation as a primarily 'technical' activity. Moreover, many definitions of evaluation refer to the 'objective assessment' of policies, programmes and activities, the assessment of the extent to which given objectives have been achieved, and to the application of such knowledge to improve the effectiveness of means in achieving given ends (see, for example, European Commission 1997).

Indeed, prevailing notions of evaluation can be seen as heavily conditioned by a strong top-down control imperative in the British state (Bovaird and Gregory 1996). Thus, discussion of the purpose of evaluation conventionally emphasizes two key reasons: first, to promote accountability for performance in the use of public funds; and second, to improve management and allocation of resources (European Commission 1997: 14; HM Treasury 1997). This perspective marries instrumental rationality to a political context in which the ends and values embedded in public policies and programmes are subject to strong top-down influence from central government. The importance of the requirement for 'accountability upwards', attendant upon this strong top-down control, explains the dominance of 'summative evaluation' of a primarily quantitative nature.

An alternative view sees evaluation as a form of 'practical reason', in the sense of intelligence and argument directed to practical, and especially moral, outcomes (MacIntyre 1984; Dryzek 1990). This perspective rejects 'positivist-objectivist' notions of valid knowledge and the role of the evaluator as 'technician' and, instead, sees evaluation as a process of knowledge production, embedded in a particular sociopolitical context, in which assessments of the 'value' of policies and programmes involve judgement informed by a wide range of cognitive and valuative influences. It also rejects instrumental rationality and sees evaluation as an essentially critical, normative activity which questions the ends and goals behind policies and programmes, thus ensuring that the assessment of their 'value' embodies a broad conception of 'social welfare'. From this point of view, therefore, we can question both the 'cognitive' and 'normative' bases of evalution; that is, both the basis upon which 'valid knowledge' can be derived and the ends and values which govern public policies and programmes.

Evaluation, realism and 'practical reason'

Over the past decade the evaluation community has been engaged in a lively debate between, on the one hand, the positivist-empiricist tradition which emphasizes quantification and the 'cold, rational calculations' of the experimental method and, on the other hand, the phenomenological-constructivist tradition which emphasizes a qualitative, 'hermeneutic' process through which understanding of the meaning of 'constructed reality' can be achieved (Pawson and Tilley 1997: 6). Much of the debate has focused on Guba and Lincoln's (1989) *Fourth Generation Evaluation* which has been extremely influential in criticizing positivist experimentation and promoting what they term the 'responsive constructivist' approach which seeks to involve all stakeholders in an 'interactive, negotiated process' of meaning construction.

However, it has been argued that this debate is posited upon an unrealistic choice between 'either a conceptually impoverished and deconceptualizing empiricism, or a hermeneutics drained of causal import and impervious to controls' (Bhaskar quoted in Julnes *et al.* 1998: 485). Pawson and Tilley (1997), supported by Julnes *et al.* (1998), argue that the realist tradition in the philosophy of science provides a basis for evaluation which progresses beyond the 'positivist versus constructivist' debate and develops our understanding of the effect of our interventions in a complex social world, addressing those structural and institutional features of society which are in some respects independent of the individuals' reasoning and desires (Julnes *et al.* 1998: 23).

In realist evaluation, social programmes are seen as open systems comprising various 'levels' of social processes which interrelate at the micro level (the conscious action of individual and group 'agents') and the macro level (institutional rules and structures) such that action at the micro level is 'socially structured' – *embedded* in deeper social processes. The way in which programmes work must therefore be understood in terms of underlying *mechanisms* operating at both micro and macro levels to produce outcomes, such mechanisms referring to 'stakeholders' choices (reasoning) and their capacity (resources) to put these into practice' (Pawson and Tilley 1997: 66).

However, the way in which causal mechanisms operate to produce outcomes is contingent upon the *context* into which programmes are introduced, not just the geographical and institutional location, but 'the prior set of social rules, norms, values and interrelationships gathered in these places which sets limits on the efficacy of programme mechanisms' (Pawson and Tilley 1997: 70). The effects or outcomes of a programme can then be understood as the product of mechanisms operating in particular contexts – i.e. *'outcome = mechanism + context'*. The task for the evaluator in studying the success or failure of a programme is to identify how its various mechanisms have operated to cause change and how they have been sustained or constrained by the social and cultural conditions of the programme's context. The key question is: 'what works for whom in what circumstances' (Pawson and Tilley 1997: 74–7). Such understanding, albeit conditional and contingent in an open systems context, allows judgements to be made about how programmes can be developed and delivered in the future.

A key feature of theory-driven realist evaluation, with its focus on explanation, is that methods of data collection and analysis become means to this end. It is the task of evaluation design to 'tailor' the choice of methods carefully to the particular circumstances; there is no presumption that any particular method is inherently superior. This provides a coherent basis for a 'pluralist' approach to method and for the use of 'mixed method' or 'multi-method' designs in the evaluation of complex social phenomena (see Waysman and Savaya 1997). This position is also advocated by Connell and Kubisch (1997) in their 'theory of change' approach to evaluation of comprehensive community initiatives which has a realist focus in the 'systematic and cumulative study of the links between activities, outcomes and contexts of the initiative' (p. 5). They argue that this approach to evaluation 'relies upon and uses many methodologies that have been developed and refined over the years – quantitative and qualitative, impact and process oriented, traditional and non-traditional, and so on – for information collection, measurement and analysis' (p. 7).

However, we need to broaden our conception of evaluation in other ways if it is to fulfil its potential in improving human welfare. Thus, evaluation must be perceived as an essentially normative activity which questions the 'rationality' of the ends and values that govern collective action. This point is made by Julnes *et al.* (1998: 498–500), who argue that realist evaluation must go beyond knowledge construction to facilitate the 'valuing' of programmes and policies. This position is reflected in Schwandt's (1997) notion of 'critical intelligence' which, in questioning the value of the ends of human practices, is fundamentally an exercise in practical-moral reasoning. From this perspective, the purpose of evaluation is not simply to assess the 'correctness' (effectiveness) of actions in achieving defined ends but rather to form a judgement of the 'appropriateness' of actions in particular circumstances with reference to both empirical and normative aspects (Fischer 1980).

In this enterprise, then, we face two key questions. First, to what extent are the objectives and values which govern the development of a policy or programme appropriate to the treatment of the social problems and needs which underpin its rationale? Second, to what extent are the measures implemented in the policy or programme appropriate in terms of producing outcomes which address the defined problems and needs? The indexing of 'appropriateness' to social problems and needs in this way emphasizes the nature of evaluation as an instance of 'practical reason' directed to ethical/moral ends – namely, enhancing human welfare or 'changing the world for the better'. Moreover, it requires a theory-driven approach to evaluation, as discussed above, which is capable of developing our understanding of how and why policies and programmes 'work' (or do not 'work') in addressing problems and needs as the basis for learning and improvement in the quest for social reform (see Pawson and Tilley 1997: xiv).

Conceptualizing interventions to address social exclusion: an evaluation framework

The problematical nature of the task of conceptualizing social exclusion underpins the difficulties faced by evaluators. Issues surrounding the definition of social exclusion were discussed in Chapter 1 where the complexity of the concept was emphasized. Thus, it is evident that social exclusion is multidimensional, refers to a set of dynamic processes and is a 'relational' concept. The complexity is captured in Room's definition of social exclusion as 'multidimensional disadvantage, which is of substantial duration and which involves dissociation from the major social and occupational milieux of society' (quoted in Berghman 1995: 25). Exclusionary processes may arise in four key 'societal systems': civic (democratic participation); economic (labour market); social (welfare state); and interpersonal (social networks of family and friends) (Dunn *et al.* 1998: 4). These processes interact over time in complex and imperfectly understood ways and different degrees of exclusion arise which are difficult to capture in measurable outcome states.

Policies and programmes to address aspects of social exclusion are, in effect, based upon hypotheses and assumptions about how they will 'work'. They embody a 'programme theory' or 'intervention logic' which informs the design of policy instruments and the specification of the desired or intended outcomes and effects (European Commission 1997; Pawson and Tilley 1997). This intervention logic will have some degree of evidential support from previous research but the complex nature of social exclusion processes means that the evidential base for many policy responses is limited. This is particularly so in the case of cross-sectoral and cross-agency initiatives which seek to address the various dimensions of exclusion in a 'holistic' way. In this context there is a strong case for a theory-based approach to evaluation which seeks to 'test' or assess the validity of the 'intervention logic' so as to improve our understanding of how policies and programmes are working (or not). This will ensure that evaluation contributes to learning about how to improve policy responses and thereby promotes 'evidence-based' policy making.

Therefore, it is important to clarify at the outset the intervention logic which underpins the policy or programme to be evaluated; to identify the hypotheses, assumptions and theories which have informed its design. In essence, the intervention logic for a particular programme comprises three key elements:

- In a particular set of contextual circumstances, a situation is defined as a 'problem' which is in need of public policy intervention (e.g. unacceptably high youth unemployment).
- Programme instruments are designed and implemented which are intended to provide mechanisms to address the defined 'problem' (e.g. job search advice, training and work experience).
- Anticipated outcomes are specified which indicate a degree of improvement in the defined 'problem' (e.g. reduction in youth unemployment) which justifies the intervention.

Testing the intervention logic then involves analysing to what degree and in what way the programme 'mechanisms' are effective (or not) in addressing the defined problem so as to improve our understanding of 'how it works' as well as assessing 'how well it works'. It also involves developing a broader view of the 'appropriateness' of the programme given the values underpinning it (e.g. that reducing youth unemployment in the defined context is a 'good thing').

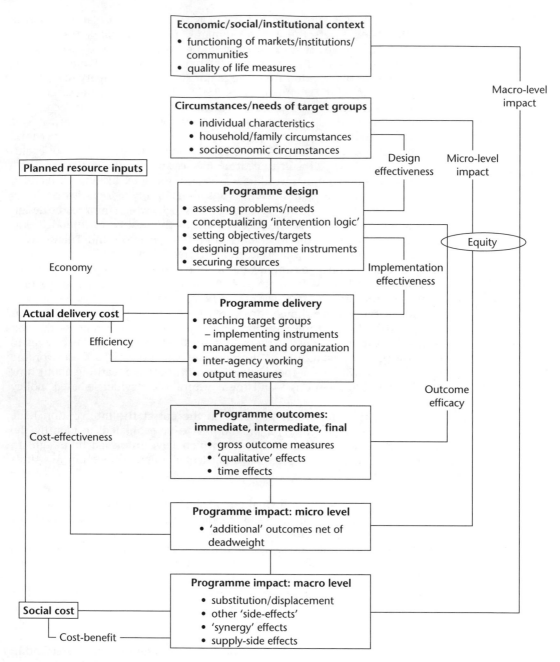

Figure 12.1   A framework for programme evaluation

Figure 12.1 presents a framework for evaluation which can help to clarify the intervention logic of programmes to address social exclusion. This specification is widely used in evaluation in the form of the systems model of 'production of welfare' (Knapp 1984); elsewhere we have termed it the 'production of value' approach (Sanderson *et al.* 1998). It specifies how a set of resource inputs and activities are organized and managed so as to produce defined outputs which in turn lead to desired outcomes and impacts, the latter comprising effects on the degree of social exclusion experienced by the target individuals, groups or geographical areas. The framework also seeks to achieve the realist objective of understanding how (well) programmes 'work' for particular groups in particular circumstances and contexts.

In seeking to implement such an approach to evaluation we face four sets of problems: first, problems of *capturing* and measuring key variables; second, problems of *attributing* measured effects to programmes; third, problems of *explaining* how effects are produced (caused) by programme measures (mechanisms); and, fourth, problems of *valuing* the net contribution of the programme to social welfare. These will now be considered briefly in turn.

'Capturing' and measuring outcomes and effects

Of particular significance in theory-driven evaluation is the need to 'capture' and measure key variables in such a way as to provide a valid test of the underpinning conceptual model. It is in the area of outcomes and effects of social policy interventions that the greatest difficulties arise in capturing and measuring the 'phenomena of interest' (Smith 1996) as specified in the intervention logic. The difficulties are discussed by Connell and Kubisch (1997) in the context of the evaluation of Comprehensive Community Initiatives (CCIs): neighbourhood-based, cross-sectoral initiatives which emphasize community capacity-building in seeking 'improved outcomes for individuals and families as well as improvements in neighbourhood circumstances' (Connell and Kubisch 1997: 2). They argue that outcomes need to be measured at different *levels* – community, organizational/institutional, family/personal network, and individual; that many *community attributes* that need to be captured (such as the strength of social capital, shared values and networks) are 'elusive'; and that many outcomes and effects take considerable *time* to develop (pp. 17–19). A key problem for quantitative approaches to evaluation is the omission or neglect of essentially *qualitative* effects which cannot be captured adequately through measurement (Sanderson 1998).

The basis for identifying and measuring outcomes is the set of objectives specified for a programme, because these represent the desired or intended outcomes and effects which should be made explicit in the intervention logic. However, as Knox (1995) argues, policy initiatives frequently proceed without precise objectives both 'to indulge politicians' and to allow flexibility in implementation. When considering community relations programmes in Northern Ireland, Knox found an 'evaluation morass' which required basic concept mapping techniques. Moreover, public programmes are characterized by multiple stakeholders each with different interests and possibly conflicting views on objectives (Thomas and Palfrey 1996). As Smith (1996: 9) argues:

It is rare to find consensus about what constitutes the objectives of a public sector programme. Thus, in making a choice of outcome measures, the outcome measurer is implicitly reflecting the objectives of one group of stakeholders, possibly at the expense of another group. That is, no outcome measurement scheme can be free of values, and any evaluation of outcome must be in respect of a particular set of objectives.

In relation to programmes addressing social exclusion there will often be a complex pattern of stakeholder interests covering target recipients, related representation groups, the wider community, the implementing agencies and funding and commissioning agencies. Barr et al. (1996: 21–2) argue that the philosophy of community development which should underpin such programmes requires 'partnership working which indicates the importance of negotiated agreement over the evaluation criteria'. This requires an approach to evaluation which promotes full stakeholder participation. This is illustrated by Pitcher et al. (1998) in an evaluation of a local programme aimed at improving the life chances of disadvantaged young people. The approach adopted deliberately set out to elicit the perspectives of all stakeholders – managers, staff, agencies and young people themselves – and to develop alternative ('bottom-up') performance indicators to those implied by the 'official' ('top-down') objectives. Thus, in addition to qualifications and job outcomes, indicators capturing (for example) increased self-confidence, independent decision making and increased leisure activities were established.

A further problem arises because even where there are clear objectives it is comparatively rare for them to state explicit outcomes which are amenable to direct measurement. Thus, Smith (1996: 10) argues that measures 'usually cannot embrace the complexity of the underlying objective', commonly substituting output indicators as proxies for outcomes. Dunn et al. (1998: 7) argue that because the effects of public policies to address poverty and disadvantage are indirect, diffuse or intangible, most available quantifiable measures are proxy indicators. Due to the complexity of the issues it has been difficult to derive indicators which are suitable for assessing and evaluating policies. Considerable effort has gone into the development of 'composite' indicators, such as the Department of the Environment, Transport and the Regions' (DETR) Index of Local Deprivation (Robson et al. 1998), which combine several variables and are seen as having better explanatory powers than single variable indicators (Dunn et al. 1998: 10). However, while such composite indicators have considerable value in mapping deprivation and need for resources, they are less useful in monitoring the effects of policies and programmes due to the lack of any direct relationship between policy interventions and changes in the indicators. This point is made by Howarth et al. (1998) who propose a set of single variable indicators for monitoring the effect of policies to address social exclusion, grouped according to the life stages of people affected and incorporating variables relating to finance, education and qualifications, unemployment and pay, health, crime and housing conditions.

Although the problem of capturing and measuring outcomes specified in defined objectives is likely to be difficult enough, it is important that evaluation is not restricted in scope to the intended effects expressed in explicit objectives. Rather, as was argued earlier, the task is a broader one of assessing the value and effectiveness of a programme in addressing the social problems and needs which provide its rationale. A programme may have significant unintended or unanticipated effects and it is important that these are identified and captured. However, the fact that these are labelled 'unintended' indicates inadequacies in the underpinning programme theory or intervention logic which provides the specification of intended outcomes. As argued in the previous section, it is an essential task of evaluation to critically test this intervention logic and to seek to identify all significant effects of a programme, but it may be that many unintended effects can be captured only in qualitative terms. For example, a housing initiative might have adverse effects on community relations which are unanticipated because the underpinning programme theory is too narrow, neglecting cross-sectoral linkages. If performance indicators are not specified in advance, such effects would be identifiable only through 'open-ended' qualitative research.

Another important factor which influences the role of quantitative measures and indicators is the level at which effects are manifested. A basic distinction can be made between micro and macro levels (see Figure 12.1). At the micro level the focus is on the effects on target client groups comprising individuals, households or organizations who are commonly the intended beneficiaries of policies and programmes. Most quantitative indicators capture micro level effects (e.g. individual employment status, household income, organizational membership) and there is often a reasonably close relationship between programme instruments and changes in such indicators (although see the next section on attribution and 'deadweight' effects). However, at the macro level we are concerned to assess the broader impact of programmes on communities or 'localities' taking into account aggregate effects on economic and social welfare and unintended effects (positive and negative). Generally, at the macro level, indicators of social exclusion (measuring, for example, aggregate levels of income, unemployment, health status) may be of limited use in assessing the effects of particular programmes since such effects are likely to be 'swamped' by broader factors causing change. Therefore a key evaluation problem is how to identify the macro level changes attributable to programmes, and we return to this in the next section.

A further issue to be addressed in the use of quantitative indicators derives from the distinctive nature of the concept of social exclusion, referring to social, institutional, economic and political processes that exclude people from the major societal systems which promote a sense of citizenship and belonging in society. Given that considerable effort and time may be needed to achieve an impact on these processes, it is not easy to capture the effects of programmes in measurable 'outcomes'. For example, the most disadvantaged young people who are suffering problems of homelessness and drug abuse may require considerable help before they can engage with programmes to provide qualifications and employment, and the effects of such help – to 'build capacity' – are difficult to capture in quantitative indicators. Another potentially important aspect of social exclusion that is difficult to measure is the degree of support provided by family, friends and the local community. In order to capture fully the effects of programmes in addressing these processes, evaluation is likely to require an element of qualitative research.

A final concern in seeking to capture effects and outcomes is the time taken for policies and programmes to achieve change, given that many of the processes causing social exclusion are deep-seated and difficult to modify.

The significance of time to the definition and measurement of social exclusion has been emphasized by Walker (1995: 103–4) who argues that: 'failure to take adequate account of time causes us to understate the extent to which poverty touches the lives of people, to misunderstand the real nature of social exclusion and thereby to continue with policies that are at best ameliorative and, at worst, exacerbate the problem'. This criticism has important implications for evaluation, which needs to be capable of identifying, capturing and explaining how the effects of programmes are produced over time. In particular, as Barr *et al.* (1996: 26–7) argue, it needs to be capable of distinguishing between 'short term alterations to previous conditions and long term, systemic change which redefines the status quo'. Longitudinal measurement over a sustained period of time is likely to be required in order to capture 'capacity-building' effects, the development of longer-term macro level effects and the sustainability or 'durability' of outcomes at both micro and macro levels.

Hence there are a number of problems and issues that need to be addressed in seeking to capture and measure the outcomes and effects of a programme addressing social exclusion. In the next section we go on to look at the task of identifying what part of the measured 'gross' effects are directly due to (or 'attributable' to) the programme.

Attributing effects to programmes

Even if we accept that our 'gross measures' (e.g. qualifications and jobs obtained by individuals, change in unemployment in a locality) capture all the key effects of a programme, we must address the problem that they do not indicate the 'net additional' effect of the programme – i.e. the change attributable to the programme which would not have occurred in its absence. In order to estimate the latter we require an assessment of the 'counterfactual' situation. Measures of gross outcome will need to be adjusted for *deadweight* – i.e. that part of the gross effect which would have occurred anyway even in the absence of the programme. Deadweight reflects a failure to restrict receipt of a programme's benefits to its intended beneficiaries – those who could not have secured the benefits in any other way. This may be unavoidable (due, for example, to spatial targeting or inability to means-test) or alternatively may be due to poor programme design (ineffectiveness) or delivery (inefficiency). Because of deadweight effects, gross outcome measures can be very misleading in assessing programme effectiveness and more detailed research is required to estimate the 'additional effects' attributable to the programme.

A commonly adopted approach to evaluation is to establish a baseline situation comprising measures or indicators relating to the conditions that the programme is seeking to improve (for example, qualifications, employment and health levels of target groups, housing conditions and crime levels in a locality) and then monitor change over the lifetime of the programme. However, such a 'before and after' design does not isolate non-programme effects and therefore cannot estimate deadweight. This is illustrated in an evaluation of a community-based speech and language project in a deprived area of Plymouth which was designed to improve the communication skills of preschool children (Cooper *et al.* 1998). Five consecutive year intakes were assessed and the results were compared to a baseline and, although the results were regarded as significant, it was not possible to isolate the effect attributable solely to the intervention because it was acknowledged that 'there are factors outside the boundaries of the current study which may well have had an impact' (Cooper *et al.* 1998: 531). The ideal approach to addressing this problem within 'conventional evaluation research' (Schmid *et al.* 1996) is the 'experimental design'.

In a *true experimental evaluation design*, people eligible for the programme are allocated randomly to one of two groups: the participant group and the remainder (the control group) who do not achieve a place on the programme. The net effect of the programme is obtained by comparing the mean value of a defined outcome variable for participants and the control group of non-participants (Bjorklund and Regner 1996). The validity of the true experimental design relies on the ability to create a control group through random assignment that overcomes selection bias (i.e. allocation to 'participant' or 'control' group on the basis of decisions by administrators or eligible persons themselves). However, the circumstances in which it is feasible to use a true experimental design are relatively limited. First, there are obvious ethical objections to excluding some people from participating in public programmes which are intended to be beneficial. Second, there are various practical difficulties, notably the requirement to design the evaluation in advance of the implementation of the programme, and the relatively high cost.

Because of these problems recourse is often made to a *'quasi-experimental design'* involving the use of a matched comparison group in place of a control group. The matched comparison group comprises people specially chosen on the basis of their similarity in key respects to the participants (i.e. in terms of the key characteristics which are likely to affect job outcomes). Statistical methods can be used to control for characteristics that are not matched in the construction of the comparison sample (Payne *et al.* 1996).

Experimental and quasi-experimental designs can therefore provide estimates of the net intended effect of programmes which are more or less reliable according to the degree of conformance with the 'technical' requirements of sampling and statistical analysis. In technical parlance this can overcome a number of 'threats to internal validity' which lie behind deadweight. In particular, it allows for the influence of other causal factors, for 'maturation effects' as individuals improve their conditions by ageing or maturing, and for 'regression to the mean' as people find jobs of their own accord through 'normal' processes (Gaude 1996; Farrington 1997). Moreover, according to Payne *et al.* (1996: 2) 'results are based on a comparison of like with like, and hence are intrinsically more persuasive'.

The use of experimental or, more usually, quasi-experimental approaches is quite common in the evaluation of labour market programmes in the UK. For example, they have been used to evaluate the Training for Work programme (Payne *et al.* 1999), a number of 'job placing' programmes such as job clubs and work trials (White *et al.* 1997) and experimental schemes by the Employment Service to facilitate the transfer from benefits into work (Sanderson and Sheppard 1997). However, they are difficult to apply to comprehensive programmes, as is illustrated by the fact that it has not been possible to use them in the evaluation of the New Deal for young people because of universal entitlement for the eligible client group (Hall and Reid 1998). Schmid (1997: 422) argues that they are most suited to small-scale programmes of limited duration, designed to achieve well-specified changes – a context which does not map well onto the territory of social exclusion.

Moreover, experimental designs involving programme client groups cannot address directly the effects at the macro level. Thus, the effects of a programme for its client group (e.g. securing jobs for the long-term unemployed) may be secured at the expense of other groups (e.g. short-term unemployed and those in work) and this *substitution effect* will not be identified directly. There may also be other positive or negative *side-effects* which will not be captured (e.g. social and environmental effects). The identification of attributable effects at the macro level will either require supplementary research among affected 'non-target' groups and agents to identify such effects directly, the use of assumptions based upon research elsewhere in similar circumstances, or the use of macroeconomic modelling techniques to simulate a 'counterfactual'. The latter is being used as one element in the evaluation of the New Deal programme in the UK although it is recognized that it has limitations due to three factors: first, the potential small size of the New Deal impact relative to the total labour market; second, the number of observations available at the macro level; and third, the size of the sampling error in the relevant data sets (Hall and Reid 1998: 551).

A more general critique of experimental approaches to evaluation has developed which addresses their limitations where we are seeking to go beyond the tasks of measurement and attribution to the task of *explaining how* programme measures produce outcomes and effects, and to provide, on this basis, an understanding of how the programme might be improved. It is to this evaluation task that we now turn.

Explaining how outcomes and effects are caused by programme 'mechanisms'

A key argument of this chapter is that the task of evaluation is not simply to identify and measure the effects of a policy or programme and assess whether it has achieved its objectives and intended effects – but rather, more fundamentally, to seek to understand *how* the effects have been produced and *how well* the programme has 'worked' in relation to both its intended beneficiaries and its broader socioeconomic impact. Explanation is the central task of theory-based evaluation and, from a realist perspective, this involves analysing how 'causal mechanisms' in programmes produce particular outcomes and effects in particular contexts. Only through such understanding can we learn how programmes might be developed and applied in particular circumstances and how they might be improved to 'work' more effectively.

In the context of poverty and social exclusion, Walker (1995) has emphasized the importance of a 'causal' approach to analysis of the 'triggers that precipitate poverty' (p. 121) and of the need to identify how causal mechanisms are influenced by context. Thus, he argues that although the events that can trigger poverty are widespread, the actual incidence of poverty is comparatively rare. Therefore, the key to explanation is understanding 'the interactions between the triggers and the structural circumstances in which people find themselves' (p. 121), the latter relating to personal circumstances, social position and spatial location. According to Walker, the task of explanation is to 'disentangle the effects of personal and structural factors, and to construct theories that span micro and macro explanations' (p. 121).

As regards the methods for achieving such explanation, I argued above for a 'pluralistic', multi-method approach that recognizes the limits of alternative paradigms in respect of their claims to produce 'valid knowledge'. From this perspective, the privilege accorded to the experimental paradigm can be challenged, a task undertaken with some style by Pawson and Tilley (1997). They argue that the fundamental problem for the experimental approach derives from the underpinning 'successionist' theory of causation – namely that causation must be inferred on the basis of observational data. In neglecting the 'internal' characteristics of phenomena, which constitute their 'transformative potential', the experimental approach 'seeks to discount in design and evidence precisely that which needs to be addressed in explanation' (Pawson and Tilley 1997: 31). In practical terms, a programme will be effective in achieving outcomes if it provides forms of help which are appropriate to the particular circumstances and characteristics of participants under the right conditions, and experimental evaluation cannot provide an explanation of success in these terms.

In effect, the programme is treated as a 'black box' which can be highly problematical unless it comprises instruments which can be clearly and easily specified and measured. Whereas this is usually the case in the medical field, which is held up as the model of the experimental approach (with treatment protocols defined very precisely), it does not apply widely in social and economic policy areas. This is particularly problematical in the case of programmes addressing social exclusion which commonly comprise a range of specific projects and 'policy instruments' provided by a range of agencies. Since these are designed to be complementary, with the intention of achieving synergy benefits, their relative contribution to the programme outcomes is difficult to disentangle. An experimental design is incapable of addressing this issue. The problem is also acute where services or programmes of support involve a high degree of 'interaction' between provider and client, especially when the form of support is adapted and 'tailored' to meet clients' particular circumstances and needs. For example, various studies have indicated that it is precisely this 'tailoring' which is a key factor in the success of local initiatives to address the long-term unemployment (Campbell *et al.* 1998; Sanderson *et al.* 1999). Yet in the experimental approach, this 'within-programme' variation is averaged out; it may be able to show that a programme is effective (in the sense of attributable net effects) but 'it does not tell us which elements of a successful programme make the difference' (Gaude 1996: 54).

The fundamental problem with the experimental approach is that it abstracts the evaluation of a programme from the social and institutional context that is fundamental to explaining its effectiveness (Schmid *et al.* 1996). In the circumstances of programmes designed to address social exclusion it is likely that 'sealed' experimental environments will differ considerably from the way programmes are normally operated. Programmes 'work' when they provide appropriate forms of help which address the needs and circumstances of individuals in the particular prevailing contextual conditions. The 'environment' of relevant policies and services in which a programme is located is also an important consideration in explaining programme effectiveness and since experimental evaluations fail to address this context, they cannot tell us to what extent results can be generalized to inform policy development under different contextual circumstances. This is the problem of *external validity*. The result is the 'so what?' syndrome – results are interesting as far as they go but are hedged round with provisos about their wider applicability. This is evident in the conclusions of White *et al.*'s (1997: 124) evaluation of job placing programmes: 'It is not possible to assess, from the results of a single cross-sectional study, what would be the effect of the programmes under changes in the set of policies, services and labour market conditions'.

In thinking about alternatives to the experimental approach, Heckman and Smith (1996: 83) argue that 'the assumptions required to justify experiments are often ignored or downplayed, while those required to justify nonexperimental methods are often overstated'. Among the latter, Schomann (1996: 117) argues for the use of longitudinal designs as the basis for 'theory-driven evaluation': 'The purpose of longitudinal studies is not just to describe different situations at different points in time but also to explain why there has or has not been a change in situations. This purpose thus has to do with explaining the processes involved in such a change'. Longitudinal designs therefore allow 'the time-ordered study of processes' which is a key element in explaining how the 'mechanisms' in policy interventions help people to achieve outcomes. Moreover, such designs can overcome the common problem of 'short-sightedness' of programme evaluation which often seeks to assess outcomes too soon after participation and can neglect the longer-term effects of 'institutional reforms' (Schomann 1996: 136). In relation to labour market programmes, Schomann emphasizes the need to understand 'the process of implementing a *specific* programme' (p. 138) and to obtain 'more detailed knowledge about a person's labour market experience and other parts of the life course' (p. 137) in seeking to understand the effectiveness of programmes. However, longitudinal designs have their problems, notably relatively high cost and administrative complexity, the danger of high attrition rates from 'panel' studies and the problem of recall errors in retrospective studies (Schomann 1996: 118–23).

The potential value of longitudinal research has been emphasized in the work to develop an evaluation framework for the Scottish Social Inclusion Strategy which can promote understanding of the dynamic and multiple aspects of exclusion as well as how and why action to promote social inclusion is successful or otherwise (Scottish Social Inclusion Network 1999). From a perspective which is clearly consistent with a 'realist' approach to evaluation, longitudinal designs are seen as permitting the combination of quantitative and qualitative approaches to the analysis of:

- dynamic effects over time, with temporal ordering providing a key to causation;
- effects at different 'levels' (individual, household and community) and linkages between them;
- 'transition' processes between life stages of school, work and retirement and states within these stages (e.g. in and out of work);
- contextual processes that influence or determine change (Scottish Social Inclusion Network 1999).

Notwithstanding the limitations of quantitative evaluation designs, it is clear that they do contribute important elements of the broader explanatory picture which we seek to achieve through a multi-method approach. Thus, as Julnes *et al.* (1998) argue, experimental methods can be valuable as a preliminary to in-depth 'process-oriented' investigation by analysing the empirical implications of hypothesized mechanisms and thereby suggesting lines for further investigation. This would be particularly valuable where it is possible to combine experimental and longitudinal approaches in a 'comparative time series' design (Mohr 1995). This is the approach adopted by Bagley and Pritchard (1998) in an evaluation of an experimental programme of school social work to reduce school exclusions in two schools serving deprived estates in Dorset. Data was collected over three years in the project schools and two control (or, more strictly) 'comparison' schools which permitted both the estimation of the 'net attributable effect' of the project and an understanding of how the intervention produced the effects (i.e. how it 'worked'). This study illustrates the point that there is ultimately a limit to the scope of quantitative designs in relation to the realist task of understanding cause and effect mechanisms and processes; as Moulaert (1995: 186) argues, this requires 'detailed qualitative analysis of structures, institutions and behavioural patterns'.

If we are interested in 'formative' evaluation 'to suggest actions to change the program in certain ways to make it more successful' (Mohr 1995: 33) and to understand how it may be applied in other settings, then we need to undertake detailed analysis of how programme activities and instruments are implemented and applied to individuals and groups experiencing particular circumstances within a particular social and institutional context. Of particular interest will be 'synergy' effects in multi-instrument/agency programmes and the way in which instruments are applied to particular individuals or groups where there is a significant degree of discretion and/or 'personal interaction' (e.g. counselling and advice measures). Such in-depth analysis requires qualitative methods and Mohr (1995: 260–72) makes a strong case for the validity and utility of such methods in 'causal reasoning' as a basis for 'understanding the method or mechanism by which the causation came about' (p. 271).

Therefore, it can be argued that there is a convincing rationale for a 'pluralistic' approach to the methodology of realist evaluation, with each of a range of methods able to 'capture' a particular aspect of the broader causal picture and contributing to a 'construction' of this picture, the robustness of which is strengthened by virtue of the multi-method design. In this sense, there can be no methodological guarantees of 'truth' – only good reasons for accepting a 'construction' of the causal picture. Thus, a multi-method approach to evaluation might employ the following design which addresses three basic 'levels' of analysis:

1 The first level of analysis is the most 'superficial' and requires the establishment of a comprehensive *programme monitoring* system based upon performance measures and indicators relating to the programme's objectives and to relevant contextual social and economic conditions. The value of such a monitoring system is indicated by Auer and Kruppe (1996) in the labour market context. They argue that, given appropriate indicators and measurement intervals, a monitoring system can play a valuable role not

only in adjusting programme design and implementation but also in providing indications of how outcomes and effects are being produced, thus guiding the focus of evaluation research. Julnes *et al.* (1998) also discuss the value of analysis at this level in realist evaluation using both classification and monitoring.

2 The second level of analysis proceeds in the context of the analysis of monitoring data. It involves the establishment of *quantitative evaluation* designs which are appropriate to the particular characteristics of the programme in question and to the practical circumstances in which the evaluation is to be carried out (including the interests and requirements of the various stakeholders). If a realist approach is to be followed, it is vital to continually bear in mind that the ultimate aim is to understand 'what works, for whom, in what circumstances' and to 'craft' the evaluation design accordingly. The philosophy here is 'horses for courses' balancing the above aim against such practicalities as the commissioner's requirements, the funding available for the evaluation and what is ethically and feasibly possible in relation to the programme in question (e.g. whether the evaluation is designed-in at the commencement of a programme permitting longitudinal 'tracking'; the feasibility of control or comparison groups). I have argued that longitudinal designs are likely to be particularly appropriate to realist evaluation.

3 The third level of analysis follows from the second level and involves in-depth *qualitative research* to develop 'causal understanding' of how the programme 'triggers' mechanisms to produce particular outcomes for individuals and groups in particular circumstances. Such analysis will often proceed under the guise of 'case study evaluation' which provides the opportunity to focus on key instances of 'context-mechanism-outcome' configurations to explain how they came about. Of particular value in such analysis is the comparative investigation of instances to identify how the operation of mechanisms in different 'contextual' circumstances produces different outcomes in terms of states of social exclusion.

Such a multi-method, multi-level approach is consistent with the realist notion of the 'stratified nature of social reality' and embodies progressively 'deeper' analysis of the way programmes work in such a way that our 'delving' to 'lower' levels of quantitative and qualitative evaluation research is guided and focused by analysis at the level above. This can fulfil our requirement for explanation but, as argued previously, evaluation as a practical activity of knowledge construction and utilization involves more than explanation. It also involves assessing the 'worth' of public action in the absence of a market to provide a valuation, in order to inform decision making as to whether such action is justified in relation to the resources it requires.

Valuing the net 'worth' to society

Inherent in the definition of evaluation is the notion of 'assessing value', so a key element in the evaluation process involves the identification of how a programme can be judged as 'adding value for society'. It should be emphasized that the task for evaluators is to clarify and elaborate the criteria by which 'value' can be assessed, to set out how a programme 'performs' in relation to those criteria and to present justifiable and transparent judgements on this basis. Ultimately, in a democratic society, it is for those accountable through democratic political processes to make decisions about the 'social worth' of policies and programmes (which may or may not be informed by evaluation findings!).

I have discussed various issues around the estimation of the outcomes and effects which are attributable to a programme with a view to identifying and capturing the changes to the world which would not have occurred if the programme had not been implemented. The questions which now face us are: do these changes represent a net improvement to our welfare, and did the programme represent a 'good' use of resources? These are complex questions and only a brief overview of some issues can be provided here.

A number of criteria are conventionally used in answering these questions. These can be considered in two groups, the first representing criteria of 'effectiveness' and the second representing criteria of 'value for money'. As regards the first group, 'effectiveness' itself is conventionally defined as the extent to which the programme achieves its objectives – i.e. its planned or intended outcomes. Certain 'intermediate' criteria might be used as 'proxies' for effectiveness – for example, 'coverage' (or 'take-up') (the proportion of the target population 'treated' by the programme) and 'satisfaction' or 'perceived benefit' (based upon participants' assessments). However, a broader measure of effectiveness in relation to the problems or needs that the programme is intended to address might be termed 'utility' (European Commission 1997: 22) or 'adequacy' (Mohr 1995: 7–8). Mohr's 'adequacy ratio' expresses the percentage difference between the outcome and baseline value of a defined measure of programme effect.

Criteria of value for money require the comparison of measures of the effect or benefit of a programme with its costs. As Figure 12.1 indicates, there are various 'levels' at which cost can be defined. The ratio between actual and planned delivery costs provides the criterion of 'economy' but this is not a true value for money indicator. The comparison of measures of programme outputs with actual delivery costs gives indicators of 'efficiency'. The most commonly used efficiency measures are unit costs (e.g. cost per training place provided) while measures of productivity express the ratio of outputs to non-cost resource inputs (e.g. persons advised per counsellor). The cost per unit outcome from the programme is a measure of 'cost-effectiveness' (e.g. cost per job provided).

Assessing the 'value' of a programme from such measures requires comparators, either change over time from a baseline or towards a target, or performance relative to other programmes or organizations which provide a valid comparison. Such comparisons are achieved through 'data benchmarking' exercises which are becoming increasingly important in public services in the context of the growing requirement to demonstrate improving performance (Bullivant 1994). However, there are two fundamental requirements for effective benchmarking to ensure 'like with like' comparisons. First, there must be similar policy/institutional contexts such that the relative costs express broadly similar levels and priorities of provision. Second, costs must be defined according to similar accounting conventions – for example, in respect of the allocation of 'overhead' costs.

Such an approach to assessing the 'value' of programmes to address social exclusion has severe limitations. Thus, it is applicable only to narrow, sectoral programmes which have measurable outcomes that are comparable with other programmes implemented in similar policy and institutional contexts. Even under these conditions there are limited prospects for achieving meaningful measures of, for example, cost per qualification or cost per job for valid comparative analysis. Under the conditions of multi-sectoral programmes with the kinds of complex effects and outcomes which we have discussed above (and potentially severe problems of cost attribution), measures of cost-effectiveness will provide a very limited picture of their 'value'.

A broader measure of value for money is provided through a cost-benefit framework. From the perspective of welfare economics, cost-benefit analysis (CBA) represents the ideal approach to 'valuing' a programme since the calculation of 'net social benefit' provides an assessment of the extent to which a programme contributes to allocative or social efficiency (Levacic 1987; Williams 1993). However, the use of CBA is controversial because of the requirement that benefits are measured in monetary units and valued in terms of what individuals would be willing to pay for them. It is assumed in the Paretian value system that the existing distribution of income is to be taken as given, thus neglecting the incidence of gains and losses between different individuals and groups. It is now widely argued that, in many contexts, these assumptions are not appropriate and, moreover, monetary valuation of benefits on the basis of willingness to pay is neither achievable nor desirable (Williams 1993). This argument has considerable force in the context of multi-strand initiatives to address social exclusion.

However, as an alternative to Paretian CBA it is possible to consider what has been termed the 'decision-making' or *framework* approach. This approach seeks to retain the capacity to determine whether or not a project or programme contributes a net benefit to society but rejects the Paretian framework for calculating this in monetary terms, first because of the impracticability of monetary valuation of all relevant benefits and second because of the failure to take account of distributional effects. The framework approach seeks to identify and set out all relevant costs and benefits, where appropriate valued in monetary terms, but alternatively measured in relevant 'natural' units or even expressed in 'qualitative' terms. Moreover, all groups (stakeholders) affected by the project or programme are identified and the incidence of the costs and benefits is disaggregated by such groups. On the basis of all this information, a judgement can be made about the net benefit of projects or programmes; such judgement requires explicit weighting of different objectives and different items of cost and benefit as they affect different groups, thus incorporating equity issues. Fundamental to this approach, then, is the requirement that such weightings and the value judgements embodied in them should be made explicit and transparent (Williams 1993).

A key advantage of the framework approach is that it deals explicitly with the different (and perhaps conflicting) interests and values of all stakeholders in a programme, recognizing that different stakeholders may make very different judgements as to the 'value' of the programme. In initiatives to address social exclusion this is likely to be an important area for attention, given the wide range of stakeholders in multi-sectoral programmes and the considerable scope for value conflict in relation to the underlying issues. It indicates the need for a participatory approach to evaluation but raises questions about how trade-off judgements are to be made where there are value conflicts. The key issue concerns the potential for establishing an institutional framework which can support the construction of consensus through free discussion among all stakeholders; this is, at the very least, debatable.

Conclusion: evaluation and 'social improvement'

Conceived as an instance of 'practical reason', evaluation is inherently 'political' (in the classical sense) as part of our efforts to direct our collective affairs towards social improvement. However, there has been extensive soul-searching among the evaluation community about the perceived lack of impact of evaluation research on the world of politics and practice (Albaek 1995). From the realist perspective, Pawson and Tilley (1997: 213) express 'a healthy scepticism rather than a wholesale cynicism about the policy potential of evaluation research'. Notwithstanding 'the presence of power play in policy making' they argue that well-crafted research into 'what works for whom in what circumstance' can make a significant impact on policy and practice.

We have seen that it is this kind of *formative* evaluation that Mohr (1995: 32–3) advocates as the basis for action to improve programmes, founded upon answering the question: why? The key to the power of formative evaluation to engage with practice is the realist objective of understanding 'the mechanisms by which a treatment has its impact'; this provides the basis of 'external validity' – the applicability of evaluation results to other settings. Consequently, the more that evaluations are able to provide well-founded evidence of 'what works' and its applicability to particular contexts, settings and circumstances, the more likely it is that they will gain the attention of policy makers and make a positive impact on the practical activity of changing our world for the better.

With a view to promoting this aim, I have argued for a theory-based, 'pluralistic' approach to evaluation in the context of social exclusion which goes beyond demonstrating and measuring the effects of programmes to seek to explain and understand their impact. I have argued for an approach which is comprehensive or 'integrative' in terms of methodology (combining quantitative and qualitative approaches), in terms of substantive focus (addressing outcome and process) and in relation to 'stakeholder involvement'. I have argued that such an approach needs to address effects at different 'levels' (micro/macro) and the dynamic nature of effects over time. I have argued that the 'top-down' view of evaluation as a 'technical' enterprise neglects the way in which it engages with, and impacts upon, the various interests or 'stakes' in a policy or programme. In particular, if the values embodied in the prevailing power structure are taken as given, beyond the scope of 'rational deliberation', evaluation can alienate and disempower those disadvantaged groups whom the programme is intended to help. In the context of programmes in which measures are themselves implemented in a 'top-down' way and involve 'doing things to recipients', evaluation can simply reinforce the 'culture of passivity'.

For programmes which are intended expressly to promote community development and capacity building, as is increasingly the case in initiatives to address social exclusion, such a 'top-down' approach to evaluation presents a glaring contradiction. This point is made forcefully by Barr *et al.* (1996: 21), who argue: 'It is inconsistent to invest in an activity which has the declared aim of responding to community perceptions of need and appropriate action but impose criteria for evaluation of its performance which come from elsewhere'. This philosophy is also embedded in the framework for evaluating the Scottish Social Inclusion Strategy which emphasizes the need to involve those experiencing social exclusion in the process of deciding evaluation criteria (Scottish Social Inclusion Network 1999).

Barr *et al.* (1996: 31–4) argue that the approach adopted for evaluation in such contexts must embody the principles of partnership working and the 'ideals of collective empowerment for social change' and capacity building. It is therefore essential that the basis for evaluation is negotiated with the community concerned, that the process of undertaking evaluation involves community members and 'contributes to community emancipation' and that the perspectives and experiences of the community are captured through qualitative methods. Indeed, it may be possible to provide the means and support for the community to undertake self-evaluation (Barr *et al.* 1996: 34–8). The application of such a participatory approach is illustrated by Heritage (1996) in the evaluation of a community health development project in Norwich which sought to work closely with the project's participants. The justification for such a participatory approach to evaluation is as much practical as ideological in that it can help to promote the 'utilization of systematically collected and socially constructed knowledge' in policy making as well as promoting democratic participation (Cousins and Earl 1995: 10).

These principles are embodied in what Fetterman (1996) terms 'empowerment evaluation' in which evaluators work in a collaborative, partnership way to facilitate and support participants in undertaking their own evaluation with the dual objective of promoting programme improvement and encouraging participant self-evaluation and self-determination. However, Floc'hlay and Plottu (1998) emphasize the need for capacity building as the basis for effective involvement and participation of community groups, especially those experiencing the greatest disadvantage and therefore the highest levels of need in relation to policy interventions. Thus it is evident that this conception of 'democratic' or 'empowerment' evaluation rests upon two key assumptions. First, it assumes that evaluators, and the agencies commissioning them, are fully committed to, and capable of, promoting the empowerment of such groups to the degree required to give them a meaningful voice. Second, it assumes that once their voices are brought 'into the conversation' (Vanderplaat 1996: 92) then consensual processes operate. Clearly, both these assumptions are contentious given that evaluation proceeds in a wider institutional context that structures what is possible.

Nevertheless, it is important that evaluations of policies and programmes to address social exclusion are designed and executed with a clear understanding of the 'political' context and implications. At each stage in the evaluation process it is necessary to ask: do we understand the different 'stakes' or interests involved here and to what extent are they being incorporated into the process? The approach adopted is likely to have significant implications for the 'quality' of evaluation – in terms of its capacity to 'build a picture' of how a programme is working; in terms of its 'acceptability' and perceived legitimacy; and in terms of its capacity to make a difference in the world of practice.

References

Albaek, E. (1995) Policy evaluation: design and utilization, in R.C. Rist (ed.) *Policy Evaluation: Linking Theory to Practice*. Aldershot: Edward Elgar.

Auer, P. and Kruppe, T. (1996) Monitoring of labour market policy in EU member states, in G. Schmid, J. O'Reilly and K. Schomann (eds) *International Handbook of Labour Market Policy and Evaluation*. Cheltenham: Edward Elgar.

Bagley, C. and Pritchard, C. (1998) The reduction of problem behaviours and school exclusion in at-risk youth: an experimental study of school social work with cost-benefit analysis. *Child and Family Social Work*, 3(4): 219–26.

Barr, A., Hashagen, S. and Purcell, R. (1996) *Monitoring and Evaluation of Community Development in Northern Ireland*. Belfast: Voluntary Activity Unit, Department of Health and Social Services.

Berghman, J. (1995) Social exclusion in Europe: policy context and analytical framework, in G. Room (ed.) *Beyond the Threshold: The Measurement and Analysis of Social Exclusion*. Bristol: The Policy Press.

Bjorklund, G. and Regner, H. (1996) Experimental evaluation of European labour market policy, in G. Schmid, J. O'Reilly and K. Schomann (eds) *International Handbook of Labour Market Policy and Evaluation*. Cheltenham: Edward Elgar.

Bovaird, A.G. and Gregory, D. (1996) Performance indicators: the British experience, in A. Halachmi and G. Bouckaert (eds) *Organizational Performance and Measurement in the Public Sector*. Westport, CT: Quorum Books.

Bullivant, J.R.N. (1994) *Benchmarking for Continuous Improvement in the Public Sector*. Harlow: Longman.

Campbell, M. with Sanderson, I. and Walton, F. (1998) *Local Responses to Long-Term Unemployment*. York: Joseph Rowntree Foundation.

Connell, J.P. and Kubisch, A.C. (1997) Applying a theory of change approach to the evaluation of comprehensive community initiatives: progress, prospects and problems. Paper presented to UK Evaluation Society seminar, Tavistock Institute, London, 19 September.

Cooper, M., Pettit, E. and Clibbens, J. (1998) Evaluation of a nursery based language intervention in a socially disadvantaged area. *International Journal of Language and Communication Disorders*, 33 (supplement): 526–31.

Cousins, J.B. and Earl, L.M. (1995) The case for participatory evaluation: theory, research, practice, in J.B. Cousins and L.M. Earl (eds) *Participatory Evaluation in Education: Studies in Evaluation Use and Organizational Learning*. London: Falmer Press.

Dryzek, J.S. (1990) *Discursive Democracy: Politics, Policy and Political Science*. Cambridge: Cambridge University Press.

Dunn, J., Hodge, I., Monk, S. and Kiddle, C. (1998) *Developing Indicators of Rural Disadvantage*, Research Report no. 36. Salisbury: Rural Development Commission.

European Commission (1997) *Evaluating EU Expenditure Programmes: A Guide*. Brussels: European Commission.

Farrington, D. (1997) Evaluating a crime prevention programme. *Evaluation*, 3(2): 157–73.

Fetterman, D.M. (1996) Empowerment evaluation: an introduction to theory and practice, in D.M. Fetterman, S.J. Kattarian and A. Wandersman (eds) *Empowerment Evaluation: Knowledge and Tools for Self-Assessment and Accountability*. Thousand Oaks, CA: Sage.

Fischer, F. (1980) *Politics, Values and Public Policy: The Problem of Methodology*. Boulder, CO: Westview Press.

Floc'hlay, B. and Plottu, E. (1998) Democratic evaluation: from empowerment evaluation to public decision making. *Evaluation*, 4(3): 261–77.

Gaude, J. (1996) Evaluating public training and employment programmes. *Evaluation of European Training, Employment and Human Resource Programmes*. Thessalonika: CEDEFOP.

Guba, E.G. and Lincoln, Y.S. (1989) *Fourth Generation Evaluation*. Newbury Park, CA: Sage.

Hall, J. and Reid, K. (1998) New Deal for the young unemployed: monitoring and evaluation. *Labour Market Trends*, 106(11): 549–53.

Heckman, G. and Smith, J. (1996) Experimental and non-experimental evaluation, in G. Schmid, J. O'Reilly and K. Schomann (eds) *International Handbook of Labour Market Policy and Evaluation*. Cheltenham: Edward Elgar.

Henkel, M. (1991a) *Government, Evaluation and Change*. London: Jessica Kingsley.

Henkel, M. (1991b) The new 'evaluative state'. *Public Administration*, 69 (spring): 121–36.

Heritage, Z. (1996) Evaluating community health development: aims, methods and dilemmas. *Community Health Action*, 41: 4–5.

HM Treasury (1997) *Appraisal and Evaluation in Central Government: Treasury Guidance*. London: HMSO.

Howarth, C., Kenway, P., Palmer, G. and Street, C. (1998) *Monitoring Poverty and Social Exclusion: Labour's Inheritance*. York: Joseph Rowntree Foundation.

Julnes, G., Mark, M.M. and Henry, G.T. (1998) Promoting realism in evaluation: realistic evaluation and the broader context. *Evaluation*, 4(4): 483–504.

Knapp, M. (1984) *The Economics of Social Care*. London: Macmillan.

Knox, C. (1995) Concept mapping in policy evaluation: a research review of community relations in Northern Ireland. *Evaluation*, 1(1): 65–79.

Levacic, R. (1987) *Economic Policy Making*. Brighton: Harvester Wheatsheaf.

MacIntyre, A. (1984) *After Virtue: A Study in Moral Theory*. Notre Dame: University of Notre Dame Press.

Martin, S. and Sanderson, I. (1999) Evaluating public policy experiments: measuring outcomes, monitoring processes or managing pilots? *Evaluation*, 5(3): 245–58.

Mohr, L.B. (1995) *Impact Analysis for Program Evaluation,* 2nd edn. Thousand Oaks, CA: Sage.

Moulaert, F. (1995) Measuring socioeconomic disintegration at the local level in Europe: an analytical framework, in G. Room (ed.) *Beyond the Threshold: The Measurement and Analysis of Social Exclusion*. Bristol: The Policy Press.

Patton, M.Q. (1982) *Practical Evaluation*. Newbury Park, CA: Sage.

Pawson, R. and Tilley, N. (1997) *Realistic Evaluation*. London: Sage.

Payne, J., Lissenburgh, S., White, M. and Payne, C. (1996) *Employment Training and Employment Action: An Evaluation of the Matched Comparison Method*, Research Series no. 74. London: Department for Education and Employment.

Payne, J., Payne, C., Lissenburgh, S. and Range, M. (1999) *Work Based Training and Job Prospects for the Unemployed: An Evaluation of Training for Work*, Research Report no. 96. Sheffield: Department for Education and Employment.

Pitcher, J., Green, A.E. and Geddes, M. (1998) Evaluating programmes to combat disadvantage: alternative methodologies. *Bulletin*, 43. University of Warwick: Institute for Employment Research.

Robson, B., Bradford, M. and Tomlinson, R. (1998) *Updating and Revising the Index of Local Deprivation*. London: Department of the Environment, Transport and the Regions.

Sanderson, I. (1998) Beyond performance measurement? Assessing value in local government. *Local Government Studies*, 24(4): 1–25.

Sanderson, I. and Sheppard, B. (1997) Experimental evaluation and policy relevance: a case study in labour market policy. Paper presented to the UK Evaluation Society national conference, 'The Utilisation of Evaluation: Being Useful or Being Used?' Royal Institute of British Architects, London, 8–9 December.

Sanderson, I., Bovaird, T., Davis, P., Martin, S. and Foreman, A. (1998) *Made to Measure: Evaluation in Practice in Local Government*. London: Local Government Management Board.

Sanderson, I., Walton, F. and Campbell, M. (1999) *Back to Work: Local Action on Unemployment*. York: Joseph Rowntree Foundation.

Schmid, G. (1997) The evaluation of labour market policy: notes on the state of the art. *Evaluation*, 3(4): 409–34.

Schmid, G., O'Reilly, J. and Schomann, K. (eds) (1996) *International Handbook of Labour Market Policy and Evaluation*. Cheltenham: Edward Elgar.

Schomann, K. (1996) Longitudinal designs in evaluation studies, in G. Schmid, J. O'Reilly and K. Schomann (eds) *International Handbook of Labour Market Policy and Evaluation*. Cheltenham: Edward Elgar.

Schwandt, T.A. (1997) Evaluation as practical hermeneutics. *Evaluation*, 3(1): 69–83.

Scottish Office (undated) *Social Inclusion: Opening the Door to a Better Scotland*. Edinburgh: Scottish Office.

Scottish Social Inclusion Network (1999) *Progress Report, Social Inclusion Strategy Evaluation Framework Action Team*. Edinburgh: Scottish Office.

Smith, P. (1996) A framework for analysing the measurement of outcome, in P. Smith (ed.) *Measuring Outcome in the Public Sector*. London: Taylor & Francis.

Social Exclusion Unit (1998) *Bringing Britain Together: A National Strategy for Neighbourhood Renewal*, Cm 4045. London: The Stationery Office.

Thomas, P. and Palfrey, C. (1996) Evaluation: stakeholder-focused criteria. *Social Policy and Administration*, 30(2): 125–42.

Vanderplaat, M. (1995) Beyond technique: issues in evaluating for empowerment. *Evaluation*, 1(1): 81–96.

Walker, R. (1995) The dynamics of poverty and social exclusion, in G. Room (ed.) *Beyond the Threshold: The Measurement and Analysis of Social Exclusion*. Bristol: The Policy Press.

Waysman, M. and Savaya, R. (1997) Mixed method evaluation: a case study. *Evaluation Practice*, 18(3): 227–37.

White, M., Lissenburgh, S. and Bryson, A. (1997) *The Impact of Public Job Placing Programmes*. London: Policy Studies Institute.

Williams, A. (1993) Cost-benefit analysis: applied welfare economics of general decision aid?, in A. Williams and E. Giardina (eds) *Efficiency in the Public Sector: The Theory and Practice of Cost Benefit Analysis*. Aldershot: Edward Elgar.

INDEX